AF607848

Interactions of Vowel Quality and Prosody in East Slavic

Advances in Optimality Theory
Series Editors: Vieri Samek-Lodovici, University College London and Birgit Alber, Free Univerity of Bozen-Bolzano

Optimality Theory is an exciting new approach to linguistic analysis that originated in phonology but was soon taken up in syntax, morphology, and other fields of linguistics. Optimality Theory presents a clear vision of the universal properties underlying the vast surface typological variety in the world's languages. Cross-linguistic differences once relegated to idiosyncratic language-specific rules can now be understood as the result of different priority rankings among universal, but violable constraints on grammar.

Advances in Optimality Theory is designed to stimulate and promote research in this provocative new framework. It provides a central outlet for the best new work by both established and younger scholars in this rapidly moving field. The series includes studies with a broad typological focus, studies dedicated to the detailed analysis of individual languages, and studies on the nature of Optimality Theory itself. The series publishes theoretical work in the form of monographs and coherent edited collections as well as pedagogical texts and reference texts that promote the dissemination of Optimality Theory.

Published:

Blocking and Complementarity in Phonological Theory
Eric Baković

Conflicts in Interpretation
Petra Hendriks, Helen de Hoop, Irene Krämer, Henriätte de Swart and Joost Zwarts

Harmonic Grammar and Harmonic Serialism
Edited by John J. McCarthy and Joe Pater

Hidden Generalizations
Phonological Opacity in Optimality Theory
John J. McCarthy

Inflectional Morphology in Harmonic Serialism
Gereon Müller

Layering and Directionality
Metrical Stress in Optimality Theory
Brett Hyde

Linguistic Derivations and Filtering
Minimalism and Optimality Theory
Edited by Hans Broekhuis and Ralf Vogel

Modeling Ungrammaticality in Optimality Theory
Edited by Curt Rice and Sylvia Blaho

Optimality Theory, Phonological Acquisition and Disorders
Edited by Daniel A. Dinnsen and Judith A. Gierut

Phonological Argumentation
Essays in Evidence and Motivation
Edited by Steve Parker

Prosody Matters
Essays in Honor of Elisabeth Selkirk
Edited by Toni Borowsky, Shigeto Kawahara, Takahito Shinya and Mariko Sugahara

The Phonology of Contrast
Anna Łubowicz

Understanding Allomorphy
Perspectives from Optimality Theory
Edited by Eulàlia Bonet, Maria-Rosa Lloret and Joan Mascaró

Interactions of Vowel Quality and Prosody in East Slavic

Janina Mołczanow

SHEFFIELD UK BRISTOL CT

Published by Equinox Publishing Ltd.
UK: Office 415, The Workstation, 15 Paternoster Row, Sheffield, South Yorkshire S1 2BX
USA: ISD, 70 Enterprise Drive, Bristol, CT 06010

www.equinoxpub.com

First published 2022

British Library Cataloguing-in-Publication Data

A catalogue record for this book is available from the British Library.

ISBN-13 978 1 80050 234 5 (hardback)
978 1 80050 235 2 (ePDF)
978 1 80050 263 5 (ePub)

Library of Congress Cataloging-in-Publication Data
Names: Mołczanow, Janina, author.
Title: Interactions of vowel quality and prosody in East Slavic / Janina Mołczanow.
Description: Bristol, CT : Equinox Publishing Ltd, 2022. | Series: Advances in optimality theory | Includes bibliographical references and index. | Summary: "This book develops an Optimality-theoretic model of the interaction of phonological tone with segmental sonority, arguing that tone can interact directly with vowel quality without mediating factors such as syllable structure or duration. The proposal is tested against rich and complex patterns of vowel reduction in East Slavic dialects. This book will be of use to students and scholars interested in phonology, Slavic languages, and the theory of grammar in general"-- Provided by publisher.
Identifiers: LCCN 2022018294 (print) | LCCN 2022018295 (ebook) | ISBN 9781800502345 (hardback) | ISBN 9781800502352 (pdf) | ISBN 9781800502635 (epub)
Subjects: LCSH: Slavic languages, Eastern--Vowel reduction. | Slavic languages, Eastern--Sonorants. | Slavic languages, Eastern--Versification.
Classification: LCC PG411 .M65 2022 (print) | LCC PG411 (ebook) | DDC 491.7--dc23/eng/20220930
LC record available at https://lccn.loc.gov/2022018294
LC ebook record available at https://lccn.loc.gov/2022018295

Typeset by Sparks – www.sparkspublishing.com

Contents

Acknowledgements **ix**

List of abbreviations **xi**

1 Theoretical background **1**

1.1. Introduction 1

1.2. OT model: outline 4

1.2.1. Extreme reduction 7

1.2.2. Tone-driven reduction 9

1.3. Typology of tone–vowel interactions 12

1.4. The interaction of tone and vowel quality in East Slavic: preview 17

2 East Slavic vowel patterns: basic generalizations **19**

2.1 Overview 19

2.2. Segmental inventory 22

2.2.1. Vowels in stressed syllables 23

2.2.2. Consonants 24

2.3. Extreme reduction 25

2.4 Non-dissimilative vowel reduction 27

2.4.1. Reduction after non-palatalized consonants 27

2.4.2. Reduction after palatalized consonants 28

2.5. Dissimilative vowel reduction 30

2.6. Compound dissimilative vowel reduction 36

2.7. Assimilative-dissimilative vowel reduction 38

2.8. Dissimilative reduction in C^jVC^j contexts 41

2.9. Summary 42

3 East Slavic metrical system **45**

3.1. Introduction 45

3.2. Russian word stress: basic facts 46

3.3. Foot form 49

3.4. Foot as a domain 56
3.5. Formal representation of stress 58
3.6. Rhythmic structure of dialects with dissimilative reduction 63
3.6.1. Descriptive generalizations 63
3.6.2. Foot structure 66
3.7. Summary 71

4 Extreme reduction 73
4.1. Introduction 73
4.2. Analysis 74
4.3. Blocking of extreme reduction 76
4.4. Previous approaches to Russian vowel reduction 81
4.5. Summary 85

5 Tone-driven reduction 86
5.1. Introduction 86
5.2. Background 86
5.3. Non-dissimilative reduction 88
5.4. Dissimilative reduction 93
5.4.1. Preliminaries 93
5.4.2. Analysis 94
5.5. Pretonic length dialects 99
5.5.1. Basic generalizations and previous studies 99
5.5.2. Aŭciuki: an OT analysis 104
5.6. Typology 111
5.7. Interim conclusion 115

6 Harmonic systems 119
6.1. Introduction 119
6.2. Backness harmony (compound dissimilative patterns) 120
6.3. Height harmony (assimilative-dissimilative patterns) 137
6.4. Interim conclusion 146

7 Vowel reduction in the context of palatalized consonants 150
7.1. Introduction 150
7.2. Feature assimilation in *C'V* contexts 152
7.2.1. [e]-reduction 152
7.2.2. [i]-reduction 156
7.2.3. Interim summary 160
7.3. Feature assimilation in *C'VC'* contexts 162
7.4. Reduction after non-palatalized stridents 169

7.4.1. Introduction 169
7.4.2. Basic facts 170
7.4.3. Analysis 173
7.5. Conclusion 177

8 Concluding remarks **178**

References **181**

Language index **199**

Subject index **201**

Acknowledgements

The sound structure of East Slavic has been at the forefront of phonological investigation since the establishment of phonology as an independent field of study. This book builds on the ground-breaking work of Roman Jakobson, Morris Halle, Christina Bethin, Katherine Crosswhite, Jerzy Rubach, and many other scholars, whose numerous insights into the phonology of East Slavic languages have advanced the field in many significant ways. Though the ideas developed here often depart from their views, the influence of these prominent linguists is seen throughout the book. The present study also owes much to the dialectologists who have provided comprehensive descriptions of East Slavic dialects, and whose extensive fieldwork has yielded detailed documentation of many interesting sound patterns which are analysed in the subsequent pages.

The research was supported by the National Science Centre (Poland), grant 2017/27/B/HS2/00780. Preliminary work on the book was carried out at the University of Marburg in 2011–2012. I would like to express gratitude to the Alexander von Humboldt Foundation for the scholarship which made this research stay possible. The theoretical model presented in this book was first laid out in Mołczanow (2015) and further elaborated on in my post-doctoral dissertation (Mołczanow, 2017), I wish to thank Elsevier and the Institute of Applied Linguistics, University of Warsaw, for permission to use copyright material from these studies in the current book. The present work extends on the previous studies by covering a greater array of empirical facts and by thoroughly revising and modifying the theoretical base of the analysis.

I am indebted to a number of people who have contributed to the final result in various ways. First and foremost, I would like to express my gratitude to two anonymous reviewers and the Editor of the series Birgit Alber for their valuable feedback, numerous suggestions, and constructive criticism, which have led to a considerable improvement of both the content and the presentation of the ideas in this book. I would also like to thank Beata Łukaszewicz, who has read and re-read the manuscript, offering many insightful comments and providing much encouragement during the years I have been working on the topic. I am also grateful to Paula Orzechowska,

Richard Wiese, and Eugeniusz Cyran for their helpful suggestions and a number of stylistic improvements of the manuscript. Needless to say, any remaining errors and shortcomings are solely my responsibility.

Finally, my warmest and sincerest thanks go to my family. This book would never have been written without their unfailing love and support.

List of abbreviations

acc. – accusative
adj. – adjective
adv. – adverb
dat. – dative
dim. – diminutive
fem. – feminine
gen. – genitive
imp. – imperative
inf. – infinitive
instr. – instrumental
loc. – locative
masc. – masculine
nom. – nominative
pers. – person
pl. – plural
sg. – singular
expr. – expressive
pejor. – pejorative
perf. – perfective
imperf. – imperfective
pres. – present
OT – Optimality Theory
μ – mora
σ – syllable
ω – prosodic word
Δ – head
-Δ – non-head
H – High tone
L – Low tone
M – Mid tone
/ / underlying representation
[ ] – surface representation
ˈ – stress

^{j}	– palatalization
+	– morpheme boundary
#	– word boundary
>>	– ranked higher than
>	– more prominent than
≻	– more harmonic than
⇒	– a winning candidate
⇐	– a winner that is not the attested form
😐	– the attested form that is not the winner in a tableau
*	– ungrammatical form

Selected symbols of transliteration:

y	– ы; a high back vowel
j	– й; a front glide
c	– ц; a voiceless alveolar affricate
š	– ш; a voiceless postalveolar fricative
ž	– ж; a voiced postalveolar fricative
č	– ч; a voiceless palatalized alveolar affricate
x	– х; a voiceless velar fricative
jo	– ё; a front glide followed by a mid back vowel
ja	– я; a front glide followed by a low back vowel
ju	– ю; a front glide followed by a high back vowel
'	– ь; palatalization

Chapter 1

Theoretical background

1.1. Introduction

The patterns of vowel reduction found in East Slavic are typologically isolated and extremely complex compared to reduction types attested in the world's languages. Typically, unstressed vowels are neutralized in favour of the central vowel schwa, as in English and Dutch (Gimson, 1970; Booij, 1995). A characteristic feature of standard Russian and of many East Slavic dialects is that they exhibit two-degree vowel reduction: neutralization to corner vowels is found in pretonic positions and centralization to schwa in atonic (pre-pretonic and post-tonic) contexts (Avanesov, 1984).[1] It is noteworthy that the operation of vowel reduction varies only slightly from dialect to dialect. For instance, in the dialects with the so-called dissimilative reduction, [ə] occurs in pretonic syllables if the stressed vowel is [a], e.g. *slona* [slə'na] 'elephant' (gen. sg.), whereas [a] is found before stressed high vowels, e.g. *slony* [sla'nɨ] id. (nom. pl.). Depending on a dialect, either [a] or [ə] is used before stressed mid vowels, so that the word *slone* id. (loc. sg.) can be pronounced as either [sla'nʲe] or [slə'nʲe] (Kuznecov, 1960; Požarickaja, 2005; Avanesov and Orlova, 1965; Kasatkin, 2005).

The picture is further complicated by the fact that the outcome of reduction is conditioned not only by the position in a word but also by the quality of the preceding segment. After palatalized consonants, [e], [a], and [o] are

[1] The present book employs the terminology widely used in the Slavic literature in denoting different prosodic positions within a word, e.g., Jakobson (1929, *et seq.*), Bethin (2006), and many others). The term 'tonic' refers to primary lexical stress, the term 'pretonic' is employed to refer to positions immediately preceding the stressed syllable, and 'post-tonic' designates positions following the stressed syllable. The term 'atonic' indicates positions not immediately preceding the stressed syllable, while 'unstressed' collectively refers to all positions which are not marked for stress.

reduced to [i] in standard Russian, to [a] in the southern Russian dialects, as well as Belarusian, and to [e] in the central Russian dialects. Hence, depending on a dialect, the word *reka* 'river' can be pronounced [rʲiˈka], [rʲaˈka] or [rʲeˈka] (compare the gen. pl. form *rek* [ˈrʲek]).

Furthermore, East Slavic dialects may exhibit either dissimilative or moderate [a]-reduction. In the dissimilative [a]-reduction, lowering to [a] is blocked before [a] in the following stressed syllable. In the moderate [a]-reduction, [a] is found before non-palatalized consonants, whereas [i] appears before palatalized consonants, as illustrated by the pronunciation of the words /nʲeˈsla/ 'carry' (past fem.) and /nʲeˈsi/ id. (imp.) in the two dialects, given in (1).

(1)	*dissimilative [a]-reduction*	*moderate [a]-reduction*	
	[nʲiˈsla]	[nʲaˈsla]	/nʲeˈsla/ 'carry' (past fem.)
	[nʲaˈsʲi]	[nʲiˈsʲi]	/nʲeˈsi/ (imp.)

Both reduction types are unusual from the typological perspective. First, the reduction to the back vowel [a] after non-back palatalized consonants (dissimilative [a]-reduction) is at odds with the basic generalization about the phonology of the Slavic languages which show an agreement in backness between vowels and consonants (Halle, 1959; Lightner, 1972; Rubach, 2000). In turn, the reduction to [i] attested in the moderate [a]-reduction takes place *before* palatalized consonants. This, however, is problematic because in Slavic vowels typically agree in backness with the preceding, not the following, segments.

This brief overview is meant to demonstrate that East Slavic dialects offer a rich material for the study of vowel reduction because they display minimal patterns of variation in the same contexts and in the presence of similar underlying vowel inventories. The model of vowel reduction developed in the present book unifies these apparently disparate phenomena by proposing a limited set of optimality-theoretic constraints (Prince and Smolensky, 1993/2004; McCarthy and Prince, 1995), whose minimal re-rankings yield the attested East Slavic vocalic patterns. Building on the fundamental insight of Bethin (2006), the present book advocates the view that vowel alterations attested in the immediately pretonic position in different East Slavic dialects is directly connected with the presence of High tone. More specifically, I argue that that different patterns of reduction in pretonic syllables arise due to the interaction of phonological tone with segmental quality. Current phonological theory does not provide a fully developed formal mechanism that would relate tone to sonority (but see the analysis in Becker and Jurgec, 2017); in fact, some authors explicitly deny a possibility of such an interaction (Hombert *et al.*, 1979; Hombert, 1977; Schuh, 1978; Fox, 2000; de Lacy, 2007). In particular, it has been suggested that in many cases of tone–vowel interactions, tone affects vocalic quality indirectly through syllable structure, foot structure, or duration (Jiang-King, 1999; Gussenhoven and Driessen, 2004; Köhnlein, 2017; Kehrein, 2017). Based on the evidence from various East Slavic dialects, the present book argues that tone can interact directly with vowel quality, the basic assumption being that tonally prominent units co-occur with prominent segments. Though the idea that tone constitutes a part of the phonological system of some Slavic languages has been around for decades (e.g., Jakobson, 1929, 1931, *et seq.*; Halle, 1997; Bethin, 2005, 2006; Dubina, 2012), its relation to vowel reduction has received little attention in the previous literature.[2]

On the descriptive side, this study formulates novel generalizations and presents linguistic data not previously discussed in the generative literature. More importantly, besides providing a descriptive characterization of the East Slavic vocalic system, the aim of the present book is to develop a theoretical model which would derive numerous and at times contradictory phenomena from general principles governing the organization of phonological structure.

The book is organized as follows. This chapter sets the theoretical scene for the remainder of the study by presenting the model of the tone-sonority interaction which is employed in the analyses of vocalic neutralization in the subsequent chapters. In particular, I suggest that the interaction between tone and vowel quality is regulated by a set of constraints derived through the harmonic alignment of the sonority scale with the tonal prominence scale. Furthermore, conflation of sonority scale with prosodic prominence is employed in the analysis of vowel reduction which is not related to tone. Chapter 2 introduces different patterns of vocalic neutralizations attested in East Slavic. Next, Chapter 3 presents the most important facts concerning East Slavic metrical system, whereas Chapter 4 develops an analysis of vowel reduction in unstressed positions not affected by the presence of tone. Chapter 5 demonstrates how the constraints that directly relate High tone

---

[2] The exception is constituted by Bethin (2006) and Dubina (2012). Bethin (2006), who employs tone to analyse pretonic lengthening, points to a possibility that vowel reduction in pretonic syllables may be connected to the tone-induced increased duration (cf. Bethin 2006: 149). Dubina (2012) proposes a tone-based analysis of vowel reduction in Belarusian and suggests that Russian vowel reduction can also be analysed in similar terms. The model of East Slavic vowel reduction developed in this book differs substantially from Dubina's (2012) work, both in scope and in the implementation of the assumption that reduction is driven by tone. Let us also note that the ideas presented here were developed independently and were first presented in Mołczanow (2012a, b), prior to the publication of Dubina's (2012) book.

to sonority levels account for vowel neutralizations occurring in immediately pretonic positions in systems with non-dissimilative and dissimilative reduction. Next, Chapter 6 extends the tonal analysis to the more complex patterns of reduction attested in different East Slavic dialects with the so-called compound dissimilative and assimilative-dissimilative reduction. It is demonstrated that these systems are accountable for by minimal re-rankings of constraints generating vowel reduction in non-dissimilative and dissimilative patterns analysed in Chapter 5. I argue that these additional patterns instantiate vowel harmony systems in which stressed syllables serve as triggers of harmony for the vocalic features [back] and [low]. The constraints driving vowel harmony are shown to work in concert with the constraints on the association of High tone with vocalic elements to generate complex neutralization patterns. Chapter 7 considers cases in which High tone fails to trigger the lowering of a vowel in the immediately pretonic position. This happens in the contexts of adjacent palatalized consonants and after non-palatalized stridents, where non-high vowels undergo fronting and/or raising. An OT analysis developed in this chapter builds on the two generalizations about the Slavic phonology concerning the tendency of consonants and the following vowels to exhibit the agreement in backness and in height. I adduce evidence demonstrating that the agreement in backness and height is observed not only in consonant-vowel sequences, as has been usually assumed in the literature, but is also operative in mirror image contexts, where a vowel changes to accommodate in backness and/or height to the following consonant. Finally, Chapter 8 summarizes the main results.

1.2. OT model: outline

This section introduces basic theoretical assumptions which lie at the core of the model of the tone-sonority interaction developed in the rest of the book. The present study employs the theoretical apparatus of Optimality Theory (OT; Prince and Smolensky, 1993/2004; McCarthy and Prince, 1995) to express grammatical generalizations. The choice of the theory is motivated by the nature of the phenomena which are subject to the analysis: East Slavic dialects display rich patterns of vocalic alternations which vary only slightly from dialect to dialect. It is generally agreed that 'the fundamental descriptive and explanatory goals of OT are (i) to derive complex patterns from the interaction of simple constraints and (ii) to derive language typology by permuting rankings' (McCarthy, 2011: 5). From this perspective, OT appears to be well-suited to deal with the East Slavic data, and, in turn, these data constitute an excellent testing ground for the premises of the theory.

This section begins with a presentation of the formal schemas which are employed in the construction of the Optimalitytheoretic generalizations.[3] Next, a set of OT constraints which are derived by harmonic alignment of natural linguistic scales will be presented. As we will see below, these constraints play a crucial role in the formal expression of the generalization that tonally prominent units are expected to co-occur with prominent segments.

Originally employed to match syntactic and prosodic constituents (Selkirk, 1986), the notion of alignment has been adopted to relate the edges of morphological and phonological constituents (McCarthy and Prince, 1993). Alignment constraints are stated using the following general format.

(2) *Generalized alignment*
Align(Cat1, Edge1, Cat2, Edge2) $=_{def}$
$\forall$ Cat1 $\exists$ Cat2 such that Edge1 of Cat1 and Edge2 of Cat2 coincide.
Where
Cat1, Cat2 $\in$ PCat $\cup$ GCat
Edge1, Edge2 $\in$ {Right, Left}

Generalized alignment as defined in (2) above demands that an element standing at the Edge of any Cat_1 also stands at the Edge of some Cat_2. Typically, alignment constraints map the edges of grammatical categories, such as words and morphemes, onto the edges of prosodic categories, e.g. prosodic words or syllables. For instance, ALIGN (Stem, R, σ, R) requires that the right edge of a stem coincides with the right edge of a syllable. McCarthy and Prince (1993) point out that alignment constraints can also be extended to compare phonological categories, such as syllables, feet, features, or subsegmental nodes. Alignment constraints of the latter type are employed to map tonal units onto prosodic constituents in the present study.

Another general technique of constraint construction concerns the expression of implicational universals and natural scales in OT. One example of a natural scale is constituted by a sonority hierarchy, which orders segments on a scale from the most to the least prominent. As is well known, languages employ sonority in determining the position of syllable nuclei and margins: the greater the sonority the better nucleus that segment makes, and, conversely, the lesser the sonority, the more likely the segment is to occur in a syllable margin. This generalization is expressed in OT by combining the sonority hierarchy (vowel > liquid > nasal > fricative > stop) with the

[3] The discussion of the OT machinery in this section is limited to the issues which bear directly on the model of East Slavic vocalic alternations. For a detailed overview of OT, the reader is referred to Kager (1999) and McCarthy (2002); the tenets of autosegmental phonology are presented in Goldsmith (1976, 1990) and in numerous subsequent contributions.

syllable-position prominence scale (Peak > Margin) to form universal constraint hierarchies (Prince and Smolensky, 1993/2004: 147–148):

(3) a. *Peak Hierarchy*: *P/*t* >> ... >> *P/*i* >> *P/*a*
b. *Margin Hierarchy*: *M/a >> *M/i >>... >> *M/a

The rankings derived from natural linguistic scales are universally fixed. This assumption allows for an expression of cross-linguistic implicational generalizations.[4] For instance, the ranking in (3a) reflects the fact that languages can only have vocalic nuclei, or vocalic and liquid nuclei, and languages which, for example, have nasal nuclei, also allow liquid and vocalic nuclei (e.g. English, Czech), whereas there are no languages which would allow liquid and vocalic nuclei but not vocalic nuclei.

The technique for scale combination, referred to as harmonic alignment, is formally defined in (4) below (after Prince and Smolensky, 1993: 149). (Note: the symbol '>' means 'is more prominent than', '≻' stands for 'is more harmonic than', and '>>' indicates a dominance relation.)

(4) *Harmonic alignment*
Suppose given a binary dimension D_1 with a scale X > Y on its elements {X, Y}, and another dimension D_2 with a scale a > b > ... > z on its elements. The *harmonic alignment* of D_1 and D_2 is the pair of harmony scales:
H_X: X/a ≻ X/b ≻ ... ≻ X/z
H_Y: Y/z ≻ ... ≻ Y/b ≻ Y/a
The *constraint alignment* is the pair of constraint hierarchies:
C_X: *X/z >> ... >> *X/b >> *X/a
C_Y: *Y/a >> *Y/b >> ... >> *Y/z

Originally designed to analyse Imdlawn Tashlhiyt Berber syllabification (Prince and Smolensky, 1993), harmonic alignment has been employed to deal with sonority-driven stress (Kenstowicz, 1997), tone-driven stress (de Lacy, 2002b), and different types of segmental neutralizations (Crosswhite, 1998; Gouskova, 2003; de Lacy, 2006; among others).

The present study uses harmonic alignment in the analysis of the East Slavic vocalic neutralization. Building on the work of Crosswhite (2001) and de Lacy (2006), extreme vowel reduction (i.e., reduction taking place in atonic positions) is accounted for in terms of the constraints derived through

---

[4] Another way to express implicational generalisations in OT is to state the constraints in the form of context generalisations, which stand in a subset or 'stringency' relation (Prince, 1998; de Lacy, 2002a, *et seq.*).

the harmonic alignment of the sonority scale with two prosodic prominence scales. These constraints require prosodically dominant positions (foot and syllable heads) to favour high-sonority segments, and prosodic non-heads (unstressed syllables) to prefer low-sonority segments.

The harmonic alignment of linguistic scales is also employed in the analysis of various reduction patterns found in pretonic positions in East Slavic. The proposal developed in this book in based on the constraints formed by the conflation of sonority scale and tonal scale.

1.2.1. Extreme reduction

Crosswhite (2001) proposes to analyse reduction involving raising and/or centralization of non-high vowels in terms of prominence reduction, driven by the pressure to reduce sonority in prosodically recessive positions. In this conception, unstressed syllables disfavour sonorous vowels, and, as a result, the latter are neutralized into less sonorous high and central vowels, usually [i u ə]. This type of reduction is frequently attested cross-linguistically. For instance, Crosswhite (2001) demonstrates that this mechanism is responsible for vowel reduction in a number of languages, including Bulgarian, Sri Lankan Portuguese, and English; prominence-reducing neutralization is also employed in the analysis of Russian extreme reduction.

De Lacy (2006) further suggests that prominence reduction instantiates a more general markedness reduction mechanism. In his model, prosodic heads and prosodic non-heads impose conflicting demands as to the sonority of the melodic content they contain: prosodic heads favour high-sonority segments, such as the low vowel [a], whereas prosodic non-heads prefer low-sonority high central vowels, such as [ɨ]. Unstressed syllables constitute both prosodic heads and prosodic non-heads. As heads of the syllabic constituents, they demand vowels associated with them to be sonorous. As occupants of the dependent positions within prosodic words, and hence non-heads, unstressed syllables prefer less sonorous vowels. De Lacy (2006) formalizes this idea in terms of the OT constraints relating sonority markedness scales with prosodic prominence scale. Sonority hierarchy ranks segments on a scale ranged from the most to the least sonorous (Sievers, 1881; Jespersen, 1904; Vennemann, 1972; Selkirk, 1984).[5] The following partial ranking of vowels has been adapted from de Lacy (2006: 68).

---

[5] There is no generally accepted definition of sonority and the phonetic basis of sonority distinctions is a debatable issue. See Szpyra-Kozłowska (1998) and Parker (2002) for an overview of the different proposals and discussion.

(5) a. *Sonority scale*

low peripheral vowels		mid-low peripheral vowels		mid-high peripheral vowels		high peripheral vowels		mid central vowels		high central vowels
{a}	>	{ɛ,ɔ}	>	{e,o}	>	{i,u}	>	{ə}	>	{ɨ}

b. *Prosodic prominence scale*
prosodic heads > prosodic non-heads

The conflation of the two scales produces two constraint sets in (6), from de Lacy (2006: 288). Note: the symbol '-Δ_{ω}' stands for prosodic non-heads and 'Δ_{σ}' represents syllable heads. For instance, *Δ_{σ}≤{ɨ,ʉ} reads as follows: 'Assign a violation mark for every head of a syllable that contains a segment with sonority less than or equal to {ɨ, ʉ}', whereas *-Δ_{ω}≥{a} is a shortcut for: 'Assign a violation mark for every non-head of a word that contains a segment with sonority greater or equal to {a}'.

(6) a. *-Δ_{ω}≥{a}, *-Δ_{ω}≥{ɛ,ɔ}, *-Δ_{ω}≥{e,o}, *-Δ_{ω}≥{i,u}, *-Δ_{ω}≥{ə}, *-Δ_{ω}≥{ɨ,ʉ}
b. *Δ_{σ}≤{ɨ,ʉ}, *Δ_{σ}≤{ə}, *Δ_{σ}≤{i,u}, *Δ_{σ}≤{e,o}, *Δ_{σ}≤{ɛ,ɔ}, *Δ_{σ}≤{a}

De Lacy (2006) employs the constraints on prosodic (non-)heads and sonority to explain various phenomena, including stressed and unstressed vowel inventories, the quality of epenthetic vowels, as well as sonority-driven stress.[6]

In the present book, I employ the constraints displayed in (6) in the analysis of the extreme reduction taking place in the atonic positions in standard Russian and in East Slavic dialects. As we will see in Chapters 4 and 5, East Slavic features both low-sonority vowels in atonic positions, [ə] and [ɨ] (e.g., [ə] in standard Russian, [ɨ] in the Žizdra reduction pattern), as well as the sonorous vowel [a] (e.g., standard Belarusian and some pretonic length dialects discussed in Chapter 5). These facts are accounted for based on different rankings of the constraints in (6a) in (6b). In general terms, systems with [ə]-reduction and [ɨ]-reduction rank (6a) above (6b), thus requiring vowels in unstressed syllables to minimize sonority. In contrast, systems with [a]-reduction have the opposite ranking, requiring syllable heads to contain maximally sonorous vowels.

The present proposal, while adopting the idea that extreme reduction is driven by the markedness constraints regulating sonority in prosodic heads and non-heads, differs in suggesting a separate mechanism to account for

---

[6] Although de Lacy has made an extensive use of the constraints on prosodic (non-)heads and sonority in his earlier work (e.g., de Lacy, 2002a, 2002b, 2007)), he has questioned the existence of sonority-driven stress in more recent work (Shih and de Lacy, 2019). I am grateful to the anonymous reviewer for pointing this out.

[a]-reduction attested in pretonic positions in East Slavic. As further explained in the following section, I suggest analysing this neutralization in terms of the interaction of sonority scale with tonal prominence.

1.2.2. Tone-driven reduction

One of the central claims of this books is that the complexity of the vowel reduction systems attested in different East Slavic dialects arises due to the influence of tone. The objective of this section is to present a formal model of the interaction of phonological tone with segmental quality, which will lie at the core of the analysis of vowel reduction developed in the remainder of the present study.

As in the case of the conflation of the markedness scale with prosodic prominence, I suggest employing harmonic alignment to form new constraints that conflate the markedness scale with tonal prominence. The prominence scales which are relevant to the analysis of tone–vowel relation are the sonority hierarchy depicted in (5a) in the previous section and the tone hierarchy. De Lacy (2002b) assumes the following scale of tone types, which expresses the idea that High tone is more prominent than lower tones.

(7) *Tonal prominence scale*
H > M > L

It has been noted previously that the formal mechanism of prominence alignment crosses the most and the least prominent elements of the two scales, one of which should be binary (Prince and Smolensky, 1993/2004). I suggest that only High and Mid tones combine with sonority hierarchy. As a result, there are constraints banning the combination of vowels of different sonority levels with High tones and Mid tones, but not with Low tones. The markedness constraints which are produced by crossing the sonority scale with the tonal scale are formulated in (8). The constraints are stated in the form of context generalizations, which stand in a subset or 'stringency' relation (Prince, 1998; de Lacy, 2002b; Rubach, 2003).[7]

[7] Another way to state implicational generalizations in OT is to postulate universally invariant ranking (Kenstowicz, 1997). The combination of sonority hierarchy with tonal prominence would produce the following ranking: *H/ɨ >> *H/ə >> *H/i,u >> *H/e,o >> *H/ɛ,ɔ >> *H/a. The fixed ranking can account equally well for the Russian facts as the context generalisation constraints. However, the stringency approach is chosen here as it has been demonstrated in the literature that in many cases fixed ranking fails to render an empirically adequate account (Rubach, 2003; de Lacy, 2006).

(8) a. *H/ɨ: Assign a violation mark for every high central vowel associated with a High tone.
*H/ɨ;ə: Assign a violation mark for every high or mid central vowel associated with a High tone.
*H/ɨ;ə;i,u: Assign a violation mark for every central or high peripheral vowel associated with a High tone.
*H/ɨ;ə;i,u;e,o: Assign a violation mark for every central, high, or mid-high peripheral vowel associated with a High tone.
*H/ɨ;ə;i,u;e,o;ɛ,ɔ: Assign a violation mark for every central or non-low peripheral vowel associated with a High tone.
*H/ɨ;ə;i,u;e,o;ɛ,ɔ;a: Assign a violation mark for every vowel associated with a High tone.

b. *M/a: Assign a violation mark for every low vowel associated with a Mid tone.
*M/a;ɛ,ɔ: Assign a violation mark for every low or mid-low peripheral vowel associated with a Mid tone.
*M/a;ɛ,ɔ;e,o Assign a violation mark for every mid or low peripheral vowel associated with a Mid tone.
*M/a;ɛ,ɔ;e,o;i,u: Assign a violation mark for every low, mid, or high peripheral vowel associated with a Mid tone.
*M/a;ɛ,ɔ;e,o;i,u;ə: Assign a violation mark for every mid central or non-high peripheral vowel associated with a Mid tone.
*M/a;ɛ,ɔ;e,o;i,u;ə;ɨ: Assign a violation mark for every vowel associated with a Mid tone.

The constraint schemata in (8a) express a generalization that low vowels are better carriers of High tone than mid vowels, and that mid vowels are better carriers of High tone than high vowels, etc. In contrast, the ranking in (8b) states that mid tones favour higher vowels over low vowels. The absence of constraints against the association between vowels and Low tone ensures that Low tone can freely combine with any vowel, which makes it the least marked tone. Furthermore, it predicts that the Low tone will not induce the change of vowel quality. The tableaux in (9) serve to illustrate the point. It can be seen that the number of violation marks increases as more vowels are included in the constraint statement. For compactness, '≤' is used instead of listing all the vowels; so that *H/ɨ;ə;i,u;e,o;ɛ,ɔ;a is *H/≤a, and *M/a;ɛ,ɔ;e,o;i,u;ə;ɨ is *M/≥ɨ. For instance, a low vowel [a] associated with the High tone violates only one constraint, a mid-high [e] incurs violations of three constraints, while a high central vowel [ɨ] runs afoul of all six constraints formulated in (8a).

(9) a. *High tone interacting with vocalic sonority*

	*H/≤ɨ	*H/≤ə	*H/≤i,u	*H/≤e,o	*H/≤ɛ,ɔ	*H/≤a
H a. ɨ	*	*	*	*	*	*
H b. ə		*	*	*	*	*
H H c. i, u			*	*	*	*
H H d. e, o				*	*	*
H H e. ɛ, ɔ					*	*
H f. a						*

b. *Mid tone interacting with vocalic sonority*

	*M/≥a	*M/≥ɛ,ɔ	*M/≥e,o	*M/≥i,u	*M/≥ə	*M/≥ɨ
M a. ɨ						*
M b. ə					*	*
MM c. i, u				*	*	*
MM d. e, o			*	*	*	*
MM e. ɛ, ɔ		*	*	*	*	*
M f. a	*	*	*	*	*	*

The constraints favouring the association between H tone and sonorous segments are functionally grounded. It is well known that tonal contours are attracted to long vowels: as a pitch rise takes longer time to produce than a pitch fall, a tonal contour is expected to be better expressed phonetically on a long segment (Ohala, 1978). Moreover, there is a correlation between tone and vowel height, which is rooted in physiological properties of the vocal apparatus. Low vowels are inherently longer because they are produced with a wider aperture than mid and high vowels (Lehiste, 1970). As tonal contrasts, especially High tone, favour long segments, low vowels are predicted to constitute a better docking site for High tone than high vowels. Based on this reasoning, Bethin (2006) suggests that lexical tone can be manifested phonetically by adjusting vowel quality. Since low vowels are intrinsically longer, vowel lowering can be used as another strategy to increase vowel duration, and, as a result, to render it a better docking site for a phonological tone.

The following section discusses the attested cases of the interconnection between tone and vowel quality and explores the implications of the present theory for typology.

1.3. Typology of tone–vowel interactions

Tone is a suprasegmental feature which frequently occurs in prosodic systems. It is manifested phonetically by a change in the fundamental frequency F_0. Languages with pitch distinctions have been traditionally classified as tone languages and pitch-accent languages. In the former, the occurrence of contrastive pitch contours is unrestricted, while in the latter, there is an association between pitch and accent. Typical representatives of pitch-accent languages are Swedish and Serbo-Croatian, where tonal contrasts occur on or near a stressed syllable.

The relation between tone and prosodic units has been well documented in the literature. It has been demonstrated that tone can interact with stress placement (de Lacy, 2002b), duration (Zhang, 2002), and syllable structure (Gordon, 2006). Furthermore, the literature is replete with examples of the interrelation between tone and the laryngeal properties of consonants (Hombert, 1978; Bradshaw, 1999; among others). In contrast, the interaction between tone and vowel quality is not widely attested. Nevertheless, there are languages which exhibit tone-driven vowel alternations. For instance, High tone is reported to have a raising effect on vowels in Fuzhou (Yip, 1980; Jiang-King, 1999; Myers and Tsay, 2003), Foochow (Chen and Norman, 1965) and Lahu (Matisoff, 1973). Similarly, Becker and Jurgec (2017) report a synchronic interaction of tone with vowel quality in Slovenian, where High tone co-occurs with tense vowels and low tone co-occurs with lax vowels. The opposite pattern is also attested. In Shuijingping Mang, lower tones induce vowel raising (Mortensen, 2013). High tone is correlated with low vowels in Ngizim, where the vowel [a] in the first syllable of verbs is predictably associated with High tone (Schuh, 1971). Similarly, High tones avoid high vowels in a number of Japanese dialects (Haraguchi, 1984).

The model of tone-sonority interaction laid out above assumes that the interaction between tone and vowel quality is directly regulated by two sets of constraints, *H/≤a and *M/≥ɨ, which are formed by conflating the sonority scale with the tonal scale. This theory predicts the following patterns of vowel-tone interaction:

(10) a. High tone favouring lower vowels
b. Mid tone favouring higher vowels
c. Low tone not interacting with vowel quality

The correlation of the High tone with a lower vowel is attested in a number of languages exhibiting vowel-tone interactions. In Taiwanese, for instance, High tone is associated with lower vowels (Zee, 1980). Lax (lower) vowels co-occur with higher tones in Rengao (Gregerson, 1976) and Western Cham (Edmondson and Gregerson, 1993). Verbs in Ngizim (Schuh, 1971) have a predictable High tone on the vowel [a].[8]

The interaction of the Mid tone with vocalic quality, as predicted by (9b), is attested in Shuijingping Mang (Mortensen, 2013). The vowels are raised when correlated with the underlying Mid tones (mid falling ML tones and low rising LM tones).

The historical development of vowel contrast in West Germanic Limburgian dialects provides an example of the interaction of both High and Mid tones with vowel height.[9] In the conservative tonal dialects of Maastricht, there is a tonal contrast between Accent 1 (a fall from high to low, HL) and Accent 2 (a mid level tone (M) or a weak rise to mid (LM), both followed by a late fall). This contrast has brought about differences in vowel qualities in other Limburgian dialects. In Weert, the diphthongs /ɛi, œy, ɔu/ were decomposed into a sequence of low vowels and glides /æj, œj, ɑβ̞/ when they co-occurred with a HL tonal contour (Accent 1). No such change took place when the diphthongs were associated with the Mid level tone or with a weak rise to mid (Accent 2). In the tonal dialect of Sittard, higher vowels are associated with Accent 2, while lower diphthongs co-occur with Accent 1. The Mechelen-aan-de-Maas dialect exhibits a similar pattern: mid vowels change into a lower vowel in syllables with Accent 1 and into a higher vowel in syllables with Accent 2. In terms of the theory of the vowel-tone interaction presented in this book, all these alternations can be analysed as a result of the interaction of markedness *H/≤a and *M/≥ɨ with feature faithfulness constraints.

Furthermore, the lack of constraints on the association of vowels with the Low tone predicts that it should freely combine with all vowels and not be phonologically active in triggering vocalic change. This prediction is borne

---

[8] Similar morphologically-conditioned interaction between tone and vowel quality exists in Eastern Maninkakan (Spears, 1968) and Kinande (Mutaka, 1994). For further examples, see Becker and Jurgec (2017).

[9] The discussion of the Limburgian dialects is based on Gussenhoven and Driessen (2004); see references therein for individual dialects.

out as there are no documented cases of vowel-tone interaction, where the Low tone would require a vowel of a particular quality, whereas the High and Mid tones would combine with any vowel.

Finally, the system of constraints which link sonority with tones predicts that there should be no systems with the High tone favouring high vowels and/or Mid tone favouring low vowels. However, there is a number of languages in which High tone is correlated with high vowels, the cases reported in the literature include Lahu (Matisoff, 1973), Foochow (Chen and Norman, 1965), and Matsue Japanese (Nitta, 2001).[10] Experimental studies reveal a phonetic affinity between High tones and high vowels: higher vowels have higher fundamental frequency than lower vowels (Ladefoged, 1968; Ohala, 1973; Hombert, 1978). It might then be the case that there is a constraint which forces high tones to be associated to high vowels. This type of constraint, *H[-ATR -low], has been postulated by Becker and Jurgec (2017) to account for a synchronic interaction of tone with vowel quality in Slovenian, where High tone co-occurs with tense vowels and low tone with lax vowels. Incorporated into the analysis developed in this book, this constraint either outranks or interacts with the markedness constraints *H/≤a and *M/≥ɨ.

An account prohibiting the association of the High tone with low vowels is suggested by Myers and Tsay (2003) in their analysis of Fuzhou. This analysis is grounded in articulatory facts, which indicate that 'raising pitch can reduce the energy required to produce a rise in vowel height' (Myers and Tsay, 2003: 120). However, this motivation for the constraints on the tone–vowel association is not entirely convincing because the opposite pattern with the high pitch favouring low vowels can also be grounded in articulation. In particular, phonetic studies show that high pitch raises the larynx, which shortens the vocal tract and raises F1, which correlates with a lower vowel (Hombert *et al.*, 1979; Archangeli and Pulleyblank, 1994). In the face of the contradictory articulatory-based evidence, it might be assumed that the acoustic correlation between the higher F_0 of the high vowels and the High tone plays a role in attracting the High tone to high vowels.

To summarize briefly, the generalizations expressed by the constraints *H/≤V and *M/≥V only in part explain the attested patterns of vowel-tone interaction. However, the full typological coverage of such a complex phenomenon as tone is certainly beyond the scope of the current book, and

---

[10] Becker and Jurgec (2017) list and discuss more systems in which High tone co-occurs wth higher vowels.

more empirical research on tonal and pitch-accent languages is needed to validate the model of tone-sonority interaction proposed here.

The analysis of vowel reduction developed in this book is based on the idea that H tone interacts with vowel quality in East Slavic. I suggest that the constraints of the *H≤V family generate vowel reduction in immediately pretonic positions both in standard Russian and in a variety of East Slavic dialects. The assumption that lexically accented vowels are associated with High tone is an old and a relatively uncontroversial one. Tone has played an important role in the development of Slavic, and its presence is manifest in the present-day Slavic languages (Jakobson, 1929, 1931, *et seq.*; Inkelas and Zec, 1988; Halle, 1997; Bethin, 1998, 2006; Dubina, 2012; and others). Contrastive tone is employed in the dialects of Serbian and Croatian (Lehiste and Ivić, 1986). Non-contrastive tone has been postulated for East Slavic dialects (Bethin, 2006), for standard Belarusian (Dubina, 2012) and for Moscow Russian (Mołczanow, 2015). High tone plays a crucial role in deriving various East Slavic reduction patterns in the model of vowel reduction to be developed in this book. In the present work, I subscribe to the position of Halle (1997), who assumes that High tone, which is interpreted as stress phonetically, serves as a diacritic mediating between the highest grid prominence and stress assignment. In his model, the head of the word is assigned a High tone, while all other positions are supplied with low or neutral tones.

Keeping in mind that High tone in the present analysis is a theoretical construct having a diacritic status, let us note that the distribution of High tone in Russian is limited by the position of the stressed syllable, which parallels closely the behaviour of tone in the prosodic systems of languages commonly referred to as pitch-accent or tonal accent, in that in all of them the location of a H tone is fully predictable from the position of accent. There are several ways in which tone can relate to stress in systems allowing tonal contrasts only on stressed syllables. In languages such as Japanese, underlying tone supposedly does not interact with stress, whose assignment is independent of tone (Poser, 1984). Other prosodic systems show an interplay between tone and metrical system. Tone is assigned on the basis of the underlyingly accented syllables in Norwegian (Withgott and Halvorsen, 1984), while stress is predictable from the lexical tone in Golin (Hayes, 1995). The bilateral interaction between tone and stress is present in the Neo-Štokavian dialect of Serbian or Croatian, as analysed in Zec (1999), where stress sets limitations on the distribution of tone, and tone influences the structure of metrical feet.

There has been much debate in the literature as to the classification of the systems in which the location of tone is predictable from the location of accent. In general, the question is whether such systems should be identified as tonal, accentual, or both. Whereas most researchers go for the third option, the classification of such languages is often subject to much disagreement and methodological vagueness. To give one example, the prosodic system of Tokyo Japanese has been analysed using a tonal accent approach, a pitch-accent approach, and a restricted tone approach (for further discussion and references, see van der Hulst, 1999: 66). The problem lies in distinguishing stress from tone in a language which makes a distinctive use of phonetic pitch, since it is not clear whether pitch expresses phonological tone or is used as a cue to stress. As Odden (1999: 189) expresses it, 'The question is whether there is ever any hope of being able to hear a difference between tone and stress: the answer seems to be that there is not.' Despite this analytical indeterminacy, numerous attempts have been made in the literature to establish a typology based on the relationship between accent and tone (e.g., see Hyman (2006: 237)).

As noted previously, the present study assumes that tone is present in the output representation of Russian, and the question then arises whether this language should be grouped together with the stress-accent or pitch-accent languages. There are several phonetic and phonological cues pointing to the presence of stress in Russian. On the phonological side, all words in Russian contain only one prominent syllable (thus fulfilling the basic requirements of obligatoriness and culminativity), and only this syllable can support a full set of vowel contrasts. Phonetically, Russian stress is manifested by vowel duration, quality and intensity (Bondarko, 1977; Zlatoustova, 1981). According to Beckman (1986), the latter are definitional properties of a stress accent language. In contrast, pitch-accent languages, such as Serbo-Croatian or Swedish, use F_0 to mark prominent syllables (Beckman, 1986). As there are no conclusive instrumental measurements which would allow us to state that pitch rises are identified with word stress, Russian cannot be legitimately classified as a pitch-accent language.[11] To conclude, in the absence of evidence for the use of F_0 to mark word-level prominence in Russian, High tone in the present analysis is employed as a theory-internal diacritic devise.

[11] It is noteworthy though that there exists an interesting point of similarity between standard Russian and pitch accent languages, which lies in their lack of ability to licence additional degrees of stress. Levi (2005: 74) points out that 'perhaps the most important difference [between stress and pitch languages] is that PA [pitch accent] languages do not show a secondary level of prominence, whereas many stress languages do'. Interestingly, neither Russian nor Belarusian, the two East Slavic languages with phonological tone, have secondary stress, whereas a closely related Ukrainian, for which phonological tone has not been postulated in the literature, does exhibit secondary degrees of prominence (Łukaszewicz and Mołczanow, 2018 a, b; Mołczanow and Łukaszewicz, 2021). See, however, section 3.3, in which instances of secondary stress are discussed in some East Slavic dialects with lexical stress.

1.4. The interaction of tone and vowel quality in East Slavic: preview

The remainder of this book illustrates the theory of tone–vowel interaction using the data from East Slavic. I demonstrate that the constraints of the *H≤V family are active both in standard Russian, where they generate vowel reduction in immediately pretonic positions, and in East Slavic dialects, which exhibit an unusual pattern of vowel reduction, in which the quality of a reduced vowel in the pretonic position depends on the quality of the stressed vowel.[12] Such patterns, traditionally referred to as dissimilative types of reduction, are widespread in the South Russian dialect area, as well as in the Eastern Belarusian dialects and in the dialects spoken in the north-eastern part of Ukraine. In a typical case, [ə] occurs if the stressed vowel is low (see (11a) below), whereas [a] is found before high stressed vowels (11b), and, depending on a dialect, either [a] or [ə] are used before stressed mid vowels (11c). The input quality of the unstressed vowel is determined based on the alternation with the word [ˈvodɨ] 'water' (nom. pl.), in which the vowel [o] appears when stressed.

(11) a.	/voˈda/	[vəˈda]	'water' (nom. sg.)
b.	/voˈdɨ/	[vaˈdɨ]	id. (gen. sg.)
c.	/voˈdoi̯/[13]	[vaˈdoi̯]/[vəˈdoi̯]	id. (instr. sg.)

In addition, some dialects exhibit types of reduction in which dissimilation before non-low vowels is combined with assimilation before the low vowel [a]. For instance, mid vowels trigger reduction to [ə] (12c), while high and low vowels induce reduction to [a] in the preceding syllable (12a–b):

(12) a.	/voˈda/	[vaˈda]	'water' (nom. sg.)
b.	/voˈdɨ/	[vaˈdɨ]	'id.' (gen. sg.)
c.	/voˈdoi̯/	[vəˈdoi̯]	'id.' (instr. sg.)

Also, there exist dialects with dissimilative reduction which draw a distinction between back and front mid vowels. Back mid vowels are grouped together with high vowels in triggering [a]-reduction (13a), while front mid vowels and low vowels induce [i]-reduction in the pretonic syllable (13b).

---

[12] Unless indicated otherwise, data description is based on the standard sources such as Kuznecov (1960), Avanesov and Orlova (1965), Vajtovič (1968), Avanesov (1974), Kasatkin (2005), Požarickaja (2005).

[13] The word-final glide comes from the underlying high front vowel. As this issue is not relevant to the present analysis, the underlying form is shown with the final glide here and below to simplify the presentation.

(Note: the form [ˈsʲelʲskʲɪj̯] ‘village’ (adj.) demonstrates that the input vowel in the first syllable is /e/.)

(13)	a.	/sʲeˈlʲitʲ/	[sʲaˈlʲitʲ]	‘to settle’
		/sʲeˈlo/	[sʲaˈlo]	‘village’ (nom. sg.)
	b.	/sʲeˈlʲe/	[sʲiˈlʲe]	id. (dat. sg.)
		/sʲeˈla/	[sʲiˈla]	id. (gen. sg.)

Overall, there are over fifteen distinct types of dissimilative reduction described in the literature. The present analysis assumes that numerous and complex reduction patterns attested in East Slavic arise due to two major factors. First, minimal permutations between HEAD=H and the members of the *H≤V family of constraints yield basic dissimilative types of [a]-reduction and [ja]-reduction. Second, the dissimilative systems can exhibit assimilation in vowel quality, both in height and in backness, which gives rise to further patterns of vowel neutralizations.

Only the dialects exhibiting assimilation in height are called assimilative in the traditional descriptions of Russian dialects, whereas the dialects which show assimilation in backness are not considered to be assimilatory in nature. Instead, they are classified together with dissimilative patterns (*cf.* Kuznecov, 1960; Avanesov, 1974; Kasatkin, 2005; Požarickaja, 2005). Furthermore, Crosswhite (2000, 2001) argues that pretonic vocalic patterns in these dialects are not dependent on the vowel in the tonic syllable but are caused by a palatalized consonant which immediately follows the pretonic vowel. I suggest an alternative interpretation which builds on the assumption that the East Slavic dialects instantiate vowel harmony systems in which stressed syllables serve as triggers of harmony for the vocalic features [back] and [low]. The constraints driving vowel harmony work in concert with the constraints on the association of High tone with vocalic elements to generate complex neutralization patterns.

Finally, let us note that the term ‘vowel reduction’ can refer to both phonetic and phonological reduction in the literature. Phonetic reduction results from the undershoot of vocalic targets, which is dependent on speech tempo, style, prosodic and segmental context. Phonetic reduction is gradient and typically leads to the shrinkage of vocalic space, without the concomitant reduction of the number of vowel contrasts. Phonological reduction, in turn, refers to stress-dependent neutralization of the lexical distinctions which is categorical and not affected by factors such as speech rate or register. The present book is concerned with phonological reduction, and the terms ‘vowel reduction’ and ‘neutralization’ are used interchangeably to refer to categorical substitution of vocalic qualities in unstressed positions.

Chapter 2

East Slavic vowel patterns: basic generalizations

2.1 Overview

This chapter introduces the patterns of East Slavic vocalic neutralizations which are analysed in the subsequent chapters of this book. The characteristic feature of many East Slavic dialects, including standard Russian, is that they exhibit two-pattern vowel reduction. As an illustration, let us consider the alternation of vowels in stressed and unstressed syllables in the following morphologically related words.

(1) a. [ˈfon] 'phone'
  b. [faˈnolək] 'phonologist'
  c. [fənaˈlogʲɪjə] 'phonology'
  d. [fənəlaˈgʲi t͡ʃʲɪskʲɪi̯] 'phonological'

We can observe that the vowel [o] which appears in the stressed syllable in the word [ˈfon] (1a) is reduced to [a] in the immediately pretonic position in [faˈnolək] (1b) and to [ə] in [fənaˈlogʲɪjə] (1c) and [fənəlaˈgʲi t͡ʃʲɪskʲɪi̯] (1d), in which the first syllable is removed from stress by one and two syllables, respectively. Similarly, stressed [o] in [fənaˈlogʲɪjə] (1c) surfaces as [ə] in the post-tonic position in [faˈnolək] (1b). Reduction to [a] attested in pretonic positions is traditionally called 'moderate' reduction, whereas reduction to [ə] taking place in atonic (pre-pretonic and post-tonic) contexts is referred to as 'extreme' reduction.

Whereas extreme reduction does not exhibit much variation across different East Slavic dialects which distinguish two degrees of neutralization, many different patterns of moderate reduction have been described in the literature. These patterns are traditionally called non-dissimilative and dissimilative vowel reduction, depending on whether the quality of the stressed syllable influences the outcome of reduction in the preceding syllable. A typical example of a non-dissimilative reduction pattern is found in standard Russian, in which the pretonic vowel /o/ is reduced to [a] before all stressed syllables illustrated in (1) (cf. also 2a). In dissimilative reduction, the quality of the vowel in pretonic position depends on the quality of the vowel in the stressed syllable. In the majority of cases, the vowel [a] in the stressed syllable cannot be preceded by [a] in the pretonic syllable, and stressed high vowels cannot be preceded by the high vowel [i] or [ə] (cf. 2b). The two patterns are illustrated below with the gen. sg. and the nom. pl. forms of the word [ˈstol] 'table' (nom. sg.).

(2) a. *Non-dissimilative reduction*
[staˈla] – [staˈlɨ]
b. *Dissimilative reduction*
[stəˈla] – [staˈlɨ]

As pointed out by Crosswhite (2001: 65), the term 'dissimilative' is traditionally used by the Russian dialectologists without implying either a synchronic featural dissimilation or a historical development of the vocalism in these dialects. The same use of the term 'dissimilative' is adopted in the present study, where it is employed to label any pattern in which the quality of the tonic vowel affects the outcome of pretonic reduction.

In most dissimilative patterns, the low vowel [a] occurs in pretonic position before the high vowels and, depending on the quality of the preceding consonant, either [ə] or [i] is found in pretonic position if the vowel in the stressed syllable is low (cf. 2b). Three main types of dissimilative reduction can be distinguished depending on the quality of the reduced vowel appearing before mid vowels in the stressed syllable. These types, named Žizdra, Obojan', and Don patterns, are exemplified in (3) (see also Figure 2.2 at the end of this chapter). Let us note that the names refer to reduction patterns and not to dialects, as one pattern is usually attested in several dialects.

(3) *Types of dissimilative reduction*

a.	[a] before mid vowels:	[staˈlɔm]	'table' (instr. sg.)	(Žizdra)
b.	[ə] before mid vowels:	[stəˈlɔm]		(Don)
c.	[ə] before open mid vowels:	[stəˈlɔm]		(Obojan')
	[a] before close mid vowels:	[staˈlʲe]	id. (loc. sg.)	

In addition, several other patterns of reduction are reported in the literature. Among these, four types (called Ščigry, Sudža, Mosal'sk, and Dmitrov) are described under the heading 'other dissimilative reduction patterns', and five further types (Novoselki, Kidusovo, Orexovo, Kultuki, and Bel'sk) are referred to as assimilative-dissimilative types of reduction (*cf.* Avanesov,

1974; Kasatkin, 2005; among others). These patterns share one common trait: besides dissimilation, they exhibit an additional change, conditioned by the quality of the preceding consonant and the following consonant and/or vowel. To illustrate, let us compare different forms of the word [s^{j}aˈlo] 'village' in dissimilative, compound dissimilative, and the assimilative-dissimilative pattern, shown in (4) below. Let us observe that the compound dissimilative reduction in Mosal'sk (4b) is similar to the reduction in Žizdra (4a) in all contexts except before the mid front vowel [ɛ] in the stressed syllable. In Mosal'sk, [i] appears in the context in which Žizdra has [a]. In Kultuki, in turn, [a] surfaces in [s^{j}aˈla], in which the other two patterns (Žizdra and Mosal'sk) have the non-low vowel [i]. Apart from this, the reduction patterns in Mosal'sk and Kultuki are parallel. The model developed in this book builds on the idea that compound dissimilative and assimilative-dissimilative patterns illustrated in (4b) and (4c) are generated by the same ranking of constraints as in dissimilative patterns in (4a), and the differences are accounted by the presence of the harmony in backness in (4b) and the harmony in height in (4c). That is, Mosal'sk reduces the pretonic vowel to [i] in [s^{j}iˈl^{j}ɛ] because this vowel is followed by a front vowel [ɛ] in the stressed syllable. Kultuki, in turn, in addition to exhibiting harmony in backness, as in [s^{j}iˈl^{j}ɛ], also shows harmony in height in [s^{j}aˈla].

(4) *Dissimilative reduction: illustration*

a. Dissimilative (Žizdra)	b. Compound dissimilative (Mosal'sk)	c. Assimilative-dissimilative (Kultuki)	
[s^{j}aˈlu]	[s^{j}aˈlu]	[s^{j}aˈlu]	'village' dat. sg.
[s^{j}aˈlɔ]	[s^{j}aˈlɔ]	[s^{j}aˈlɔ]	id., nom. sg.
[s^{j}aˈl^{j}ɛ]	[s^{j}iˈl^{j}ɛ].	[s^{j}iˈl^{j}ɛ]	id., loc. sg.
[s^{j}iˈla]	[s^{j}iˈla]	[s^{j}aˈla]	id., gen. sg.

Furthermore, [a]-reduction is sometimes blocked in the contexts of adjacent palatalized consonants and after non-palatalized stridents, where, instead of the expected lowering, non-high vowels undergo fronting and/or raising. This can happen both in non-dissimilative and in dissimilative patterns. Different types have been attested across East Slavic dialects, including [i]-reduction, [e]-reduction, and [ja]-reduction in the C^j_ context, e.g. [r^{j}iˈka], [r^{j}eˈka], [r^{j}aˈka] 'river', moderate [ja]-reduction in the C^j_C^j and C^j_C contexts, e.g. [r^{j}iˈk^{j}i], [r^{j}aˈka]. Unlike the Mosal'sk pattern illustrated above, where the change to [i] in [s^{j}iˈl^{j}ɛ] is conditioned by the quality of the stressed vowel and not by the following palatalized consonant, these reduction patterns are not dependent on the quality of the vowel under stress, but can be straightforwardly attributed to the influence of the neighbouring palatalized consonants. Neutralization patterns found in the context of palatalized consonants in different East Slavic dialects are summarized below, with the inflected forms of the word *reka* 'river' serving as illustrations.

(5)	Context	Examples	
a.	[i]-reduction	[i]/C^j_	[r^j^i'ka]
b.	[e]-reduction	[e]/C^j_	[r^j^e'ka]
c.	[ja]-reduction	[a]/C^j_	[r^j^a'ka]
d.	moderate [ja]-reduction	[i]/C^j_C^j, [a]/C^j_C	[r^j^i'k^j^i], [r^j^a'ka]
e.	moderate [e]-reduction	[i]/C^j_C^j, [e]/C^j_C	[r^j^i'k^j^i], [r^j^e'ka]
f.	Čuxloma [ja]-reduction	[i]/C^j_C^j, [a]/C^j_$CV_{[-low]}$, [e]/C^j_$CV_{[+low]}$	[r^j^i'k^j^i], [r^j^a'ku], [r^j^e'ka]

Let us note that different types of reduction after palatalized consonants do not correspond in a one-to-one fashion to the patterns of reduction attested after non-palatalized consonants. For instance, the lowering of /o/ to [a] after non-palatalized consonants co-occurs either with the raising of the unstressed /a/ to [e] ([e]-reduction) or to [i] ([i]-reduction) after palatalized consonants in central Russian dialects. For this reason, the reduction patterns in the context of palatalized consonants and analysed separately in Chapter 7.

This chapter is organized as follows. First, I present the vocalic and consonantal inventory of East Slavic dialects (section 2.2). Next, section 2.3 describes the reduction pattern in atonic positions (extreme reduction). Section 2.4 looks at non-dissimilative reduction attested in standard Russian, which will serve as a reference point for the presentation of other reduction patterns. Dissimilative reduction types are discussed in section 2.5, followed by the descriptions of compound dissimilative and assimilative-dissimilative patterns in sections 2.6 and 2.7. The neutralization types found in the contest of palatalized consonants are depicted in section 2.8. Finally, section 2.9 summarizes and provides some road signs connecting the material presented in this chapter with the analysis developed in the remainder of the book.

2.2. Segmental inventory

Data and basic generalizations presented in this chapter come from standard descriptions of Russian phonetics, such as Jones and Ward (1923/1969), Avanesov and Ožegov (1959), Avanesov (1984), Timberlake (2004), Knjazev (2006), and others. Descriptions of dialects are based, among others, on Avanesov and Orlova (1965), Kuznecov (1973), Avanesov (1974) and Kasatkin (1989, 1999b, 2005).

2.2.1. Vowels in stressed syllables

Present-day East Slavic dialects vary in having a six-, seven, or an eight-vowel system in stressed positions (Kasatkin, 2005: 31).

(6) *East Slavic vowel systems*

(a)				(b)				(c)			
	i	ɨ	u		i	ɨ	u		i	ɨ	u
	e		o		e				e		o
	(ɛ)				ɛ		ɔ		ɛ		ɔ
		a				a				a	

A given vowel system is not an attribute of geographically-delimited areas, but can occur in any type of a dialect group (Avanesov and Orlova, 1965). The most widespread is the six-vowel system (6a) which historically developed from the eight-vowel system by merging high and low mid vowels into one vowel quality. The seven and eight-vowel systems (6b, c), referred to as archaic in traditional grammars, are less common. In most southern Russian dialects with eight-vowel system (6c), the high mid vowel /o/ can be optionally realized as [ɔ] (Savinov, 2013a). Kasatkina (2000: 98) reports that archaic systems are attested in the 10% of the texts in the corpus of recordings collected in the southern Russian dialectal area during the second half of the 20th century.

The six-vowel system shown in (6a) is found in standard Russian. The front mid vowel [ɛ], shown in parentheses, is a positional variant of the half-closed vowel [e], appearing after [t͡s], [ʃ], or [ʒ] and in word-initial position. The mid back vowel [o] has been described as falling 'between half-open and half-close but nearer to half-open than to half-close' (Jones, 1923/1969: 55). For standard Russian, it has been a well-established practice to use the IPA symbols [e] and [o] because the Russian mid vowels are tense. I will adopt this convention and transcribe the mid vowels as [e] and [o] in the dialects with six-vowel systems, which have lost the etymological distinction between [e]/[o] and [ɛ]/[ɔ]. If the symbols [ɛ]/[ɔ] are used in the descriptions of a particular system in the literature, without indication whether the system preserves the contrast between [e]/[o] and [ɛ]/[ɔ], then the original transcription will be given.

It should be noted that the high vowels [i] and [ɨ] occur in complementary distribution in standard Russian, the former is found after palatalized consonants and the latter after non-palatalized consonants. There has been a long debate in the literature whether the segments in question are different phonemes or allophones of one phoneme. I assume, after Lightner (1972), Melvold (1989), and Plapp (1996), that the underlying high unrounded /ɨ/ is a separate phoneme of Russian.

The following binary features which have been standardly used to describe Russian vowels will also be employed in the analysis of the dialectal data:

(7) *Feature specifications of Russian vowels*

	i	u	ɨ	e	o	a
high	+	+	+	−	−	−
low	−	−	−	−	−	+
back	−	+	+	−	+	+
round	−	+	−	−	+	−

2.2.2. Consonants

Russian consonants are either palatalized or velarized. In the palatalized consonants, the tongue moves forwards and its upper part is raised towards the front of the hard palate, while in the velarized segments, the tongue moves backwards and raises its dorsum at different heights towards the soft palate (Kochetov, 2002: 58–59).[14] The Russian consonantal inventory, which will serve as a reference point for the description of other dialects, is presented in (8) below. It does not include contextual variants resulting from voice assimilation; for a more detailed description, see Timberlake (2004) and Yanushevskaya and Bunčić (2015). Palatalization is shown with a superscript [ʲ], velarization is not marked. Palatalization is contrastive for most consonants except for the dental affricate [t͡s], which is non-palatalized, and the (alveo-)palatal affricate [t͡ʃʲ] and the palatal glide [j], which are always palatalized.

(8) *Russian consonantal inventory*

	bilabial	labio-dental	dental	(alveo-)palatal	velar
voiceless stop	p pʲ		t tʲ		k kʲ
voiced stop	b bʲ		d dʲ		g gʲ
voiceless affricate			t͡s	t͡ʃʲ	
voiceless fricative		f fʲ	s sʲ	ʃ ʃʲː	x xʲ
voiced fricative		v vʲ	z zʲ	ʒ	
nasal stop	m mʲ		n nʲ		
lateral			l lʲ		
trill			r rʲ		
glide				j	

[14] Palatalized consonants are also referred to as soft, and velarized consonants are also called hard, plain, or non-palatalized. For the clarity of presentation, the terms palatalized/non-palatalized are used in the present book.

2.3. Extreme reduction

The full set of vocalic contrasts presented in (6) is found only in stressed syllables.[15] Two degrees of reduction are observed in unstressed syllables in standard Russian. In immediately pretonic positions, the inventory is reduced to four vowels [i], [ɨ], [u], and [a] (moderate reduction). Extreme reduction occurs in post-tonic and not immediately pretonic positions, as shown in (9a) and (9b), respectively. In these positions, all vowels, with the exception of /u/ and /ɨ/, are centralized to [ə] after non-palatalized consonants and to a front vowel [ɪ] after palatalized consonants. The unstressed vowels [ʊ] and [ᵻ] do not lose their timbre, though they are shorter and lower than their stressed counterparts /u/ and /ɨ/.[16] (Note: 'V' stands for a vowel. In the input forms here and below, palatalization is shown before /i/ and /e/ – this is a simplification, as palatalization is predictable before front vowels. The division into morphemes is not indicated.)

(9) a. *Post-tonic positions*
V – [ə]
/vo'los/ [va'los] 'hair' (gen. pl.) – /'volos/ ['voləs] 'hair' (nom. sg.)
/go'lov/ [ga'lof] 'head' (gen. pl.) – /'nagolovu/ ['nagələvʊ] '(defeat) utterly'
/zʲer'kal/ [zʲir'kal] 'mirror' (gen. pl.) – /'zʲerkalo/ ['zʲerkələ] (nom. sg.)
/ska'zatʲ/ [ska'zatʲ] 'tell' – /'vyskazatʲ/ ['vɨskəzətʲ] 'outspeak'

b. *Not immediately pretonic positions*
V – [ə]
/'gorod/ ['gorət] 'town' – /goro'dok/ [gəra'dok] 'small town'
/'golos/ ['goləs] 'voice' (nom. sg.) – /golo'sov/ [gəla'sof] (gen. pl.)
/'parus/ ['parʊs] 'sail' (nom. sg.) – /paru'sa/ [pəru'sa] (nom. pl.)
/'maska/ ['maskə] 'mask' – /maska'rad/ [məska'rat] 'masquerade'

---

[15] In the present study, the term "accent" is employed for an abstract prosodic feature, whereas "stress" refers to the surface properties of utterances. These terms are further discussed in section 3.5, Chapter 3.

[16] The reduction of atonic /u/ and /ɨ/ is not suspended in casual speech, where both vowels neutralize to [ə] (Zemskaja, 1973).

Extreme reduction is blocked in absolute word-initial position, where /a/ and /o/ neutralize to the low vowel [a] instead of the expected schwa. Some examples are given below.[17]

(10) *odinokij* /odiˈnokʲɪ̯/ [adʲiˈnokʲɪ̯] *[ədiˈnokʲɪ̯] 'lonely'
okružat' /okruˈʒatʲ/ [akruˈʒatʲ] *[əkruˈʒatʲ] 'surround'
akvarel' /akvaˈrʲelʲ/ [akvaˈrʲelʲ] *[əkvaˈrʲelʲ] 'watercolour'
arendovat' /arʲendoˈvatʲ/ [arʲɪndaˈvatʲ] *[ərʲɪndaˈvatʲ] 'rent'

Knjazev (2006: 41) presents experimental data which demonstrates that blocking effects are found only in phrase-initial position, whereas word-initial vowels which are preceded by consonant-final words within the same phrase undergo extreme reduction.

(11) a. *ogorod* /ogoˈrod/ [agaˈrot] 'garden'
iz ogoroda /iz ogoˈroda/ [iz əgaˈrodə] 'from the garden'
vskopal ogorody /vskoˈpal ogoˈrodɨ/ [fskaˈpal əgaˈrodɨ] 'he dug gardens'
b. *Aleksandr* /alʲeˈksandr/ [alʲiˈksandr] 'Alexander'
ot Aleksandra /ot alʲeˈksandra/ [at əlʲiˈksandrə] 'from Alexander'
krax Aleksandra /ˈkrax alʲeˈksandra/ [ˈkrax əlʲiˈksandrə] 'the fall of Alexander'

In addition, the application of vowel reduction is blocked in hiatus sequences. While reduction is regular when the second member in hiatus is a high vowel, for example [nəiˈzusʲtʲ] 'by heart', [nəuˈgat] 'by guesswork', reduction to schwa does not take place in hiatus consisting of /o/ or /a/, as illustrated in (12) below. It should be noted that vowel sequences are rare in native morphemes, but they occur freely at prefix/preposition boundaries and in borrowings. Here are some examples, taken from Avanesov (1984) and Shapiro (1968).

(12) /oo/ → [aa] *voobšče* /vo+obˈšče/ [vaapˈʃʲ:e] 'generally',
sootnošenie /so+otnoˈšenʲiie/ [saatnaˈʃenʲɪ̯ə] 'ratio'
/oa/ → [aa] *poakkompaniroval* /po+akompaˈnʲiroval/ [paakəmpaˈnʲirəvəl] 'he accompanied'
/ao/ → [aa] *naobum* /na+oˈbum/ [naaˈbum] 'random'
naoborot /na+oboˈrot/ [naabaˈrot] 'conversely'
/aa/ → [aa] *zaalet* /za+aˈlʲetʲ/ [zaaˈlʲetʲ] 'grow scarlet'

---

[17] Data in (10)–(13) below are reprinted from Lingua, 163, J. Mołczanow, The Interaction of Tone and Vowel Quality in Optimality Theory: A Study of Moscow Russian Vowel Reduction, Pages No. 115–116, Copyright 2015, with permission from Elsevier.

zaaplodirovali /za+aploˈdʲirovalʲi/ [zaaplaˈdʲirəvəlʲɪ] 'they applauded'

Similarly, extreme reduction is blocked when /o/ or /a/ is preceded by /e/.[18]

(13) /eo/ → [ɪa] *ne otdam* /nʲe+otˈdam/ [nʲɪadˈdam] 'I will not give away'
neodnokratnyj /nʲe+odnoˈkratnɨi/ [nʲɪadnaˈkratnɨi̯] 'frequent'
/ea/ → [ɪa] *neakkuratnyj* /nʲe+akuˈratnɨi/ [nʲɪakuˈratnɨi̯] 'untidy'
reabilitacija /rʲeabʲiliˈtacɨia/ [rʲɪabʲɪlʲiˈtat͡sɨi̯ə] 'rehabilitation'

It should also be noted that the vowels [o] and [a] are reduced to [ə], instead of the expected [ɪ], after palatalized consonants in some grammatical endings, for example, /ˈkurʲ+at/ [ˈkurʲət] 'smoke' (3rd pers. pl.) *vs.* /ˈkurʲ+it/ [ˈkurʲɪt] 'smoke' (3rd pers. sg.), *cf.* /ˈsʲemʲdʲesʲat/ [ˈsʲemʲdʲɪsʲɪt] 'seventy'.[19]

In sum, the outcome of vowel reduction is dependent both on the prosodic as well as on the segmental context. The vowel inventory /i, ɨ, u, e, o, a/ found in stressed syllables is shrunk to the vowels [ɪ], [ɨ], [ʊ], [ə] in atonic positions (extreme reduction). In the next section, we look at the reduction patterns attested in immediately pretonic syllables (moderate reduction), in which the vocalic inventory is limited to [i], [ɨ], [u], and [a] in systems with non-dissimilative reduction.

2.4 Non-dissimilative vowel reduction

2.4.1. Reduction after non-palatalized consonants

As mentioned previously, immediately pretonic positions accommodate the inventory of four vowels [i], [ɨ], [u], and [a] (moderate reduction). The unstressed [i], [ɨ] and [u] are produced with a lower position of the tongue than their stressed counterparts. Phonetically, they are defined as high lax vowels and usually transcribed as [ɪ], [ɨ], and [ʊ], respectively (Jones, 1923/1969). In the present book, the symbols [i], [ɨ], and [u] will be used for vowels in both stressed and immediately pretonic positions, and symbols [ɪ], [ɨ], and [ʊ] will be employed for other positions.

---

[18] In informal speech, the unstressed sequence [ɪa] can be pronounced [ɪə], or further simplified to [ɪ], and sequences [aa] can be reduced to [a] (Shapiro, 1968: 24, 25). However, Avanesov (1984: 108) emphasizes that such pronunciation is non-literary and warns against it.

[19] The issues concerning morphological blocking effects will not be subject of the present investigation; see Bethin (2012) for discussion and analysis.

The quality of the reduced vowel depends on the secondary articulation of the preceding consonant. After a non-palatalized consonant or word-initially, the mid vowel /o/ is lowered and unrounded, resulting in an [a]-like sound. Traditional sources transcribe this sound as a not fully open central vowel [ʌ] (Ščerba, 1912; Jones, 1923/1969; Avanesov, 1984). However, Panov (1967) notes that 'not all speakers of literary Russian employ this pronunciation, the majority pronounce [a] instead of [ʌ].'[20] Kasatkina (2005) further reports that the pronunciation of a 'compressed' sound [ʌ] is characteristic of the standard Russian spoken in the areas, in which local dialects lack vowel reduction, such as northern Russian regions, Ural, Siberia, and Ukraine. In Moscow and surroundings, as well as areas in which local dialects neutralize the distinction between /o/ and /a/ in an unstressed syllable, a fully open sound [a] in immediately pretonic positions does not differ in quality from its stressed counterpart (see also Vysotskij, 1984: 35). Following Vysotskij (1984), Kasatkina (2005), and others, the outcome of the /o/ – /a/ neutralization in the pretonic syllable is transcribed with the symbol [a] in the present book. This process is illustrated in (14).

(14) [o]–[a]

/ˈkot/ [ˈkot] 'cat' (nom. sg.) – /koˈta/ [kaˈta] (gen. sg.)
/ˈstol/ [ˈstol] 'table' (nom. sg.) – /stoˈla/ [staˈla] (gen. sg.)
/ˈbok/ [ˈbok] 'side' (nom. sg.) – /boˈka/ [baˈka] (nom. pl.)
/ˈzorʲi/ [ˈzorʲɪ] 'dawn' (nom. pl.) – /zoˈrʲa/ [zaˈrʲa] (nom. sg.)
/koˈrolʲ/ [kaˈrolʲ] 'king' (nom. sg.) – /koroˈlʲa/ [kəraˈlʲa] (gen. sg.)

2.4.2. Reduction after palatalized consonants

Distinct types of reduction are attested in the context after palatalized consonants, where [a]-reduction is blocked in a number of East Slavic dialects. There are two ways in which palatalized consonants can affect the outcome of vowel reduction in pretonic positions. First, non-high back vowels /a/ and /ɔ/ front to [e] after palatalized consonants in the central Russian dialects. Second, vowel fronting can be accompanied by the raising to [i] in many dialects, including the standard variety of Russian (Avanesov and Orlova, 1965; Avanesov, 1984; Kasatkin, 2005). These processes, traditionally referred to as *ekan'e* ([e]-reduction) and *ikan'e* ([i]-reduction) in the literature, are schematically shown in (15).

[20] Cited after Kasatkina (2005: 31), translation is mine.

(15) a. [i]-reduction: e, a, o → i $/C^{j}\_{[\text{-stress}]}$
b. [e]-reduction: a, o → e $/C^{j}\_{[\text{-stress}]}$

As mentioned above, the vowels [a], [e] and [o] are neutralized to [i] in immediately pretonic positions in the Contemporary Standard Russian (Avanesov, 1974; Kasatkin, 2005). The illustrative data are presented below.

(16) *[i]-reduction*
a. [a] – [i]
/ˈsvʲazʲ/ [ˈsvʲasʲ] ‘connection’ – /svʲaˈzatʲ/ [svʲiˈzatʲ] ‘connect’
/xoˈmʲak/ [xaˈmʲak] ‘hamster’ (nom. sg.) – /xomʲaˈka/ [xəmʲiˈka] id. (gen. sg.)
/ˈt͡ʃʲai̯/ [ˈt͡ʃʲai̯] ‘tea’ (nom. sg.) – /t͡ʃʲaˈi/ [t͡ʃʲiˈi] id. (nom. pl.)
/oˈt͡ʃʲag/ [aˈt͡ʃʲak] ‘hearth’ (nom. sg.) – /ot͡ʃʲaˈga/ [at͡ʃʲiˈga] id. (gen. sg.)
/moˈrʲak/ [maˈrʲak] ‘sailor’ (nom. sg.) – /morʲaˈt͡ʃʲok/ [mərʲiˈt͡ʃʲok] id. (dim.)
b. [e] – [i]
/ˈdʲel/ [ˈdʲel] ‘business’ (gen. pl.) – /dʲeˈla/ [dʲiˈla] id. (nom. pl.)
/mʲesto/ [ˈmʲestə] ‘place’ (nom. sg.) – /mʲeˈsta/ [mʲiˈsta] id. (nom. pl.)
/ˈzʲemlʲi/ [ˈzʲemlʲɪ] ‘earth’ (nom. pl.) – /zʲeˈmlʲa/ [zʲiˈmlʲa] id. (nom. sg.)
/ˈlʲes/ [ˈlʲes] ‘forest’ (nom. sg.) – /lʲeˈsa/ [lʲiˈsa] id. (nom. pl.)
/ˈbʲel/ [ˈbʲel] ‘white’ (short form) – /bʲeˈlʲitʲ/ [bʲiˈlʲitʲ] ‘to whitewash’
c. [ɔ] – [i][21]
/ˈnʲes/ [ˈnʲos] ‘carry’ (past. masc. sg.) – /nʲeˈsʲi/ [nʲiˈsʲi] id. (imp.)
/ˈmʲed/ [ˈmʲot] ‘honey’ (noun) – /mʲeˈdovɨi̯/ [mʲiˈdovɨi̯] id. (adj.)
/koˈtʲel/ [kaˈtʲol] ‘pot’ – /kotʲeˈlok/ [kətʲiˈlok] id. (dim.)
/koˈlʲesa/ [kaˈlʲosə] ‘wheel’ (nom. pl.) – /kolʲeˈso/ [kəlʲiˈso] id. (nom. sg.)
/ˈt͡ʃʲernɨi̯/ [ˈt͡ʃʲornɨi̯] ‘black’ – /t͡ʃʲerˈnʲitʲ/ [t͡ʃʲirˈnʲitʲ] ‘to blacken’

[21] Historically, [o] in the stressed syllable derives from a process which turned stressed *e* into *o* before a non-palatalized consonant. As there are many [o]–[e] alternations in stressed syllables (*cf.* [ˈsʲol] ‘village’ (gen. pl.) – [ˈsʲelʲskʲɪi̯] ‘village’ (adj.)), I show /e/ in the input forms. However, it should be borne in mind that it is an open question whether the present-day alternations are to be analysed in terms of allomorphy or derived synchronically. See also discussion in section 7.4.3 in Chapter 7.

Some dialects in the northern and the central Russian dialectal area exhibit reduction patterns in which unstressed non-high vowels are neutralized into [e] when preceded by palatalized consonants. This pattern is historically older than the [i]-reduction found in the Contemporary Standard Russian and has been considered the literary norm until the first half of the 20th century (Avanesov, 1974; Kasatkin, 2005). Some examples illustrating vocalic alternations in dialects with [e]-reduction are presented below.

(17) *[e]-reduction*

a. [a] – [e]

/ˈzʲatʲ/ [ˈzʲatʲ] 'son-in-law' (nom. sg.) – /zʲaˈtʲja/ [zʲeˈtʲja] id. (nom. pl.)
/ˈpʲatka/ [ˈpʲatkə] 'heel' (dim. form) – /pʲaˈta/ [pʲeˈta] id. (nom. sg.)
/ˈt͡ʃʲas/ [ˈt͡ʃʲas] 'hour' (nom. sg.) – /t͡ʃʲaˈsa/ [t͡ʃʲeˈsa] id. (gen. sg.)
/ˈrʲad/ [ˈrʲat] 'row' (nom. sg.) – /rʲaˈda/ [rʲeˈda] id. (gen. sg.)
/ˈmʲaso/ [ˈmʲasə] 'meat' (noun) – /mʲaˈsnʲik/ [mʲeˈsnʲik] 'butcher'

b. [o] – [e][22]

/ˈsʲel/ [ˈsʲol] 'village' (gen. pl.) – /sʲeˈla/ [sʲeˈla] id. (gen. sg.)
/ˈsʲestrɨ/ [ˈsʲostrɨ] 'sister' (nom. pl.) – /sʲeˈstra/ [sʲeˈstra] id. (nom. sg.)
/ˈmʲetlɨ/ [ˈmʲotlɨ] 'sweep' (nom. pl.) – /mʲeˈtla/ [mʲeˈtla] id. (nom. sg.)
/ˈvʲesnɨ/ [ˈvʲosnɨ] 'spring' (nom. pl.) – /vʲeˈsna/ [vʲeˈsna] id. (nom. sg.)
/ˈrʲov/ [ˈrʲof] 'roar' – /rʲeˈvʲetʲ/ [rʲeˈvʲetʲ] 'to roar'

As shown above, only back vowels *a* and *o* reduce, whereas immediately pretonic *e* and *i* remain intact, as illustrated by the minimal pairs such as [lʲeˈsa] 'forest' (nom. pl.) – [lʲiˈsa] 'vixen', [mʲeˈla] 'sweep' (past. fem. sg.) – [mʲiˈla] 'kind' (fem. short form) (Avanesov, 1974: 159).

2.5. Dissimilative vowel reduction

This section describes patterns of dissimilative reduction, in which the quality of the reduced syllable depends on the quality of the vowel in the tonic syllable. Three main types of dissimilative [a]-reduction and [ja]-reduction have been described in the literature, named Žizdra, Obojan', and Don patterns; reduction after non-palatalized consonants is referred to as

22 See fn. 21 above.

dissimilative [a]-reduction (*akanie*), while reduction after palatalized consonants is traditionally called dissimilative [ja]-reduction (*yakanie*). The dialects are often spoken in different geographical areas and differ with respect to other phonological, grammatical, and semantic features. Archaic (Obojan'/Zadon) patterns have been attested in Kursk, Belgorod, Voronež, Tula, and Kaluga regions (see Figure 2.1). Žizdra, which is the most common pattern, is widespread in the north-eastern Belarus as well as in the western and eastern regions of the southern Russian dialect area (Brjansk, Tula,

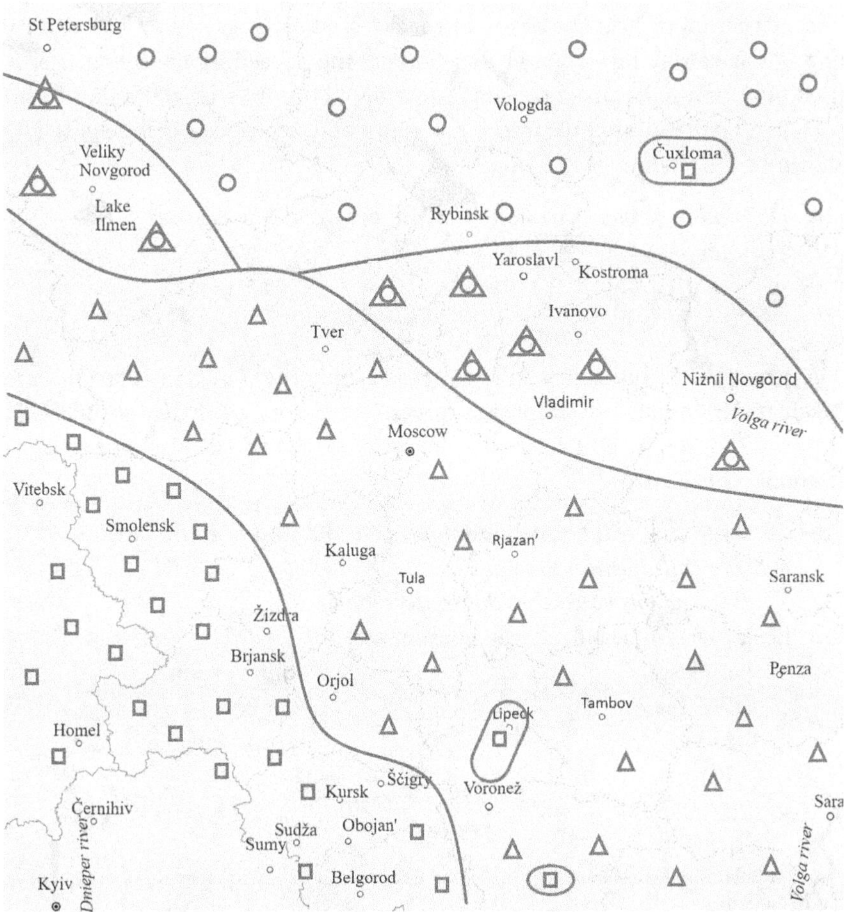

Figure 2.1: Reduction patterns (based on Kasatkin, 2005: 38).
○ No reduction
□ Dissimilative reduction
△ Non-dissimilative reduction
△ Incomplete okan'e (reduction only in positions which are not pretonic)

Rjazan', Voronež, Tambov regions) (Kasatkina, 2000; Požarickaja, 2005). The Don type is attested in isolated dialects spoken in the basin of the river Don. This type is commonly found after palatalized consonants, whereas a parallel dissimilative [a]-reduction pattern is rare after non-palatalized consonants. In fact, it has been considered unattested and dubbed theoretical in dialectology textbooks (Avanesov, 1974). However, Kasatkina (2000) presents recent fieldwork data which show this type to be present in dialects spoken in Belgorod, Lipeck, Voronež, and Kaluga regions.

All dissimilative patterns use the low vowel [a] in pretonic positions before the high vowels and, depending on the quality of the preceding consonant, either [ə] or [i] if the vowel in the stressed syllable is low. The quality of the non-low reduced vowel depends on the preceding consonant: [ə] is used after non-palatalized consonants, while [i] occurs after palatalized consonants. The reduction pattern before high and low vowels is schematically shown in (18) below.

(18) *Dissimilative vowel reduction before high and low vowels*

pretonic	tonic
a	i ɨ u
ə/i[23]	a

The reduction before high and low vowels is illustrated in (19). The data are taken from standard descriptive sources (Avanesov, 1974; Kasatkin, 2005; Požarickaja, 2005), and from the acoustic corpus of the Russian dialects (Sappok *et al.*, 2016).[24]

(19) *Dissimilative reduction before high and low vowels in the tonic syllable (all dissimilative patterns)*

a. *Before high vowels in the tonic syllable*

i. [a] after non-palatalized consonants

[va'dʲit͡sə]	'water' (dim.)
[gəva'rʲitʲ]	'say'
[tra'vɨ]	'grass' (gen. sg.)

[23] After palatalized consonants, [e] instead of [i] is used in the Zadon pattern of dissimilative [ja]-reduction.

[24] The descriptions of individual dialects found in the literature are often fragmentary, and it is not always possible to find the alternating forms which would allow to determine the segmental structure of the inputs. Therefore, only output forms are shown in the presentation of the dialectal data here and below.

[saˈvɨ] ‘owl’ (gen. sg.)
[paˈpu] ‘priest’ (dat. sg.)
[saˈʒu] ‘sit’ (1st pers. sg.)

ii. [a] after palatalized consonants
[bʲaˈlʲitʲ] ‘whiten’
[pəɣlʲaˈdi] ‘look’ (imp.)
[t͡svʲaˈtɨ] ‘flowers’
[rʲaˈbɨx] ‘pockmarked’ (gen. sg.)
[tʲaˈnu] ‘pull’ (1st pers. sg.)
[sʲmʲaˈjut͡sːə] ‘laugh’ (3rd pers. pl.)

b. *Before low vowels in the tonic syllable*

i. [ə] after non-palatalized consonants
[skəˈzal] ‘say’ (past 3rd pers. sg.)
[stəˈkan] ‘a glass’
[təˈtarʲɪn] ‘Tatar’
[vəˈda] ‘water’
[trəˈva] ‘grass’

ii. [i] after palatalized consonants
[nʲiˈsla] ‘carry’ (fem. past)
[bʲiˈda] ‘hardship’
[prʲiˈmajə] ‘straight’ (fem.)
[mʲiˈnʲatʲ] ‘change’
[ɣlʲiˈdʲat] ‘look’ (3rd pers. pl.)
[zʲiˈmlʲa] ‘earth’
[sʲiˈla] ‘village’ (gen. sg.)
[sʲiˈstra] ‘sister’
[sʲiˈdai̯ə] ‘grey-haired’ (fem.)
[rʲaˈbai̯ə] ‘pockmarked’ (fem.)
[vʲiˈlʲat] ‘order’ (3rd pers. pl.)

The difference between Žizdra, Obojan', and Don patterns consists in their treatment of mid vowels. In Žizdra, mid vowels behave similarly to high vowels, while in Don, mid vowels group together with low vowels. In Obojan', half-close mid vowels pattern with high vowels and half-open vowels with low vowels (see examples in (20) below). Žizdra and Don types are more common in dialects with five vowels, whereas Obojan' and Zadon patterns are usually attested in seven-vowel systems. Obojan' and Zadon are called archaic because they preserve the distinction between high mid and low mid vowels. Archaic types of dissimilation have been first described at the beginning of the twentieth century by Vasiljev (1904) and Durnovo (1917). Savinov (2013) reports that the results of the fieldwork conducted in 1999–2010 demonstrate that this type of dissimilation is still active in southern Russian dialects, affecting both native vocabulary as well as recent borrowings.

It should be noted that Žizdra and Don patterns are also attested in eight- and seven vowel systems, and the archaic patterns are often found in systems distinguishing five vowels under stress. In the latter, the prevocalic contrast [ə]–[a] is preserved before etymological high and low mid vowels despite the absence of any phonetic distinction (*cf.* Knjazev, 2000: 82–83). To simplify the presentation of the relevant facts, I abstract away from these variations and consider only those dialects which exhibit archaic reduction patterns in the presence of the surface contrast between [ɛ], [ɔ], and [e], [o]. The illustrative data are provided in (20) below.

(20) *Dissimilative reduction before mid vowels in the tonic syllable (Žizdra, Obojan', Don)*

a. *Žizdra: [a] after non-palatalized and palatalized consonants*

[a]

[vaˈdɔj̯]	'water' (instr. sg.)
[saˈvʲɔnʲɨʃ]	'owl' (dim.)
[daˈjɔt]	'give' (3rd pers. sg.)
[traˈvʲɛ]	'grass' (dat. sg.)
[sʲaˈlɔ]	'village' (nom. sg.)
[sʲaˈstrɔj̯]	'sister' (instr. sg.)
[ɣlʲaˈdʲɛl]	'look' (masc. past)
[lʲaˈsɔk]	'forest' (dim.)

b. *Don: [ə] after non-palatalized and [i] after palatalized consonants*

[ə]

[nəˈgʲɛ]	'leg' (dat. sg.)
[pəˈpɔm]	'priest' (instr. sg.)
[təˈkɔj̯]	'such' (masc. nom. sg.)
[vəˈrʲɔnɨj̯]	'cooked' (masc. nom. sg.)

[i]

[rʲiˈkɔj̯]	'river' (instr. sg.)
[slʲiˈpɔvə]	'blind' (masc. gen. sg.)
[slʲiˈpɔj̯]	'blind' (masc. nom. sg.)
[sʲtʲiˈnʲɛ]	'wall' (loc. sg.)
[zʲirˈnɔm]	'grain' (instr. sg.)
[vʲiˈsʲɔləj̯]	'merry' (masc. nom. sg.)

c. *Obojan': [a] before high mid vowels; [ə] after non-palatalized and [i] after palatalized consonants before low mid vowels;*

[a]

[sa'voi̯] ‘owl' (instr. sg.)
[na'gʲe] ‘leg' (dat. sg.)
[pʲat'no] ‘spot'
[rʲa'bovə] ‘pockmarked' (masc. gen. sg.)
[vʲa'lʲel] ‘order' (masc. past)

[ə]

[kə'nʲɔm] ‘horse' (instr. sg.)
[pə'jɔʃ] ‘sing' (2nd pers. sg.)
[də'jɔt] ‘give' (3rd pers. sg.)

[i]

[rʲi'bɔi̯] ‘pockmarked' (masc. nom. sg.)
[dʲi'rʲɛvnʲə] ‘village' (loc. sg.)
[nəprʲi'dʲɔm] ‘spin' (1st pl. future)

It should be emphasized that the patterns of vowel neutralizations described above are fully productive. For one thing, pretonic vowels participate in alternations in morphologically related forms, *cf.* ['travɨ] ‘grass' (nom. pl.) – [trə'va] id. (nom. sg.) – [tra'vɨ] id. (gen. sg.). Furthermore, recent borrowings undergo pretonic reduction on a par with native words, e.g. *koncert* [kən't͡sɛrt] ‘concert', *vagon* [və'gɔn] ‘wagon' in the Don pattern of reduction (Kasatkina, 2000: 101). Similarly, Vajtovič (1968: 58) reports that loanwords are subject to the same neutralization processes as native words in Žizdra, for instance *gektar* [ɣʲik'tar] ‘hectare', *materjal* [mat͡sʲi'rjal] ‘material', *sezon* [sʲa'zɔn] ‘season', *interes* [int͡sʲa'rɛs] ‘interest'. Schematically, the patterns of dissimilative vowel reduction are represented in (21) below.

(21) *Types of dissimilative vowel reduction*

i. After non-palatalized consonants

a. Žizdra

pretonic	tonic
a	i ɨ u
	ɛ ɔ
ə	a

b. Don

pretonic	tonic
a	i ɨ u
ə	ɛ ɔ
	a

c. Obojan'

pretonic	tonic
a	i ɨ u
	e o
ə	ɛ ɔ
	a

ii. After palatalized consonants

a. Žizdra

pretonic	tonic
a	i ɨ u
	ɛ ɔ
i	a

b. Don

pretonic	tonic
a	i ɨ u
i	ɛ ɔ
	a

c. Obojan'/Zadon

pretonic	tonic
a	i ɨ u
	e o
i/e	ɛ ɔ
	a

In prosodically weak positions not immediately preceding the tonic syllable, non-high vowels usually reduce to [ə] or [ɨ] after non-palatalized consonants and to the front vowel [ɪ] after palatalized consonants. South-western dialects bordering with Ukrainian and Belarusian often use [a] after non-palatalized consonants in atonic positions. There are also indications in the literature that at least in some dialects, non-high vowels in positions immediately following the tonic vowel evince the same dissimilation pattern as in pretonic positions: [a] is found after non-low stressed vowels and [ə] is attested after the low vowel [a] (Avanesov and Orlova, 1965: 68; Kasatkin, 2005: 53). Curiously, all the examples provided in the literature are stressed on the initial syllable, e.g. ['xutarʲi] 'hamlet' (loc. sg.), ['stɔranu] 'side' (acc. sg.), *vs.* ['starəmu] 'old' (dat. sg.), ['jablət͡ʃʲkə] 'apple' (gen. sg. dim.), and it is unclear what vowel patterns are found in words with the tonic syllable in non-initial position.

2.6. Compound dissimilative vowel reduction

The dissimilative systems discussed above are characterized by a reduction pattern in which [a] occurs before non-high vowels in Žizdra, before high vowels in Don, and before high and high mid vowels in Obojan'. Additional patterns of dissimilative reduction, first recorded in Ščigry, Sudža, Mosal'sk, and Dmitrov, also use [a] before high vowels and [i] before back vowels. They are different from dissimilative patterns described so far in the quality of pretonic vowels before front mid vowels in stressed syllables: [i] appears instead of [a] either before [ɛ] (Ščigry), or before [ɛ] and [e] (Sudža, Mosal'sk, and Dmitrov). In what follows, Ščigry, Sudža, Mosal'sk, and Dmitrov will be called compound dissimilative patterns for ease of reference.[25]

The Ščigry pattern is attested in the same area as the Obojan' pattern (Kursk, Belgorod, and Voronež regions) (Požarickaja, 2005: 64). The Dmitrov type has been reported to occur in the Kursk and Belgorod regions

25 I owe this descriptor to Crosswhite (2001).

(Avanesov, 1974: 152). The Sudža type is commonly found in the large part of the Southern dialect area to the east of Brjansk and to the north of Belgorod, in the southern part of the Orel region, in most of the territory in the Kursk region, and in the south-eastern Belarus (the Homel' region) (Vajtovič, 1968: 63; Požarickaja, 2005: 65). The Mosal'sk type is widespread in the eastern group of the southern Russian dialect area (Kaluga region) and in the north-eastern parts of Belarus (the Vitebsk region) (Avanesov, 1974: 152; Vajtovič, 1968: 58ff.).[26] Some examples illustrating the reduction before mid vowels in the four patterns are provided below.

(22) *Compound dissimilative pattern: Reduction before mid vowels in the tonic syllable*

Ščigry	*Dmitrov*	*Sudža*	*Mosal'sk*	*Gloss*
a. Before etymological /o/ in the tonic syllable				
[sʲaˈlo]	[sʲaˈlo]	[sʲaˈlɔ]	[sʲaˈlɔ]	'village' (nom. sg.)
[sʲaˈstroi̯]	[sʲaˈstroi̯]	[sʲaˈstrɔi̯]	[sʲaˈstrɔi̯]	'sister' (instr. sg.)
[rʲaˈkoi̯]	[rʲaˈkoi̯]	[rʲaˈkɔi̯]	[rʲaˈkɔi̯]	'river' (instr. sg.)
[slʲaˈpovə]	[slʲaˈpovə]	[slʲaˈpɔvə]	[slʲaˈpɔvə]	'blind' (masc. gen. sg.)
[pʲatˈno]	[pʲatˈno]	[pʲatˈnɔ]	[pʲatˈnɔ]	'spot'
[rʲaˈbovə]	[rʲaˈbovə]	[rʲaˈbɔvə]	[rʲaˈbɔvə]	'pockmarked'
b. Before etymological /e/ in the tonic syllable				
[sʲaˈlʲe]	[sʲiˈlʲe]	[sʲiˈlʲɛ]	[sʲiˈlʲɛ]	'village' (loc. sg.)
[vʲaˈlʲel]	[vʲiˈlʲel]	[vʲiˈlʲɛl]	[vʲiˈlʲɛl]	'order' (masc. past)
[sʲtʲaˈnʲe]	[sʲtʲiˈnʲe]	[sʲtʲiˈnʲɛ]	[sʲtʲiˈnʲɛ]	'wall' (loc. sg.)
[ɣlʲaˈdʲel]	[ɣlʲiˈdʲel]	[ɣlʲiˈdʲɛl]	[ɣlʲiˈdʲɛl]	'look' (masc. past)
c. Before etymological /ɔ/ in the tonic syllable				
[sʲaˈlɔm]	[sʲiˈlɔm]	[sʲaˈlɔm]	[sʲaˈlɔm]	'village' (instr. sg.)
[zʲarˈnɔm]	[zʲirˈnɔm]	[zʲarˈnɔm]	[zʲarˈnɔm]	'grain' (instr. sg.)
[slʲaˈpɔi̯]	[slʲiˈpɔi̯]	[slʲaˈpɔi̯]	[slʲaˈpɔi̯]	'blind' (masc. nom. sg.)
[lʲaˈsɔk]	[lʲiˈsɔk]	[lʲaˈsɔk]	[lʲaˈsɔk]	'forest' (dim.)
[pʲatˈnɔm]	[pʲitˈnɔm]	[pʲatˈnɔm]	[pʲatˈnɔm]	'spot' (instr. sg.)
[rʲaˈbɔi̯]	[rʲiˈbɔi̯]	[rʲaˈbɔi̯]	[rʲaˈbɔi̯]	'pockmarked'
d. Before etymological /ɛ/ in the tonic syllable				
[dʲiˈrʲɛvnʲə]	[dʲiˈrʲɛvnʲə]	[dʲiˈrʲɛvnʲə]	[dʲiˈrʲɛvnʲə]	'village' (loc. sg.)
[vʲiˈsʲɔləi̯]	[vʲiˈsʲɔləi̯]	[vʲiˈsʲɔləi̯]	[vʲaˈsʲɔləi̯]	'merry'
[nʲiˈsʲɔm]	[nʲiˈsʲɔm]	[nʲiˈsʲɔm]	[nʲaˈsʲɔm]	'carry' (1st pl. pres.)
[nəprʲiˈdʲɔm]	[nəprʲiˈdʲɔm]	[nəprʲiˈdʲɔm]	[nəprʲaˈdʲɔm]	'spin' (1st pl. future)

[26] Vajtovič (1968) calls this pattern the Vitebsk type of dissimilative [ja]-reduction.

The four patterns are schematically represented in (23). The mechanism at work in the four systems (compound dissimilative patterns) is the same as the one operating in dissimilative reduction: [a] is pronounced in the pretonic syllable if the stressed syllable contains high vowels and [i] is found before a low vowel in the next syllable in all these dialects. As to the mid vowels in stressed positions, a distinction is drawn between back and front vowels, as illustrated by the examples in (22). The vowel [a] is found before both back mid vowels [o] and [ɔ] in Ščigry, Sudža, and Mosal'sk. In Dmitrov, half-close [o] is preceded by [a], whereas half-open [ɔ] induces reduction to [i]. Sudža and Mosal'sk differ in terms of their treatment of the stressed [ɔ] after palatalized consonants, which originally comes from /ɛ/. In Mosal'sk, [a] is found before both the underlying and derived [ɔ], while in Sudža, like in Ščigry, [a] is pronounced before the underlying [ɔ], and [i] is pronounced before [ɔ] which comes from /ɛ/.

(23) *Compound dissimilative vowel reduction after palatalized consonants*

a. Ščigry

pretonic	tonic		
a	i	ɨ	u
	e		o
i	ɛ, ɔ (> ɛ)		ɔ
			a

b. Dmitrov

pretonic	tonic	
a	i ɨ	u
	e	o
i	ɛ	ɔ
		a

c. Sudža

pretonic	tonic	
a	i ɨ	u
i	ɛ, ɔ (> ɛ)	ɔ
		a

d. Mosal'sk

pretonic	tonic	
a	i ɨ	u
i	ɛ	ɔ
		a

2.7. Assimilative-dissimilative vowel reduction

Traditional grammars describe several other patterns of reduction, collectively referred to as assimilative-dissimilative [ja]-reduction (Kuznecov, 1960; Avanesov, 1974; Kasatkin, 2005; Požarickaja, 2005; and others). These types are attested in the eastern part of the southern Russian dialect area (the regions of Rjazan', Lipeck, Voronež, Volgograd), in the central Russian dialect area (the south-western parts of the Tver' region), as well as in the northern area (Pskov region) (Čekmonas, 1999; Požarickaja, 2005; Paschen, 2015). These dialects show reduction to [a] if the following tonic syllable contains high and low vowels. Before mid vowels, either [i] or [a] is attested, depending on a dialect. The data illustrating assimilative-dissimilative reduction patterns provided in (24) come from Avanesov (1974: 157), Kuznecov (1960: 64) and Kasatkin (2005: 47).

(24) i. *Reduction to [a] before <u>high</u> and <u>low</u> vowels in the tonic syllable (all dialects)*

a. *Before high vowels in the tonic syllable*

[nʲa'su]	'carry' (1st pers. sg.)
[lʲa'tʲit]	'fly' (3rd pers. sg.)
[sʲa'lu]	'village' (dat. sg.)
[sʲa'lʲi͡ts:ə]	'to settle'
[͡tsvʲa'tɨ]	'flowers'

b. *Before <u>low</u> vowels in the tonic syllable*

[nʲa'sla]	'carry' (fem. past)
[bʲa'da]	'hardship'
[sʲa'la]	'village' (gen. sg.)
[mʲa'nʲatʲ]	'change'
[zʲa'tʲja]	'sons-in-law'

ii. *Reduction to [a]/[i] before <u>mid</u> vowels in the tonic syllable*

Stressed vowels	[e]	[ε]	[ɔ] (>ε)	[ɔ]	[o]
Novoselki	[sʲa'lʲe]	[sʲi'lʲεnʲɪ̯]	[sʲi'lʲɔtkə]	[sʲa'lɔm]	[sʲa'lo]
Orexovo	[sʲa'lʲe]	[sʲi'lʲεnʲɪ̯]	[sʲa'lʲɔtkə]	[sʲa'lɔm]	[sʲa'lo]
Kidusovo	[sʲi'lʲε]	[sʲi'lʲεnʲɪ̯]	[sʲi'lʲɔtkə]	[sʲa'lɔm]	[sʲa'lɔ]
Kultuki	[sʲi'lʲε]	[sʲi'lʲεnʲɪ̯]	[sʲa'lʲɔtkə]	[sʲa'lɔm]	[sʲa'lɔ]
Bel'sk	[sʲi'lʲε]	[sʲi'lʲεnʲɪ̯]	[sʲi'lʲɔtkə]	[sʲi'lɔm]	[sʲi'lɔ]
	'village' (loc. sg.)	'settlement' (gen. pl.)	'herring'	'village' (instr. sg.)	'village' (nom. sg.)

The distribution of pretonic vowels in different dialects with assimilative-dissimilative reduction is schematized in (25) below.

(25) *Dissimilative patterns after palatalized consonants*

a. Novoselki

pretonic	tonic		
a	i	ɨ	u
	e		o
i	ε, ɔ (> ε)		ɔ
a			a

b. Orexovo

pretonic	tonic		
a	i	ɨ	u
	e		o
i	ε		ɔ, ɔ (> ε)
a			a

c. Kidusovo

pretonic	tonic		
a	i	ɨ	u
i	ɛ, ɔ (> ɛ)		ɔ
a			a

d. Kultuki

pretonic	tonic		
a	i	ɨ	u
i	ɛ		ɔ, ɔ (> ɛ)
a			a

e. Bel'sk

	tonic		
a	i	ɨ	u
i	ɛ		ɔ
a			a

Traditionally, Novoselki is assumed to be based on Ščigry, Kidusovo on Sudža, Kultuki on Mosal'sk, and Bel'sk on Don (Avanesov, 1974; Kasatkin, 2005). Orexovo derives from the type of dissimilation not attested among East Slavic dialects. It is similar to Novoselki, differing from the latter only in the treatment of the stressed [ɔ], which originally comes from *ɛ*, after palatalized consonants. In Orexovo, [a] is found before both underlying and derived *ɔ*, while in Novoselki, [a] is pronounced before the underlying /ɔ/ and [i] is pronounced before [ɔ] which comes from /ɛ/. The same feature differentiates Kidusovo from Kultuki: [a] is attested before both the underlying and the derived *ɔ* in Kultuki, while in Kidusovo, [a] is pronounced before the underlying /ɔ/ and [i] is pronounced before [ɔ] which is derived from /ɛ/. The Novoselki and Orexovo patterns are usually attested in seven-vowel systems distinguishing low and high mid vowels, whereas the remaining patterns are reported in systems supporting five contrastive vowel qualities (Savinov, 2013a: 318–319).

Until recently, assimilative-dissimilative types of reduction have been reported to occur only in the context of palatalized consonants in the dialectological literature (cf. Stroganova, 1955; Avanesov, 1974; Kuznecov, 1960). However, Kasatkina and Ščigel' (1995) provide data from the dialects spoken in the southern Russian dialectal area, in which the Obojan' pattern of dissimilative [a]-reduction co-exists with assimilative reduction. These systems use [ə] before low mid vowels and [a] before high, high mid, and low vowels, as shown in (26).

(26) *Assimilative-dissimilative reduction after non-palatalized consonants*

pretonic	tonic		
aː	i	ɨ	u
	e		o
ə	ɛ		ɔ
a		a	

This pattern is illustrated by the data in (27) below (Kasatkin, 2005: 40).

(27) a. [traːˈvɨ] ‘grass’ (gen. sg.)
[traːˈvu] id. (acc. sg.)
[saːˈvʲe] ‘owl’ (dat. sg.)
[saːˈvoi̯] id. (instr. sg.)
b. [traˈva] ‘grass’ (nom. sg.)
[saˈva] ‘owl’ (nom. sg.)
[vaˈda] ‘water’ (nom. sg.)
c. [ləmˈtʲɛi̯] ‘slice’ (gen. pl.)
[ləpˈtʲɛi̯] ‘bast shoe’ (gen. pl.)
[nəˈsɔk] ‘sock’
[pləˈtɔk] ‘handkerchief’

Interestingly, the vowel [a] is lengthened if the vowel in the stressed syllable is either high or high mid (27a), but not if it is low (27b). The use of [ə] before low mid vowels, e.g. *lomtej* [ləmˈtʲɛi̯] ‘slice’ (gen. pl.), but not before high mid vowels, as in *sove* [saːˈvʲe] ‘owl’ (dat. sg.), indicates that this pattern instantiates the archaic Obojan’-like system of neutralization.

2.8. Dissimilative reduction in C^jVC^j contexts

There are dialects within the southern Russian and the eastern parts of the central Russian dialectal area (Tula, Penza, Tambov and Marij-El regions) with a mixed type of vowel reduction: non-high vowels neutralize to [a] before non-palatalized consonants and to [i] or [e] before palatalized consonants (e.g., Kasatkin, 2005: 43; Požarickaja, 2005: 59). This pattern, referred to as moderate *yakan’e* ([ja]-reduction) in the traditional literature, is attested in the context of preceding palatalized consonants in systems which exhibit [a]-reduction after non-palatalized consonants. Thus, neutralization of the immediately pretonic non-high vowels in [a] is the predominant pattern in dialects with moderate [ja]-reduction, and the reduction to [i]/[e] is a contextually conditioned process, triggered by the presence of a palatalized consonant in the onset of the following stressed syllable. The illustrative data is provided below.

(28) *Moderate [ja]-reduction*
a. *Tonic vowel*
[ˈnʲos] ‘carry’ (masc. past)
[ˈlʲes] ‘forest’
[ˈpʲatʲ] ‘five’
[ˈrʲek] ‘river’ (gen. pl.)

[ˈprʲal]	‘spin’ (masc. past)
[ˈvzglʲat][27]	‘a look’

b. *Pretonic [a] before a non-palatalized consonant*

[nʲaˈsla]	‘carry’ (fem. past)
[lʲaˈsu]	‘forest’ (loc. sg.)
[pʲaˈtak]	‘five-rouble note’
[rʲaˈka]	‘river’ (nom. sg.)
[prʲaˈla]	‘spin’ (fem. past)
[glʲaˈʒu]	‘look’ (1st pers. sg. pres.)

c. *Pretonic [i]/[e] before a palatalized consonant*

[i]-reduction dialects	[e]-reduction dialects	
[nʲiˈsʲi]	[nʲeˈsʲi]	‘carry’ (imp.)
[lʲiˈsʲina]	[lʲeˈsʲina]	‘piece of wood’
[pʲiˈtʲi]	[pʲeˈtʲi]	‘five’ (gen.)
[rʲiˈkʲi]	[rʲeˈkʲi]	‘river’ (gen. sg.)
[prʲiˈdʲot]	[prʲeˈdʲot]	‘spin’ (3rd pers. sg. pres.)
[glʲiˈdʲat]	[glʲeˈdʲat]	‘look’ (3rd pers. pl. pres.)

The comparison of the forms in (28a) and (28b) shows that non-high vowels lower to [a] in the immediately pretonic position before a non-palatalized consonant in the stressed syllable. When the following consonant is palatalized (28c), the non-high vowels neutralize either into [e] or [i].

2.9. Summary

This chapter has presented basic empirical facts which are subjected to analysis in the remainder of this book. As we have seen, East Slavic dialects are characterized by rich and intricate patterns of vocalic neutralizations. In brief, the quality of the reduced vowel depends on three main factors:

(29) a. The position within a word (moderate *vs.* extreme reduction).
b. The role of the sonority of stressed vowels (non-dissimilative *vs.* dissimilative reduction).
c. The quality of the adjacent consonants (e.g, [i]-reduction and [e]-reduction).

The prosodic position (29a) plays a decisive role in that distinct reduction outcomes are seen in pretonic and atonic syllables in the East Slavic dialects

[27] The velar plosive [g] is spirantized to [ɣ] in the southern Russian dialects.

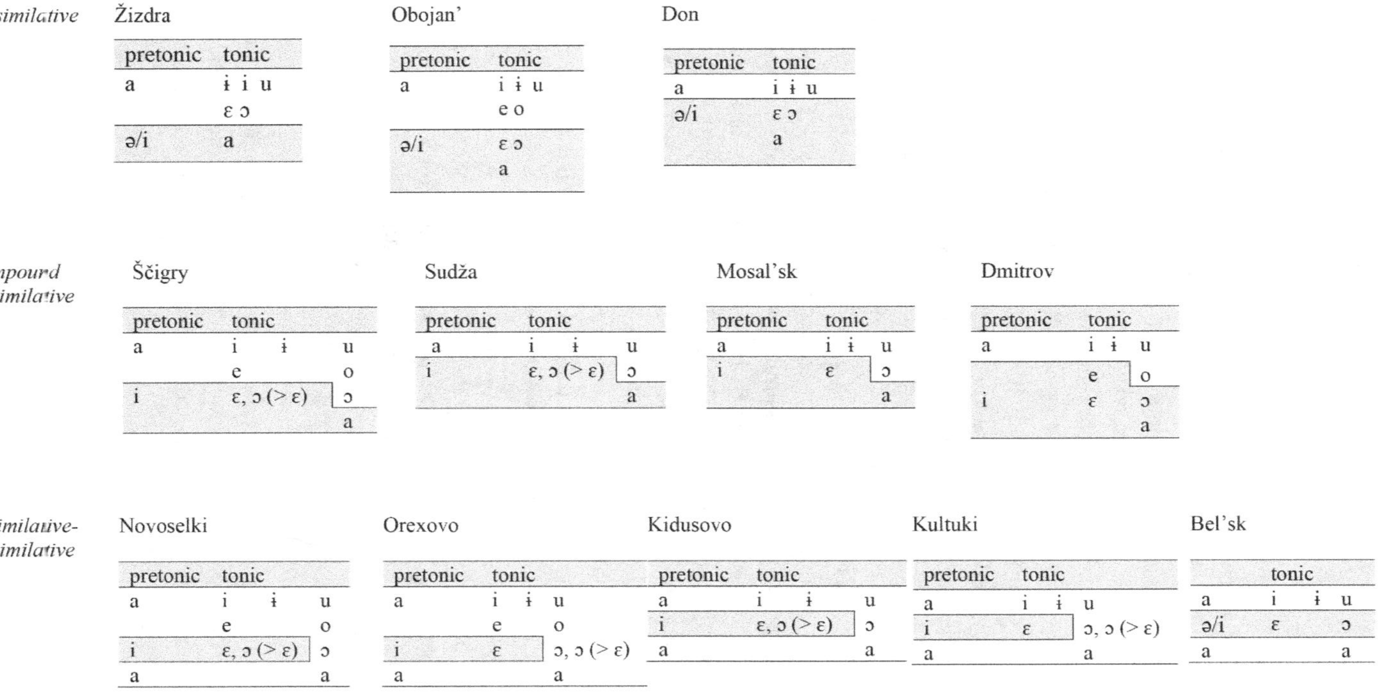

Figure 2 2: Patterns of dissimilative reduction.

with phonological reduction. In standard Russian, for instance, /o/ reduces to [a] after non-palatalized consonant in pretonic position and to [ə] in atonic positions. Extreme reduction is analysed in Chapter 4.

The second factor (29b), constituting the main focus of the present book, concerns the effect of the sonority of the vowel in the stressed syllable on the type of reduction observed in the pretonic syllable. Neutralization in pretonic positions which does not depend on the quality of vowels in the stressed syllable is called non-dissimilative reduction. Dissimilative reduction, in turn, involves the interplay between the quality of the reduced vowel with the quality of the vowel in the stressed syllable. East Slavic dialects exhibit several types of dissimilative reduction, which are summarized in Figure 2.2. Dissimilative patterns use the low vowel [a] in pretonic positions before the high vowels and [ə] if the vowel in the stressed syllable is low. Three types, Žizdra, Obojan', and Don, are distinguished depending on the effect of mid vowels in the stressed syllable on the quality of the reduced vowel. Non-dissimilative pattern attested in standard Russian and dissimilative patterns of Žizdra, Obojan', and Don are subjected to analysis in Chapter 5.

Two other patterns, compound dissimilative and assimilative-dissimilative reduction, are analysed in Chapter 6. These patterns share one common feature in that besides dissimilation, as in Žizdra, Obojan', and Don, they exhibit an additional modification. Compound dissimilative systems (Ščigry, Sudža, Mosal'sk, and Dmitrov) are analysed in section 6.2 in Chapter 6 in terms of backness harmony between the pretonic and the tonic vowel, whereas five further types, collectively referred to as assimilative-dissimilative reduction patterns (Novoselki, Kidusovo, Orexovo, Kultuki, and Bel'sk), are assumed to exhibit harmony in height (see section of 6.3 in Chapter 6).

Finally, the effect of the quality of the adjacent consonants mentioned in (29c) is the focus of Chapter 7. As we have seen in section 2.4.2 and section 2.8 in this chapter, pretonic vowels often raise and front in the context of palatalized consonants. Several types of neutralization reported in East Slavic dialects, including [i]-reduction and [e]-reduction, take place in the $C^j\_$ and $C^j\_\ C^j$ contexts. It has been noted previously that, since different types of reduction after palatalized consonants do not correspond in a one-to-one fashion to the patterns of reduction attested after non-palatalized consonants, reduction patterns in the context of palatalized consonants are treated separately in Chapter 7.

Chapter 3

East Slavic metrical system

3.1. Introduction

As the phenomenon of vowel reduction is closely related to stress, a theory of vowel reduction cannot dispense with a systematic account of metrical structure. East Slavic languages have weight-insensitive lexical stress systems, whose complexity has provided a number of analytical challenges for the phonological modelling. Most theories of lexical stress are based on standard Russian, which, being the most thoroughly described East Slavic language, will be used as a reference point in the description of East Slavic stress presented in this chapter. The scope of the present book does not allow for an in-depth presentation of the extremely complex Russian stress system, let alone of the discussion of the numerous theoretical controversies surrounding it. The goal of the present chapter is to introduce the main theoretical concepts of metrical analysis required for the modelling of various vowel reduction processes attested in East Slavic.

The stress system of East Slavic owes much of its complexity to the interaction between stress assignment and the rich morphological system. It has been standardly assumed that only some Russian stems are specified for accent in the lexicon, and the ones devoid of the underlying accent are assigned surface stress by a default rule in the grammatical component. Both the formal representation of the lexical accent as well as the nature of the default rule and the set of morphemes which are subject to it have been at the centre of attention in the literature on Russian stress (Halle, 1973, 1997; Melvold, 1990; Idsardi, 1992; Alderete, 1999; Revithiadou, 1999; Gouskova, 2010; Mołczanow *et al.*, 2013, 2019). Foot structure is another contestable issue in the analysis of the East Slavic metrical system. Different footings (trochaic/iambic, bounded/unbounded) have been postulated on theory-internal grounds (a right-headed foot has been proposed by, for example, Halle and Vergnaud (1987), Melvold (1989), Alderete (1995), Crosswhite (2001), and Crosswhite *et al.* (2003); a left-headed foot has been postulated by Idsardi (1992), Halle and Idsardi (1995), Halle (1997), Revithiadou (1999), and Lavitskaya and Kabak (2014), and others). Moreover, there are reports in the literature indicating that the metrical systems of other East Slavic languages, Belarusian and Ukrainian, are best accounted for without reference to foot structure (Dubina, 2012; Mołczanow and Łukaszewicz, 2021).

This chapter begins by presenting the most important facts concerning East Slavic stress (section 3.2). Next, sections 3.3 and 3.4 discuss controversies around the type of foot structure in Russian, arguing for iambs as default prosodic constituents for standard Russian and motivating the iambic foot as a domain of application of phonological processes. Section 3.5 lays out the main assumptions concerning the formal representation of lexical stress and outlines an account of the Russian metrical system in terms of an optimality-theoretic apparatus. Section 3.6 looks at different rhythmic patterns which are present in dialects with vowel reduction and develops a model of metrical structure for these systems.

3.2. Russian word stress: basic facts

The assignment of stress in Russian and in other East Slavic languages and dialects is not conditioned by the structural properties of a word and is not subject to obvious rules. Any syllable can be stressed in a word of more than one syllable, e.g., *ˈsintaksis* 'syntax', *deˈrevnja* 'village', *krokoˈdil* 'crocodile'. There are numerous minimal pairs where stress alone differentiates word meanings, *cf.* *ˈreki* 'rivers' (nom. pl.) – *reˈki* 'id.' (gen. sg.), *ˈmuka* 'torture' – *muˈka* 'flour', *doˈroga* 'road' – *doroˈga* 'dear' (short form). Stress location is weight-insensitive and is not circumscribed by the position within a word.[28] Russian stress is manifested phonetically by vowel duration, quality, and intensity (Bondarko, 1977; Zlatoustova, 1981).

Stress systems of East Slavic dialects whose vocalic patterns are at the centre of the current study have a similar structure to standard Russian, in that stress is free and its location is not limited by the position within a word or by syllable structure. The difference between the standard variety and dialects mainly consists in distinct stress locations in individual words, e.g, *ˈkuriš* – *kuˈriš* 'smoke' (2nd pers. sg.), *ˈsosna* – *soˈsna* 'pine', *ˈveselo* – *veseˈlo* 'merrily' (e.g, Kuznecov, 1960: 42; Kasatkin, 1989: 35 36).

---

[28] Let us note though that there are some indications in the recent literature showing that onset length is correlated with the location of stress in Russian (*cf.* Ryan, 2014; Jouravlev and Lupker, 2015; Orzechowska et al., 2018).

An important point of difference between dialects lies in the variations in rhythmic structure, which are discussed in section 3.6 later in this chapter. However, the facts concerning Russian stress presented in the current section also pertain, with minor variations, to other East Slavic languages and dialects.[29]

The assignment of stress in Russian and in East Slavic in general is morphologically-governed. Traditionally, Russian non-derived stems are divided into several classes. The accentual structure of the majority of nouns conforms to one of the following patterns.[30]

(1) a. Pattern A: stress fixed on the stem
b. Pattern B: stress fixed on the inflectional ending
c. Pattern C: mobile stress, alternating between the first syllable of the root and an inflectional ending[31]

The majority of Russian nouns (around 90%) have stress fixed on one of the stem syllables, with the same vowel stressed in all case forms (A stems).[32] For example, *'avtor* 'author' (nom. sg.) – *'avtor+u* (dat. sg.) – *'avtor+ami* (instr. pl.); *mo'roz* 'frost' (nom. sg.) – *mo'roz+u* (dat. sg.) – *mo'roz+ami* (instr. pl.). New words entering the lexicon by borrowing are usually assigned to pattern A, with stress fixed on one of the stem syllables. Nominal stems belonging to pattern B are stressed on the ending, or, when there is no inflectional suffix (zero ending), on the final syllable of the stem, for instance *ku'lak* 'fist' (nom. sg.) – *kulak+'u* (dat. sg.) – *kulak+'ami* (instr. pl.). Pattern B stems constitute about 7% of the Russian nouns. In stems with mobile stress (pattern C), the stem-initial vowel is stressed in the singular, whereas the suffix receives stress in the plural, as in *'ostrov* 'island' (nom. sg.) – *'ostrov+u* (dat. sg.) – *ostrov +'ami* (instr. pl.). Though least numerous (0.8%), this group contains items of very high lexical frequency (13% of all lexically frequent nouns), such as *golo'va* 'head', *ru'ka* 'hand', *'gorod* 'town'.

---

29 See Stankiewicz (1993) for a comprehensive review of accentual patterns of different East Slavic languages.

30 Noun stems in Russian are inflected for gender (masculine, feminine, neuter), number (singular, plural), and case (6 cases: nominative, genitive, dative, accusative, locative, instrumental).

31 In some cases of mobile stems, stress alternates between the inflection in the singular and the last syllable of the root in the plural.

32 The discussion is based on Mołczanow *et al.* (2019), the reader is referred to this study for references and further details. See also Mołczanow *et al.* (2013) and Łukaszewicz and Mołczanow (in prep.) for discussion of the theoretical issues pertaining to the Russian metrical system.

The Russian stress system has been extensively discussed in the literature (e.g, Halle, 1973, 1997; Melvold, 1990; Idsardi, 1992; and many others). It has been standardly assumed that morphemes are either inherently accented or unaccented (Jakobson, 1963; Halle, 1973; Kiparsky and Halle, 1977; Zaliznjak, 1985). In the former, accent is encoded in the underlying representation, while in the latter, surface stress is derived by rule. However, there is no agreement as to which stem types are specified for accent in the underlying representation. While pattern A stems are unanimously analysed as lexically accented, the representation of accent in pattern B and C stems has been a matter of much debate. Pattern B stems have been analysed as either lexically accented (Melvold, 1990; Idsardi, 1992; Halle, 1997; Revithiadou, 1999) or unaccented (Halle, 1973; Alderete, 1999). In the former case, pattern B stems are assumed to be stored with a floating accent, which is realized on the post-stem syllable (i.e. the syllable directly following the stem) or, when there is no overt inflectional suffix, on the final syllable of the stem. In this view, post-accenting stems form a subclass of accented morphemes. Alternatively, Halle (1973) and Alderete (1999) assume that stems of class B are not lexically accented. To derive surface stress in B stems, Halle (1973) postulates a lexically indexed rule which places accent on a vowel directly following the stem, and Alderete (1999) states a constraint forcing an insertion of accent on the inflectional ending (Post-Stem-Prominence). Pattern C stems exhibiting mobile stress have been treated as not lexically accented by most researchers, with the exception of Alderete (1999), who suggests pre-specification of initial accent in C stems. In the remaining accounts, Class C stems are lexically unaccented and receive initial stress by a default rule called Basic Accentuation Principle (Kiparsky and Halle 1977, cited from Melvold 1989: 16): 'Assign stress to the leftmost accented vowel; if there is no accented vowel, assign stress to the initial vowel.'

The Basic Accentuation Principle has been also employed to account for stress placement in morphologically complex words: if both the root and the suffix are lexically accented, the vowel of the root receives stress, if both are unaccented, the leftmost vowel of the stem gets stress (Melvold, 1989). There exist many other factors affecting stress assignment in morphologically complex words. For instance, the so-called dominant suffixes erase the lexical accents of roots, whereas recessive suffixes repel stress. The system is exceedingly complex, and as the issue of stress assignment in morphologically complex words is not directly related to the theory of vowel reduction, the details will not be presented here; for further discussion and various theoretical proposals, see, e.g., Halle (1973), Zaliznjak (1985), Melvold (1989), Revithiadou (1999), Alderete (1999), and Dubina (2012).

Default stress is another contentious issue in the descriptions of the metrical system of Russian. Different default stress placements have been postulated depending on which stems are assumed to be lexically specified for stress. Most accounts opt for an initial default based on the Basic Accentuation Principle and assuming that C stems are lexically unaccented and thus receive initial stress by default (Halle, 1973, 1997; Idsardi, 1992; Melvold, 1990; Revithiadou, 1999). In contrast, Alderete (1999) pre-specifies initial accent in C stems and assumes that B stems receive accent *via* post-stem stress, which constitutes the default. Gouskova (2010), based on her study of secondary stress assignment in compounds, postulates two phonological defaults in Russian: word-final for B stems and word-initial for C stems. Surface stress in the two patterns is derived by means of lexically indexed constraints.

Contrary to the dominant view assuming word-initial default, the findings of the empirical studies provide a strong evidence for a stem-final metrical default. Mayer (1976) reports a tendency for the last syllable of the stem to receive stress in foreign place names. Nikolaeva (1971) demonstrates that unfamiliar borrowings have penultimate stress in vowel-final words and final stress in consonant-final words. The same pattern has been observed in production studies using nonce words (D'jačok, 2002; Crosswhite *et al.*, 2003; Lavitskaya and Kabak, 2014). Further evidence comes from a study based on the data collected from speakers with acquired surface dyslexia (Mołczanow *et al.*, 2019). The analysis of errors in a word reading task showed that penultimate stress appeared in polysyllabic vowel-final words and final stress appeared in disyllabic consonant-final words, with polysyllabic consonant-final words being also likely to receive penultimate stress. Following Crosswhite *et al.* (2003), Mołczanow *et al.* (2019) argue that these results point to the rightmost stem syllable as the default stress position (the stem-final default hypothesis). That is, words with a final consonant often constitute bare stems in Russian, and, therefore, the final syllable receives default stress. The majority of words ending in final vowels are morphologically complex and can be decomposed into a stem followed by an inflectional ending, in which case the stem-final (penultimate) syllable is stressed.

3.3. Foot form

Foot structure plays an important role in the model of vowel reduction developed in this book. Based on the evidence from language games discussed below, and following other researches advocating iambs for Russian (e.g., Halle and Vergnaud, 1987; Melvold, 1990; Alderete, 1995; Crosswhite, 2001,

2003), the present study assumes right-headed feet. Let us note, however, that the structure of the Russian foot has been the subject of a long-standing debate, and both left-headed (trochaic) or right-headed (iambic) feet have been postulated in the literature on purely theory-internal grounds. An iambic foot has been proposed by Halle and Vergnaud (1987), Melvold (1989), Alderete (1995), and Crosswhite (2001, 2003), whereas a trochaic foot has been assumed by Idsardi (1992), Halle and Idsardi (1995), Halle (1997), Revithiadou (1999), and Lavitskaya and Kabak (2014).

Halle and Vergnaud (1987) based their assumption of iambic structure on the leftward stress movement, which takes place when an underlying stressed yer fails to vocalize.[33] The inflectional paradigm of the word *za'jom* 'loan' shown in (2a) serves to illustrate the point (Halle and Vergnaud, 1987: 29). The deletion of the stressed vowel *o* in the oblique forms results in the shift of stress to the preceding syllable, which is interpreted to point to right-headed pedal structure. Idsardi (1992: 121) counters this argument by observing that also rightward stress shifts are attested after the deletion of a stressed yer, as demonstrated by the forms of the word *o'tec* 'father' in (2b) below. In fact, words such as *o'tec* with the rightward shift of stress outnumber words such as *za'jom*, in which stress moves to the left after the deletion of a yer vowel.

(2)		a. leftward stress shift	b. rightward stress shift
	nom. sg.	za'jom 'loan'	o'tec 'father'
	gen. sg.	'zajma	ot'ca
	dat. sg.	'zajmu	ot'cu
	loc. sg.	'zajme	ot'ce

Therefore, since both left- and rightward stress shifts are attested in words with the deletion of the stressed yer, the direction of the stress shift does not provide an evidence for a particular (trochaic or iambic) foot structure in Russian.[34]

Revithiadou (1999) presents further arguments for trochaic footing, which are based on elision, secondary stress, and vowel reduction. However, as rightly pointed out by Dubina (2012: 68), these are 'insufficient and sometimes based on erroneous or premature generalisations'. For example, as the

---

[33] In Slavic linguistics, yers refer to vowels which are involved in vowel-zero alternations.

[34] Interestingly, in her discussion of the historical development of Slavic metrical structure, Bethin (1998: 120) notes: "One curious fact about Slavic in general is that many accentual changes (those not grammatically conditioned or analogical) were predominantly accent *retractions*, not accent *advancements*." (italicization is original). It is not clear, though, whether accent retraction is indicative of iambic footing or of some other mechanism at work.

elided form of the word *napisat'* [nəpʲiˈsatʲ] 'to write' is [nʌpˈsatʲ], Revithiadou (1999: 124) assumes that the initial syllable eschews elision because it is the head of the foot. Dubina (2012) argues that this phenomenon does not constitute a convincing piece of evidence since it could also be explained with reference to the phonotactic constraint banning the sequence [np] in onset position in Russian. Furthermore, Revithiadou (1999: 151) claims that 'audible secondary stress' appears on the initial syllable of Russian polysyllabic words, which points to initial syllables as the head elements in a trochaic foot. This generalization is factually incorrect, as non-compound polysyllabic words lack secondary stress in Russian (e.g., Lehfeldt, 2010). In turn, secondary stress in compounds can appear both on initial as well as non-initial syllables, its location being determined by the underlying accentual properties of the morphemes, e.g. [ˌvʲerəispəvʲiˈdanʲijə] 'denomination', [bʲiˌtonəmʲiˈʃalkə] 'concrete mixer', [səmʌˌlʲotəstrʌˈjenʲijə] 'airplane building' (Gouskova, 2010; see Dubina (2012) for further discussion and references). Another argument in favour of trochaic footing presented in Revithiadou (1999) is built on an incorrect descriptive generalization about vowel reduction, according to which 'mid and low vowels /a,o,e/, in pre-pre-stressed closed (CVC) syllables never exhibit the maximum degree of reduction; the vowels /a,o/ always reduce to [ʌ]' (Revithiadou 1999: 153). However, the influence of syllable structure (specifically, the presence of a coda consonant) on the outcome of reduction in Russian has not been reported in the literature to date, and words such as [pərkaˈvatʲ] 'to park' and [pəkaˈvatʲ] 'to pack' both contain the vowel [ə] in the initial (pre-pre-stressed) syllable. To conclude, the arguments presented in Revithiadou (1999) are not sufficient to legitimize trochaic footing in Russian.

Lavitskaya and Kabak (2014) argue for trochaic feet based on the results of their study of stress realizations in indeclinable novel words in Russian lacking morphological information. In their production experiment, participants assigned final stress in consonant-final words and penultimate stress in vowel-final words. The stimuli were designed to ensure that word-final vowels could not be interpreted by the speakers as inflectional endings, and the authors thus concluded that the default stress position in Russian is the trochee built at the right word edge. They also argued that consonant-final words receive final stress because they end in a degenerate trochee, headed by the word-final syllable which is followed by an empty foot-dependent position. However, let us point out that the results of this study are also consistent with the stem-final hypothesis of Crosswhite *et al.* (2003) (*cf.* section 3.2), who postulate that default stress is associated with an iambic foot aligned with the right edge of the stem. Vowel-final words used in the study ended in vowels such as /o/ and /i/ – in the former case, the participants could have interpreted this as the nom. sg. ending found in neuter nouns, e.g. *okn+o* 'window', while stress in the words ending in /i/ could be placed by analogy to existing place names such as *Tbi'lisi* or *Ta'iti.*[35]

Another study postulating trochaic feet is based on a perception-based electroencephalographic experiment using a stress violation paradigm (Mołczanow *et al.*, 2013). The results indicated a processing advantage for initially stressed disyllabic words, which was interpreted to constitute evidence for the syllabic trochee as the default foot type in Russian. In their follow-up study, Mołczanow *et al.* (2019) argue that the enhanced response to initially stressed words does not support trochaic constituency, but, rather, reflects the rhythmic structure of the carrier sentence.

To conclude, convincing evidence for a trochaic foot type in Russian is lacking. The argumentation for iambic footing found in the literature is equally unsatisfactory. Alderete (1995) limits his argumentation to the following statement 'Taking the pattern of rising amplitude over the pretonic syllable as the guide to the metrical structure (Jones and Ward, 1969, Hamilton, 1980), let us assume that the pretonic and stressed syllables together support an iambic foot in Russian.' (Alderete, 1995: 12). Crosswhite (2001), assuming that two-pattern reduction (extreme vs. moderate) is due to the iambic footing, refers to Halle and Vergnaud (1987) and Alderete (1995), and, in addition, adduces the argument of phonetic duration: 'Phonetically, the vowels within the foot are durationally different from vowels outside of the foot: the unfooted vowels are shorter than footed vowels.' (Crosswhite, 2001: 72). However, neither increased duration nor the rising amplitude of the immediately pretonic syllable constitute a convincing evidence for iambic feet. Quite the opposite, it has been observed in the literature that there is a tendency in the world's languages to maximize length distinctions within iambic feet. In Russian, however, the differences in duration between tonic and immediately pretonic syllables are only evident when a given word bears phrasal stress, whereas in non-focus positions immediately pretonic vowels are equal to or exceed the duration of the vowels in the stressed syllable (Knjazev, 2006: 50). So, in the absence of the evidence other than vowel reduction, the argument is circular: Russian iambs are motivated by vowel reduction; vowel reduction, in turn, is explained by reference to iambic foot structure.

---

[35] Lavitskaya and Kabak (2014: 382) also aduce evidence from the truncated forms of names, which have a trochaic structure, e.g. *'Vanja* > *I'van*, *'Nastja* > *Anasta'sija*. However, as these forms are decomposable into a stem and a nom. sg. suffix *-a*, they can also be analysed in terms of a stem-final hypothesis (Crosswhite *et al.*, 2003), which assumes that an iambic constituent is built at the right edge of the stem.

An indirect experimental evidence for foot structure can be potentially provided by studies investigating default stress position in Russian, mentioned in section 3.2 above. It is noteworthy that all these studies, based on stress placement in foreign place names (Mayer, 1976), unfamiliar borrowings (Nikolaeva, 1971), nonce words (D'jačok, 2002; Crosswhite *et al.*, 2003; Lavitskaya and Kabak, 2014), and aphasic productions (Mołczanow *et al.*, 2019), have demonstrated a strong tendency to stress the penultimate syllable in vowel-final words and final syllable in consonant-final words. However, these data can be analysed both in terms of trochaic footing (3a) as well as in terms of iambic footing (3b).

(3) a. Trochaic analysis
$CV(\text{'}CVCV)_F$
$CVCV(\text{'}CVC\emptyset)_F$[36]
b. Iambic analysis
$(CV\text{'}CV)_F CV$
$CV(CV\text{'}CVC)_F$

In (3a), the syllabic trochee is built at the right word edge in vowel-final words; an additional mechanism is necessary for the consonantal-final words, which presumably end in an abstract vowel. In (3b), the construction of feet is assumed to be sensitive to morphological structure. Since the majority of words ending in final vowels are morphologically complex and can be decomposed into a stem followed by an inflectional ending, the head of the iambic foot is located on the penultimate syllable in vowel-final words and on the ultimate syllable in consonant-final words.

As we have seen, the experimental data reported in the literature does not allow to adjudicate between the two theoretical options presented in (3). An external evidence for iambic footing in Russian which has not been previously discussed in the literature comes from language games. There has been general agreement that language games constitute a valuable external evidence in phonological description. For instance, Ohala (1986) rates them as second (next to experimental evidence) best source of evidence when choosing between alternative theoretical constructs (see also Bagemihl (1995) and Vaux (2014) for comprehensive overviews of the potential merits of evidence drawn from language games). Many language games (ludlings) involve transformational operations which manipulate phonological structure by infixation or syllable reversal. A number of 'secret languages' used

[36] The symbol Ø stands for an abstract vowel which is not realized phonetically.

by Russian-speaking children is described in Vinogradov (1926/2005).[37] Ludlings which are relevant for the analysis of stress in Russian are listed below (all examples come from Vinogradov 1926/2005, stress marks are original, except for (4b) and (4f), in which stress is not marked in Vinogradov (1926/2005), but the metrical pattern is explicitly commented on; the division into words is original, transliteration and translation is mine).

(4) Russian language games (Vinogradov, 1926/2005)

Type of transformation	Example
Stress on the infix	
a *zV/tV* infixation after each syllable of the target word, stress falls on the infix	ja znaju čto-to ‘I know something’ > ja ˈ*z’a* zna ˈ*za* ju ˈ*z’u* čto ˈ*zo* to ˈ*zo*
b *fVrV* infixation after each syllable of the target word, in closed syllables the coda consonant appears after the infix, stress falls on the final syllable of the infix	net ‘no’ > ne*fe* ˈ*re*t
	otpravljajtes’ na Ušakovku ‘go to Ushakovka street’ > o*fo* ˈ*ro*t pra*fa* ˈ*ra*v lja*fja* ˈ*rjaj* te*fe* ˈ*re*s’ na*fa* ˈ*ra* u*fu* ˈ*ru* ša*fa* ˈ*ra* ko*fo* ˈ*ro*v ku*fu* ˈ*ru*
Stress on the stem	
c *ver/o/šči/ša* infixation before each syllable of the target word, stress falls on the syllable of the word following the infix	ja pomnju čudnoje mgnovenje ‘I remember a wonderful moment’ > *ver*’ ˈja *ver* ˈpo *ver* ˈmnju *ver* ˈčud *ver* ˈno *ver* ˈje *ver* ˈmgno *ver* ˈve *ver* ˈnje
d *ščipa* infixation before each syllable of the target word, stress falls on the syllable of the stem following the infix[38]	ja pojdu domoj ‘I will go home’ > *šči* ˈ*paj* *ščipa* ˈpoj *ščipa* ˈdu šč*ipa* ˈdo *ščipa* ˈmoj

[37] Though the description provided in Vinogradov (1926/2005) dates one century back, some of these language games are still popular among children, which is testified by a number of YouTube films in which children teach each other to speak ‘secret languages’, usually called *kirpičnyj jazyk* ‘brick language’ or *soljonyj jazyk* ‘salty language’.

[38] Vinogradov (1926/2005: 19) comments that in this ludling stress can fall either on the first syllable of the infix or on the stem syllable, the latter pattern being more common.

	Type of transformation	Example
e	*fita/draga* infixation after each syllable of the target word, stress falls on the stem vowel	ty kuda pošla 'where have you gone (fem.)' > 'ty*fita* 'ku*fita* 'da*fita* 'pa*fita* 'šla*fita* kak vy požyvajete 'how are you (pl.) doing' > 'kak*draga* 'vy*draga* 'po*draga* 'žy*draga* 'va*draga* je'te*draga*
f	*farty/xarki* affixation after the stem, the inflectional suffix is deleted; stress falls on the stem syllable preceding the affix *farty/xarki*	žyli starik so staruxoj u samogo sinego morja 'There lived an old man and an old woman on the shore of the deep blue sea' > 'žy*farty* sta'ri*farty* so sta'ru*farty* u 'sa*farty* 'si*farty* 'mo*farty*
g	Reversal: the word is divided into two parts of comparable length, which are reversed, stress falls on the final syllable	Vasja, ty prixodi ko mne 'Vasja (proper name), come to me' > sja'va yt dipri'xo mne'ko

The inspection of the transformation rules listed in (4) reveals the following general stress pattern: stress is located either on the infix (4a,b) or on the stem vowel (4c–g). In the former case, the transformation results in the patterns of weak-strong syllables: σ'σ in (4a) and σσ'σ in (4b). The emergent structure clearly points to iambic footing. Moreover, stress is placed on the final syllable of 'new' words irrespective of the quality of the final segment, so that both open and closed syllables receive ultimate stress (e.g. *na* 'to' > *nafa'ra*, *net* 'no' > *nefe'ret*). As the words in ludlings are not decomposable into a stem and an inflectional ending, the vowel is a copy of the stem vowel in the vowel-final words, and hence, it is not analysed as an inflectional ending by the speakers. This stress placement argues in favour of the analysis in (3b), in which an iamb is built at the right edge the stems (as first suggested by Crosswhite *et al.*, 2003). In the case of the transformed forms, the right edge of the stems coincides with the right edge of the words. In contrast, the facts presented in (4) cannot be accounted for in terms of a trochaic analysis (3a), which predicts that the transformation should produce penultimate stress in vowel-final words and ultimate stress in consonant-final forms.

Transformations placing stress on the stem result in two types of patterns. In (4c,d), the infix is placed before the stem syllable, which receives stress in the transformed forms, and the resulting form is iambic (the structure σ'σ in (4c) and σσ'σ in (4d)). The right-headed foot type also emerges in (4g), in which the transformation is performed *via* the reversal of syllables. Interestingly, the underlying accent is lost and final syllables are uniformly stressed in the outcome of the transformation. In the second type (4e,f), stress is also located on the stem, but the infix in these cases is placed after the stem syllable(s), so that the resulting patterns have the structure 'σσσ in (4e) and (σ_n)'σσσ in (4f). In these transformations, the surface stress pattern can be generated by a constraint requiring the stress in the output forms to be located on the input syllables.

To conclude, the data from language games clearly point to iambic footing as the default pedal structure in Russian. Iambs emerge in all transformed forms in (4), except for the cases in which the input syllable is stressed in the output, irrespective of its position within the transformed structure (4e and 4f). In the remaining cases, the assignment of surface stress appears to be driven by a constraint requiring feet to be right-headed. A particularly compelling evidence for iambic footing is provided by the comparison of the transformations of the words *'znaju* 'I know' and *'pomnju* 'I remember': when the infix is added after the stem syllable, stress falls on the infix: *zna'za ju'z'u* (4a); when, on the other hand, the infix precedes the stem syllable, the latter receive stress: *ver'po ver'mnju* (4b).

Based on the evidence from language games discussed above, I assume that syllables are grouped into iambic feet in Russian. An iambic foot structure plays an important role in the present analysis by constraining the location of High tone and by constituting the domain of application of vowel harmony (discussed in Chapters 5 and 6). The next section provides motivation for the iambic foot as a phonological domain.

3.4. Foot as a domain

The concept of the foot domain plays a key role in the model of East Slavic vocalic alternations developed in this book. Specifically, several processes which are argued to apply within the disyllabic iambic foot are modelled employing constraints referring to foot as their domain of application. These include the positional faithfulness constraint $\text{IDENT[-low]}_{\text{HDFT}}$ (defined in (28) in section 5.5.2.2) and alignment constraints ALIGN-L([back], FT) and ALIGN-L([low], FT) (employed in the analysis of compound dissimilative and assimilative-dissimilative reduction systems, formulated in sections 6.2 and 6.3 in Chapter 6).

Positional faithfulness constraints are widely used in OT models of various neutralization processes (Beckman, 1997). Structural units which have been standardly assumed to constitute privileged positions which are resistant to neutralization comprise root-initial syllables and stressed syllables, whereas feet are not usually referred to in the formulation of such constraints. However, based on distinct vowel reduction patterns in pretonic and atonic positions in standard Russian, Alderete (1995) has argued for the head foot to constitute a salient domain, due to its strong status as a prosodic head.

In the present model, pretonic reduction arises due to the influence of H tone, which lowers the vowels attached to it in the output (which is achieved by the *H≤V family of constraints, a detailed analysis is developed in Chapter 5). The head foot plays an important role by acting as a host of H tone in the output representation (cf. HdFt = H defined in (9) in section 3.5). It will be demonstrated in section 3.5 that H tone determines the foot size in various East Slavic dialects either by shifting the foot boundary leftwards and creating a disyllabic iamb (as in standard Russian illustrated in (11) above) or, when H is linked to the head syllable, by creating a unary foot. In this view, the head foot carries two types of prominence: metrical prominence, due to the presence of the accented syllable, and tonal prominence, which might or might not coincide with metrical prominence.[39] Comparable foot-based tonal patterns have been suggested for Norwegian and Swedish, in which contrastive pitch is associated with both syllables in a trochaic foot (Rischel, 1963; Vanvik, 1963; discussed in Fox, 2000); and for Serbo-Croatian, whose tonal distribution has been argued to be defined in terms of foot structure (Zec, 1999).

Furthermore, the analysis developed in Chapter 6 relies on the assumption that the foot constitutes the domain of vowel harmony in East Slavic. Languages which restrict vowel harmony to the domain of the foot, though not numerous, have been described in the literature. For instance, an iambic foot domain delimits the application of harmony in Kera (Pearce, 2013), whereas vowels harmonize within a trochee in Ascrea Italian and Andalusian Spanish (Hualde, 1989; Rose and Walker, 2004; Archangeli and Pulleyblank, 2007; Jiménez and Lloret, 2007).[40] Likewise, I suggest that an iambic structure serves as a domain of vocalic neutralizations in compound dissimilative and assimilative-dissimilative reduction patterns attested in East Slavic.

Further evidence for the special status of the iambic foot domain in East Slavic is furnished by the data form Ukrainian, for which lengthening has been recently reported in syllables immediately preceding lexical stress

---

[39] The mismatch between metrical and tonal prominence in East Slavic is first mentioned in Bethin (2006). See also Zec (1999) for the interaction of tone and metrical structure in Neo--Štokavian, a South Slavic dialect with pitch-accent system.

[40] I owe the references to Ascrea Italian and Andalusian Spanish to Pearce (2013).

(Łukaszewicz and Mołczanow, 2018b; Mołczanow *et al.*, 2021). The detection of increased length of the syllable immediately preceding lexical stress has been unexpected because Ukrainian has duration-based rhythmic stress, whose effect is attenuated in the vicinity of the pretonic syllable due to the presence of pretonic lengthening.[41] Also, Ukrainian does not have phonological reduction, let alone a two-degree reduction comparable to Russian, in which the vowel in the pretonic syllable is both quantitatively and qualitatively distinct from other unstressed vowels. As pointed out in Mołczanow *et al.* (2021), while the functionality of pretonic lengthening in Ukrainian is unclear, the most plausible explanation is that this duration-based effect is closely related to the domain of lexical stress, which extends to the pretonic syllable. This phenomenon can be modelled by assuming that a disyllabic iamb constitutes a stress-bearing unit both in Ukrainian and in the East Slavic dialects discussed in this book. The following section addresses the issues related to foot assignment, the formal representation of stress, and its relation to tone.

3.5. Formal representation of stress

East Slavic languages have been often described as having lexical accent or lexical/free stress systems. Though the terms 'lexical stress' and 'lexical accent' are usually used interchangeably, there has been much terminological confusion concerning the use of the terms 'stress' and 'accent'.[42] For example, the term 'accent' is often employed to refer to sentence prominence or focus (e.g., Cutler, 1984); some scholars use 'accent' to represent the phonetic manifestation of 'stress', which is understood as an abstract property (e.g., Jassem and Gibbon, 1980) . The present study subscribes to the widely accepted view in which the term 'accent' is employed to refer to an underlying prosodic feature, while the term 'stress' is used for the surface representation of metrical prominence (Abercrombie, 1976/1991, Fox, 2000; van der Hulst, 2011; and many others). The way in which stress is manifested phonetically is language-specific, the commonly used acoustic cues include increased duration, intensity, and F_0. In East Slavic languages, the most conspicuous cue

[41] Traditional sources describe Ukrainian as having a 'wave-like' rhythmic pattern of alternating strong and weak syllables, and the pretonic syllable, if mentioned at all, is said to be shorter than the pre-pretonic syllable (i.e. the unstressed syllable removed by two syllables from lexical stress) (Nakonečnyj, 1969; Toc'ka, 2002).

[42] See Fox (2000: 114–150) for an extended discussion and the historical overview of the use of these terms.

to stress is vowel duration. Vowel quality plays an important role in expressing stress in Russian and Belarusian, both of which display phonological vowel reduction. Intensity and F_0, though invariably mentioned in standard sources, have not been proved to be as salient as duration in cuing stress in East Slavic (see Martynaŷ and Padlužny (1975), Vyhonnaja (1991) for Belarusian; Bondarko (1977), Zlatoustova (1981) for Russian; Łukaszewicz and Mołczanow (2018a, 2018b, 2018c), Mołczanow *et al.* (2018, 2019, 2021) for Ukrainian).

There is no agreement as to the representation of the accentual properties in the lexicon. The theoretical devices encoding underlying metrical prominence include the ones employing a diacritic feature (Melvold, 1990), parentheses (Halle, 1997), a floating autosegmental feature (Revithiadou, 1999), or a High tone (Jakobson, 1931/1971, Dubina, 2012). A detailed discussion of various proposals is beyond the scope of the present book (the interested reader is referred to Fox (2000) for general discussion; Bethin (1998) provides a comprehensive overview on the representation of accentual properties in Slavic languages; Revithiadou (1999) and Dubina (2012) review different analyses developed for Russian). Following a number of previous studies, including Halle and Vergnaud (1987), Idsardi (1992), and Alderete (1999), I assume that accent is encoded lexically as 'a prominence on the metrical grid' (Alderete, 1999: 16). As noted by Alderete (1999), the choice of this formal assumption allows for an insightful parallel between lexical accent systems and pitch-accent systems; both systems are found in Slavic languages (lexical accent in East Slavic languages and pitch-accent in some South Slavic languages). That is, formalizing lexical accent as prominence on a grid allows to explain the cumulativity of both stress and pitch-accent systems as resulting from the hierarchical structure of metrical representations (see Alderete (1999) for further arguments; the metrical system of East Slavic *vis-à-vis* pitch-accent systems is discussed in section 1.3 in Chapter 1).

Vowels which are specified with a grid mark in the underlying representation function as head elements in the hierarchical prosodic structure, which consists of syllables, feet, phonological words and phrases (Liberman and Prince, 1977; Nespor and Vogel, 1986; Selkirk, 1980, and others). In languages with lexical stress, feet are constructed with reference to the lexically accented vowel (e.g., Halle and Vergnaud, 1987), which serves as the head of the foot in the output representation. The grammar ensures that the lexically encoded prominence on the grid is realized as the head of a foot and the prosodic word in the output representation. Lexically specified accents surface on the corresponding vowels in the output due to the following prosodic faithfulness constraint (Alderete, 1999: 18).

(5) NO-FLOP-PROM
For x a prominence, y a sponsor, and z an autosegmental link,
∀x ∀y ∀z [x and y are associated via z in S1 →
∃x' ∃y' ∃z' such that (x, y, z)R(x', y', z') and x' and y' are associated via z' in S2.
'Corresponding prominences must have corresponding sponsors and links.'

NO-FLOP-PROM ensures that foot heads correspond to lexical accents, which are represented as grid marks in the input. It has been argued in section 3.3 above that Russian employs syllabic iambic footing. In OT, the following constraints are responsible for this rhythmic grouping (Prince and Smolensky, 1993).

(6) a. FTFORM=IAMB: Feet have final prominence.
b. FT=BIN: Feet are binary at some level of analysis (μ, σ).

Stress systems which do not exhibit the alternating patterns of strong and weak syllables are usually analysed by assuming non-iterative feet construction (see van der Hulst (1999) for further discussion). In languages with free stress, a foot is only built if it can be headed by a syllable which is lexically marked for accent. Thus, each prosodic word contains only one foot in Russian and in most East Slavic dialects discussed in this book.[43]

In words lacking an underlying accent (e.g., in novel or nonce words) an iambic foot is built at the right edge of the stem (*cf.* the stem-final hypothesis (Crosswhite *et al.*, 2003) discussed in sections 3.2 and 3.3 above).[44] This generalization is formalized using the alignment constraint ALIGN-R(STEM, FT) (McCarthy and Prince, 1993; the informal formulation is taken from Crosswhite *et al.*, 2003: 160).

(7) ALIGN-R(STEM, FT): The right edge of the stem coincides with the right edge of some foot.

I further assume, following Halle (1997), that the head foot is supplied with High tone in the surface representation. Alternatively, it can be assumed

[43] There are dialects exhibiting secondary stress, discussed in section 3.5, which are analysed using iterative foot construction. See also Mołczanow and Łukaszewicz (2021) for a discussion of the metrical system of Ukrainian, the East Slavic language which, besides lexical stress, exhibits secondary degrees of prominence. Mołczanow and Łukaszewicz (2021) argue that iterative foot construction (either iambic or trochaic, or mixed) fails to generate the metrical pattern attested in this language.

[44] See Crosswhite et al. (2003) for the analysis of morphologically complex words containing more than one accents or no accents (i.e., composed of unaccented morphemes, *cf.* section 3.2).

that only High tone is lexically present, and accent is assigned on the surface to the high-pitched syllable, as proposed for Belarusian by Dubina (2012).[45] In the present model, such an assumption would lead to redundancy as both accent (as a prominence on a grid) and H tone would be present in the underlying representation. There is no principled way to exclude this possibility, however, let us note that the choice between either the underlying accent or the underlying tone does not affect the core of the analysis, because surface regularity in OT is implemented through constraints on the output representation. In terms of OT, High tone (H) is assigned to the stressed syllable due to the constraint HEAD = H formulated in (8a) (adapted from Yip, 2002: 85).[46] Insertion of tone is penalized by DEP-T (8b).

(8) a. HEAD = H: Assign a violation mark to a head syllable which is not associated with H tone in the output.
   b. DEP-T: No insertion of tones.

As will be demonstrated in the ensuing chapters, the analysis of the data from East Slavic dialects relies on the assumption that the head foot domain is associated with H tone. In dialects with non-dissimilative reduction, including standard Russian, H tone lands on the non-head position in the foot. In systems with dissimilative reduction, the location of H either in the head or in the non-head foot position is determined by the quality of the vowel in prosodic head. I suggest that H tone appears in non-head positions in the output forms due to the following constraint.

(9) HDFT = H: Assign a violation mark for every head foot not associated with H tone in the output.

This constraint refers to the foot as the domain of H tone. It should be pointed out that while moras typically serve as tone-bearing units in systems with lexical tone, feet have also been argued to constitute a docking site of tone in languages such as Kera, Slave, Hausa, and Bambara (see Wee (2019: 21–28)

---

45 Floating tones have been also postulated for other languages, e.g. High tone for Serbo-Croatian (Zec, 1992) and for Ancient Greek (Golston, 1990), Low tone for Mixtecan (Goldsmith, 1990) and Bora (Yip, 2002), among others.

46 De Lacy (2002b) develops a restrictive theory of the interaction between tone and prominence, which suggests two hierarchies of negative markedness constraints: *HD/L >> *HD/H and *NON-HD/H >> *NON-HD/L. These hierarchies account for the cross-linguistic preference for stressed syllable to carry the H tone and for unstressed syllables to be linked to the L tone. While these constraints can successfully derive the surface tone distribution in languages with contrastive lexical tone, they are not employed in the present analysis because it is not immediately clear how they could force the insertion of tones in a language without an underlying tone specification.

for references and further discussion). These systems are usually analysed by requiring feet to be associated to one tone (*cf.* No Contour Ft 'The foot is only associated to one tone' used in an analysis of Kera in Pearce (2013)). In contrast to tonal languages, in which tone comes from the underlying representation, East Slavic assigns H tone in the output, and the constraint HdFt = H formulated in (9) above defines the foot as a tone-bearing unit by explicitly banning feet which do not host H tone.

The present model assumes that, in addition to being associated with the stressed syllable, High tone lands on the leftmost syllable in the foot in standard Russian and in a number of East Slavic dialects with dissimilative reduction. In OT, this is achieved by the constraint Align-L(H, Ft), adapted from Yip (2002: 83–84). This constraint plays a key role in the present model, which assumes that different reduction patterns arise in part due to differences in foot structure, which are generated by the position of Align-L(H, Ft) *vis-à-vis* Ft=Bin.

(10) Align-L(H, Ft): Assign a violation mark for every High tone which is not aligned with the left edge of a foot.

The constraints introduced so far are shown in Tableau (11), which displays an analysis of a hypothetical quadrisyllabic morphologically simple form in standard Russian. The most faithful candidate (11f) incurs a fatal violation of HdFt = H because it contains a foot which is not linked to High tone. The configuration in which High tone is associated only to the stressed syllable (11b) violates Align-L(H, Ft) because a syllable intervenes between High tone and the left edge of the foot. In (11c), a trochee is built at the right edge of the stem. This operation ensures the satisfaction of the constraint Align-R(Stem, Ft), but fatally violates a high-ranked constraint on foot form, FtForm=Iamb. Candidates (11d) and (11e) comply with Align-L(H, Ft), but incur fatal violations of No-Flop-Prom and Ft=Bin, respectively. Let us note that No-Flop-Prom is mute in forms lacking lexical accent in the input. In this case, candidate (11d) with the default stress placement (i.e., with stress located on the stem-final iambic foot) would win.

(11) *Russian metrical structure*

/σσ'σσ/[47]	No-Flop-Prom	FtForm = Iamb	HdFt = H	Ft = Bin	Align-L (H, Ft)	Head = H	Dep-T	Align-R (Stem, Ft)
H ⇒a. σ(σ'σ)σ						*	*	*
H b. σ(σ'σ)σ					*!		*	*
H c. σ σ ('σ σ)		*!					*	
H d. σ σ (σ'σ)	*!					*	*	
H e. σσ('σ)σ				*!			*	*
f. σ(σ'σ)σ			*!			*		*

Finally, let us note that in most versions of the current metrical theory, stress is defined as a head of the hierarchical prosodic structure, which constitutes a separate tier. Although there is a correlation between metrical structure and tone, the latter is represented on a tier of its own (Goldsmith, 1990). The interaction between the two tiers is evident in (11): the location of tone is circumscribed by the location of stress, and the spreading of tone is further dependent on metrical structure, in that foot structure determines the location of the docking site of H tone. In this respect, the foot constitute the domain of tone.

3.6. Rhythmic structure of dialects with dissimilative reduction

3.6.1. Descriptive generalizations

Standard Russian and most central and southern Russian dialects do not have secondary stress,[48] and their rhythmic structure is traditionally described based on the formula 1-2-3-1. This notation, known as Potebnja's formula in the Russian literature, refers to the impressionistic relative salience of syllables in different prosodic positions, and is meant to reflect the relative duration, with '3' standing for the longest (tonic) syllable, and '1' indicating the shortest (unstressed) syllable of the word; the pretonic syllable,

---

[47] Syllable structure is predictable, and, hence, is not encoded in the underlying representation. I abstract away from this fact at the moment and, for convenience, use the symbol 'σ' as a shortcut. A grave accent indicates that the following syllable is stressed.

[48] Secondary stress may appear in Russian in some compounds and in emphatic speech (see Lehfeldt (2010) for a general discussion; Gouskova (2010) and Gouskova and Roon (2013) discuss and analyse compound stress).

indicated with ‘2’, has duration intermediate between the tonic syllable (3) and the unstressed syllable (1) (Potebnja, 1865; see also Vysotskij, 1973: 26ff for critical remarks, and Knjazev (2006) for acoustic measurements and further discussion). The two prominent syllables are also referred to as the vocalic centre of the word and the overall prosodic structure is metaphorically described as ‘strong centre and weak periphery’ (Kasatkina, 1996b).

In contrast, some East Slavic dialects and languages show an alternation of strong and weak syllables. This pattern, which is also called a ‘wave-like pattern’ in the literature, is commonly attested in the northern Russian dialects (Al'muxamedova and Kul'šaripova, 1980; Knjazev, 2006) and in standard Ukrainian (Nakonečnyj, 1969; Łukaszewicz and Mołczanow, 2018a, 2018b; Mołczanow and Łukaszewicz, 2021).[49] In Ukrainian, for instance, a predictable alternating pattern of strong and weak syllables is formed by locating secondary (rhythmic) stress at the word edges and on every other syllable intervening between the lexical stress and the word edge, e.g. [ˌpɔpaˈdatɨ] ‘get’ (imperf.), [ˈlaɦɔˌdɨtɨˌmɛ] ‘repair, 3rd pers. sg.’. It is noteworthy that both Ukrainian and northern Russian dialects exhibiting this pattern lack phonological vowel reduction, and secondary stress is expressed by means of the increased duration of metrically strong syllables and not by differences in vowel quality.

It has been long observed that the southern Russian dialects with dissimilative reduction exhibit two different rhythmic patterns (Broch, 1916; Vojtovič, 1972b; Vysotskij, 1973; Kasatkina and Ščigel', 1996; among others). In the majority of these dialects, rhythm has been described to vary between 1-1-3-1 and 1-2-3-1 (Kasatkin, 2005; Savinov, 2013b). The presence of the perceptual salience (or the lack thereof) is usually attributed to prolonged duration and to the absence of reduction to [ə].[50] The type 1-1-3-1 is found in words with the low vowel [a] in the stressed syllables, whereas the

---

[49] The existence of rhythmic stress in Ukrainian has been confirmed in several acoustic studies (Łukaszewicz and Mołczanow, 2018a, 2018b, 2018c; Mołczanow et al., 2021); instrumental data concerning northern Russian dialects is presented in Al'muxamedova and Kul'šaripova (1980), Knjazev (2006), and Vysotskij (1973).

[50] Systematic acoustic measurements of the phonetic correlates of the rhythmic prominence are scarce and it is not clear which acoustic correlates the perceptual salience is based on. Instrumental measurements of the duration of pretonic vowels in dialects with dissimilative reduction reported in Vysotskij (1973), Fomina (1985), Savinov (2013b), and Kasatkina (1995) reveal differences in the duration of pretonic vowels which are related to the quality of the stressed vowel (see Mołczanow (2017: 59–62) for a detailed discussion). A recent study of Ukrainian, which is also claimed to have a wave-like pattern, has demonstrated that there is no difference in vowel quality (despite the differences in duration) between vowels which perceptually salient and those which are not – both are subject to articulatory undershoot (Mołczanow et al., 2019).

pattern 1-2-3-1 occurs in words containing non-low stressed vowels, as exemplified in (12) below (data come from Kasatkin, 2005: 25). These dialects are similar to standard Russian in that both draw an opposition between the disyllabic domain containing the tonic and pretonic and the remaining unstressed syllables.

(12) a. *1-1-3-1*
[nəkəˈpalə] 'dig up' (fem. perf.)
[prədəˈvalə] 'sell' (fem. past. imperf.)
[nəglʲiˈdʲat͡sːə] 'watch' (3rd pers. pl. future)
[vɨlʲiˈtalə] 'fly out' (fem. perf.)
b. 1-2-3-1
[pədaˈrʲilə] 'give a present' (fem. perf.)
[rəzaˈgnulsʲə] 'unbend' (masc. perf.)
[rəzdaˈbɨlə] 'procure' (fem .perf.)
[pʲirʲiˈsɨpətʲ] 'pour' (inf.)

A mixed rhythmic structure is attested in some southern Russian dialects and in the western Belarusian dialects, in which a 'wave-like pattern' (2-1-3-1) appears in words containing non-high vowels in the stressed syllable. In turn, when the vowel in the tonic syllable is high, the rhythm is 1-2-3-1 (Vajtovič, 1968; Kasatkin, 2005; Savinov, 2013b). According to various sources (Avanesov and Orlova, 1965; Fomina, 1985; Kasatkin, 2005; Savinov, 2013b), rhythmic stress is manifested by the increased duration and the absence of reduction to [ə]. The difference is illustrated by the following pairs of words from the western Belarusian dialect area (Vajtovič, 1968: 116):[51]

(13) a. *2-1-3-1*
[paluˈčaw] 'get' (masc. imperf.)
[zabʲiˈrat͡sʲ] 'receive' (inf.)
[ɣarbuˈza] 'pumpkin' (gen. sg.)
b. *1-2-3-1*
[ɣəlaˈʋɨ] 'head' (gen. sg.)
[mɨlaˈdɨ] 'young'
[stɨnaˈʋʲi] 'stop' (2nd sg. imp.)

As these examples show, the presence of secondary stress on the initial syllable in [ˌpaluˈčaw] is dependent on the presence of a non-high vowel in the tonic syllable, no secondary stress appears in [ɣəlaˈʋɨ] with a high

[51] See Kasatkin (2005: 53) and Savinov (2013b: 40) for similar patterns attested in the Southern Russian dialects.

vowel in the tonic syllable. Such systems combine the properties of non-rhythmic dialects, such as standard Russian, with the characteristics of rhythmic languages, such as Ukrainian. As in standard Russian, only the tonic and the immediately pretonic syllables receive extra length in words such as [ɣəlaˈʋɨ] 'head' (gen. sg.), *cf.* the standard Russian form [gəlaˈvɨ] 'id'. Similarly to Ukrainian, word-edge syllables are metrically strong in words such as [ˌpaluˈčaw] 'get' (masc. imperf.), *cf.* the standard Ukrainian form [ˌpɔpaˈdatɨ] 'get' (imperf.). Like the non-rhythmic dialects, and unlike Ukrainian and northern Russian, the dialects exhibiting the hybrid metrical structure also have phonological vowel reduction.

To summarize, most East Slavic dialects with non-dissimilative and dissimilative vowel reduction do not have rhythmic secondary stress and are characterized by a typologically rare structure wherein pretonic and tonic syllables are singled out as carriers of word prominence. As a result, the vowels in the two positions are qualitatively and quantitatively different from the vowels in the remaining syllables. Dialects which lack phonological reduction (most northern Russian dialects, standard Ukrainian) are reported to have a distinct prosodic structure, involving a regular alternation of strong and weak syllables, which is due to the presence of the word-edge-based rhythmic stress. A small group of dialects with dissimilative reduction displays a mixed metrical structure, combining the rhythmic and the non-rhythmic patterns. In these dialects, rhythmic stress is only present in words in which the tonic syllable contains a non-high vowel. The remainder of this section analyses the metrical structure of rhythmic and non-rhythmic dialects with dissimilative reduction, for an analysis of Ukrainian metrical structure, see Mołczanow and Łukaszewicz (2021).

3.6.2. Foot structure

It has been argued earlier in this chapter (section 3.4) that the output location of H tone is constrained by the metrical structure in that H tone is associated with the leftmost syllable in an iambic foot in standard Russian. In terms of OT, the H tone ends up linked to the pretonic syllable in the disyllabic iambic foot due to three high-ranked constraints: FtForm=Iamb, Ft=Bin, and Align-L(H, Ft).

Based on a generalization originally formulated by Bethin (2006), the current proposal models dissimilative reduction on an assumption that dissimilative dialects realize High tone on a low stressed vowel (14a) and on the pretonic vowel when the stressed vowel is high (14b).

(14) *Distribution of H tone in the dissimilative dialects*

```
        H                          H
        |                          |
a. σ'σ                  b. σ'σ
        |                          |
   [–high]                  [+high]
```

In dialects with dissimilative reduction, similarly to Russian and other lexical stress systems, the lexically accented vowel serves as the head of the foot in the output. There are several possible metrical parsings of the representations in (14), as illustrated in (15) based on a quadrisyllabic structure σ σ 'σ σ with penultimate lexical stress.

(15) a. *Iambic feet*

```
            H                        H
            |                        |
   i.  σ σ ('σ) σ              σ (σ 'σ) σ
            |                        |
        [–high]                  [+high]

            H                        H
            |                        |
   ii.  σ (σ 'σ) σ             σ (σ 'σ) σ
              |                      |
          [–high]                [+high]
```

b. *Trochaic feet*

```
             H                        H
             |                        |
   i. (ˌσ σ)('σ σ)              (ˌσ σ)('σ σ)
               |                        |
           [–high]                  [+high]

              H                           H
              |                           |
   ii. (ˌσ σ)('σ σ)             (ˌσ σ)('σ σ)
              |                         |
          [–high]                   [+high]
```

c. *Hybrid metrical structure*

```
          H                        H
          |                        |
   (ˌσ σ)('σ σ)             b. σ(σ 'σ) σ
            |                         |
        [–high]                  [+high]
```

Iambic feet in (15ai) align H with the left edge of the feet, which leads to a construction of a unary foot and a binary foot in which H is misaligned with the foot head. In (15aii), two binary iambic feet are constructed, in which H is either aligned with the stressed syllable and misaligned with the left foot edge, or, reversely, is aligned with the left foot edge and misaligned with the stressed syllable.

The quadrisyllabic form is exhaustively footed by constructing two trochees in (15bi). However, this metrical parsing generates a structure in which H associates to the vowel which is not incorporated into the same foot as the stressed syllable. Another possibility, shown in (15bii), is to align

H with the right edge of the head trochee. This option is not exploited in East Slavic, in which tone-related effects usually are observed on the pre-tonic syllable, and not on the post-tonic one. However, the rightward shift of H appears to take place in one case, discussed later in this section, where a post-tonic vowel lowers in words with initial lexical stress (*cf.* the evaluation in Tableau 20 below).

In turn, the structure in (15c) admits two foot types, whose construction is determined not only by the position of stress, but also by the location of High tone. In this setting, the foot boundary coincides with the left edge of the stressed syllable only when it hosts High tone. Otherwise, the foot boundary shifts leftwards, to align with the syllable associated with H. As a result, words which contain a non-high vowel in the stressed syllable are parsed into trochaic feet, whereas words with stressed high vowel construct an iambic foot.

Iambic footing shown in (15a) appears to be more coherent on theoretical grounds, because in both (15ai) and (15aii) H tone lands on a syllable within the same foot. In contrast, trochaic footing in (15b) fails to align H with the left foot edge, incorporate H into the head foot or to associate H with the head syllable.

Chapters 5 and 6 will demonstrate that the most adequate way to model the relationship between tone and metrical structure in East Slavic is to assume right-headed feet, as in (15ai) and (15aii) above. The proposed model will argue that the footing shown in (15ai) is employed by dissimilative and compound dissimilative dialects, whereas the footing in (15aii) is present in assimilative-dissimilative dialects. The difference between (15ai) and (15aii) arises due to different rankings of Ft=Bin and Align-L(H, Ft): (15ai) is generated by the ranking Align-L(H, Ft) >> Ft=Bin, whereas (15aii) is produced by the opposite ranking: Ft=Bin >> Align-L(H, Ft).

Foot forms presented in (15c) account for the metrical structure in systems exhibiting increased prominence in position removed from the main stress by one syllable if the stressed vowel is non-high, e.g. [ˌpadəˈʃla] 'approach' (fem. sg. past), but not if the vowel under stress is high, e.g. [pədaˈʃlʲi] id. (past. pl.), discussed in section 5.1 above. The parsing of the words [ˌpadəˈʃla] and *[ˌpadaˈʃlʲi] is provided below.

(16) *Hybrid metrical structure*

a.	b.
H (linked to ʃla)	H (linked to da)
[(ˌpadə)(ˈʃla)]	[pə(daˈʃlʲi)]
/podoˈʃla/	/podoˈʃli/

Though the majority of metrical models assume either trochees or iambs for one language, foot reversals within systems have been proposed in the literature (see Alber (2005) for a general discussion, and Hyde (2002, 2016) for a metrical theory employing both foot types within one language). It should be noted that this rhythmic pattern is only attested sporadically among the dialects with dissimilative reduction, and is only remarked upon in passing in the literature (*cf.* Kasatkin; 2005: 53; Kasatkin, 2013: 308). Also, descriptive sources usually list disyllabic and trisyllabic words, as these are most common in East Slavic. Therefore, given a dearth of reliable descriptions, a full-fledged theoretical model of the hybrid metrical structure illustrated in (16) would be premature and certainly go beyond the scope of the present book. However, see Mołczanow and Łukaszewicz (2021) for a discussion of the suitability of the proposal developed in Hyde (2002, 2016) as well as other current metrical models for analysing the data from Ukrainian, a related East Slavic language with secondary stress.

It has been previously pointed out that the majority of East Slavic dialects with dissimilative reduction (i.e., dissimilative patterns in Chapter 5 and compound dissimilative patterns in Chapter 6) will be analysed in terms of the iambic footing, as shown in (17a) below. Dialects with the assimilative-dissimilative reduction (analysed in section 6.3 in Chapter 6) are argued to employ a minimally different metrical parsing, in which, like in non-dissimilative patterns discussed in section 3.5 above, the pretonic syllable is parsed into an iambic foot, irrespective of the quality of the stressed syllable. This difference will be argued to account for distinct patterns of pretonic reduction in the word /pɔdɔˈʃla/, pronounced with pretonic [a] in assimilative-dissimilative systems and with pretonic [ə] in dialects with dissimilative and compound dissimilative reduction (see Chapter 6 for a detailed analysis).

(17) a. *Foot structure in dialects with dissimilative and compound dissimilative reduction*

H	H
[pədə(ˈʃla)]	[pə(daˈʃlʲi)]
/pɔdɔˈʃla/	/pɔdɔˈʃli/

b. *Foot structure in dialects with assimilative-dissimilative reduction*

H	H
[pə(daˈʃla)]	[pə(daˈʃlʲi)]
/pɔdɔˈʃla/	/pɔdɔˈʃli/

The bidirectional interaction between metrical structure and tone is generated by the constraints regulating the interaction of H with sonority and foot structure. This is illustrated in the tableaux in (18), which show the evaluation of the words /vɔˈda/ [vəˈda] 'water' (nom. sg.) and /vɔˈdɨ/ [vəˈdɨ] 'id.' (gen. sg.). in the dialects with dissimilative and compound dissimilative reduction.

(18) *Metrical structure in the dialects with dissimilative and compound dissimilative reduction*

i. /vɔ'da/	*H/≤i,u	*H/≤a	Head=H	Align-L(H, Ft)	Ft=Bin
H ⇒ a. və('da)		*			*
H b. (va'da)		*	*!		
H c. (və'da)		*		*!	
ii. /vɔ'dɨ/	*H/≤i,u	*H/≤a	Head=H	Align-L(H, Ft)	Ft=Bin
H ⇒ a. (va'dɨ)		*	*		
H b. və('dɨ)	*	*			*!
H c. va('dɨ)		*	*	*!	*

As shown above, AlignL(H, Ft) ranked above Ft=Bin ensures that H tone is aligned with the left edge of the foot at the cost of creating unary feet when the stressed syllable is non-high, cf. candidate (18ia). When the stressed vowel is high, as in (18ii), H lands on the pretonic syllable, and, as a result, H tone is aligned with the left edge of a disyllabic iamb in the optimal output (18iia). This is ensured by the constraint *H/≤i,u, which disallows H to be associated with the stressed syllable in (18iia), generating the alternation between [a] and [ə] in pretonic position. The ranking between Head=H and the members of the *H/≤V family of constraints cannot be established based on the evaluations in (18), ranking arguments for individual dialects will be provided in Chapters 4, 5, and 6.

Also, the ranking of AlignL(H, Ft) with respect to the *H≤V family of constraints cannot be determined on the basis of the forms shown in (18) above: Align-L(H, Ft) is ranked together with *H/≤a, but the same result would be achieved if Align-L(H, Ft) were ranked higher. However, the ranking of AlignL(H, Ft) *vis-à-vis* *H≤V plays a decisive role in the evaluation of forms with lexical stress on the initial syllable. In this case, there is no vowel preceding the main stress, so H tone can either dock on the stressed syllable or on the following unstressed syllable. If the vowel in the stressed syllable is high, its association with H runs afoul of *H/≤i,u. The rightward shift of H, in turn, violates Align-L(H, Ft). Hence, there are two predicted scenarios for forms containing a high vowel in the initially stressed syllable. If AlignL(H, Ft) outranks *H≤V, then H tone will be linked to the initial syllable irrespective of the quality of the vowel. If, on the other hand, *H≤V is ranked above ALIGN-L(H, FT), then H tone will link to the vowel in post-tonic position. In the latter case, the vowel is expected to lower in order to comply with *H/≤i,u. In fact, both patterns are attested in the dialects with dissimilative reduction. The post-tonic reduction to [ə] is observed in the majority of dialects, e.g. [ˈxutərʲi] 'hamlet' (loc. sg.) *vs.* [ˈjablət͡ʃʲkə] 'apple' (gen. sg. dim.). This indicates that H tone is linked to the initial stressed syllable, in agreement with the highranked ALIGN-L(H, FT). (See Tableau (19) for an illustration.)

(19) *Post-tonic non-dissimilative reduction*

/ˈxutɔrʲ+i/	ALIGN-L(H, FT)	*H/≤i,u	*H/≤a	HEAD=H	FT=BIN
H ⇒ a. (ˈxu)tərʲi		*	*		*
H b. (ˈxuta)rʲi	*!		*	*	

Some dialects, however, are reported to use [a] after non-low stressed vowels and [ə] after the low vowel [a], e.g. [ˈxutarʲi] 'hamlet' (loc. sg.) *vs.* [ˈjablət͡ʃʲkə] 'apple' (gen. sg. dim.) (see section 2.1). This pattern is generated by the ranking *H/≤i,u >> ALIGNL(H, FT), FTFORM=IAMB, as illustrated in (20).

(20) *Post-tonic dissimilative reduction*

/ˈxutɔrʲ+i/	*H/≤i,u	*H/≤a	ALIGN-L(H, FT)	FTFORM=IAMB	HEAD=H	FT=BIN
H ⇒ a. (ˈxuta)rʲi		*	*	*	*	
H b. (ˈxu)tərʲi	*	*!				*

To conclude, East Slavic systems with dissimilative reduction exhibit a bi-directional interaction between metrical structure and tone. High tone interferes with the metrical structure by shifting the foot boundary leftwards or rightwards. In most patterns, H is aligned with the left foot edge, both when linked to the stressed syllable and when associated to the pretonic syllable. So, on the one hand, the position of lexical stress determines the location of High tone, whereas, on the other hand, tone affects the structure of feet. Section 5.6 in Chapter 5 presents the typology of patterns generated by different ranking hierarchies involving, among others, the constraints ALIGN-L(H, FT) and FT=BIN.

3.7. Summary

This chapter has laid out the main representational assumptions concerning the tonal and metrical structure of East Slavic. I have outlined the issues pertaining to the analysis of lexical stress, including the relation between stress and accent, the form of the foot, and its role in the analysis of various neutralization patterns developed in this book. Based on evidence from language games, I have argued for an iambic footing in standard Russian. An iambic foot structure has been also assumed for most dialects with dissimilative reduction. Furthermore, I have suggested that some systems might be analysed in terms of hybrid iambic-trochaic foot forms.

It has been demonstrated that systems with dissimilative reduction show a bidirectional interaction between metrical structure and tone. On the one hand, the position of lexical stress constrains the locus of High tone, whereas, on the other hand, tone affects the structure of feet. Specifically, H tone shifts the foot boundaries leftwards or rightwards, depending on a dialect and on the quality of the vowel in the tonic syllable.

The main objective of the present book is to demonstrate that H tone is the trigger of numerous reduction systems attested in the pretonic position in East Slavic dialects. Before developing the account of pretonic (moderate) vowel reduction patterns, the next chapter presents the analysis of extreme reduction, which can be considered a more general pattern as it takes place in positions which do not immediately precede stressed syllables.

Chapter 4

Extreme reduction

4.1. Introduction

The characteristic trait of standard Russian is that it exhibits a two-pattern vowel reduction: reduction to corner vowels is found in immediately pretonic positions and centralization to schwa in atonic contexts (Avanesov, 1984). The phenomenon of Russian vowel reduction, due to its complexity and reliance on both prosodic as well as segmental context, has received a great deal of attention and has often been used as a textbook example in the phonological literature (Jakobson, 1929; Halle, 1959; Miller, 1972; Halle and Vergnaud, 1987; Gussmann, 2002; Odden, 2005; Padgett and Tabain, 2005; among others). In the framework of Optimality Theory, recent studies include Alderete (1995), Crosswhite (2000, 2001), de Lacy (2006), Mołczanow (2007), and Iosad (2012). Though these models have provided a number of descriptive and theoretical insights, they do not account for all reduction patterns found in Russian. The present study rethinks the motivation for Russian vowel reduction in a novel way, adding a new dimension to the discussion of the vocalic system of Russian. The proposal is based on the assumption that pretonic vocalic neutralizations are driven by the presence of H tone. The analysis of neutralization in positions not immediately preceding tonic syllable presented in this chapter is based on the model of prominence reduction developed by Crosswhite (2001), and is formalized in terms of the markedness constraints regulating sonority of prosodic heads and non-heads proposed by de Lacy (2006). Though the analysis draws on the data from standard Russian, the model can be also applied to other East Slavic dialects with a two-pattern reduction.

The chapter is organized as follows. First, section 4.2 develops an analysis of vowel reduction in atonic syllables. Next, section 4.3 considers the blockage of the extreme reduction in hiatus and phrase-initial positions. A brief review of the previous accounts of Russian vowel reduction is presented in section 4.4, and the main results are summarized in section 4.5.

4.2. Analysis

As we might remember, vowels in positions which do not immediately precede stressed syllables undergo extreme reduction in systems with the two-degree neutralization described in Chapter 2 (section 2.3). Typically, contrasts among non-high vowels are neutralized in [ə] after non-palatalized consonants and in [ɪ] after palatalized consonants, as exemplified below.

(1) /ˈgorod/ [ˈgorət] ‘town’ (nom. sg.) – /goroˈdok/ [gəraˈdok] ‘small town’
/ˈzʲerkalo/ [ˈzʲerkələ] ‘mirror’ (nom. sg.) – /zʲerkaˈla/ [zʲɪrkaˈlə] ‘id.’ (nom. pl.)

It has been pointed out in Chapter 1 (section 1.2.1) that previous research has modelled this type of neutralization in terms of prominence reduction driven by the pressure to reduce sonority in prosodically recessive positions (Crosswhite, 2001; de Lacy, 2006). I adopt this approach in the present study and assume that reduction in atonic syllables results from an interplay of the sonority markedness scales with prosodic positions, as proposed by de Lacy (2006) (see section 1.2.1 in Chapter 1). Specifically, de Lacy (2006) suggests that prosodic heads and prosodic non-heads impose conflicting demands as to the sonority of the melodic content they contain: prosodic heads favour high-sonority segments, such as the low vowel [a], whereas prosodic non-heads prefer low-sonority high central vowels, such as [ɨ]. In OT, this generalization is expressed by the constraints which are formed by crossing the sonority scale (ɨ,ʉ > ə > ... > a) with prosodic prominence scale (prosodic heads > prosodic non-heads) (the scales and the resulting constraints are presented in (5) and (6) in section 1.2.1).

Vowels in unstressed syllables are heads of the syllabic domain but non-heads of prosodic words. As only low-sonority vowels [ɪ], [ɨ], [ʊ], and [ə] are allowed in atonic positions in Russian, extreme reduction is driven by the following constraint exerting the pressure to reduce sonority in prosodic non-heads (adapted from de Lacy (2006: 288).

(2) $*\text{-}\Delta_{\omega}\geq\{i,u\}$: Assign a violation mark for every non-head of a word that contains a segment with sonority greater or equal to {i,u}.

The decrease in the sonority of atonic vowels takes place at the expense of violating identity constraints, such as IDENT-V[–high] and IDENT-V[+back], which are outranked by the markedness constraint $*\text{-}\Delta_{\omega}\geq\{i,u\}$. According to the sonority hierarchy (cf. (5a) in section 1.2.1), there are two vowels, [ɨ] and [ə], which are less sonorous than [i,u]. Both vowels occur in pretonic positions in East Slavic dialects. The high vowel [ɨ] is found in a number of systems with dissimilative [a]-reduction, e.g. in Žizdra (Vajtovič, 1968).[52] Given that there is a pressure to reduce sonority in prosodic non-heads, less sonorous [ɨ] makes a better reduced vowel than [ə]. However, [ə] is also found in pretonic positions, in fact, it is more widespread than [ɨ].[53]

It is often assumed in the literature that schwa is a defective vowel which is devoid of a melodic content (Anderson, 1982; van Oostendorp, 1995; Cyran, 2010; among others). In this view, schwa is represented as an empty root node, defined only for the major class feature [-cons]. Consequently, reduction of a full vowel to [ə] does not lead to the violation of IDENT constraints because there is no value of a given feature in the output which can be compared to the input. In dialects which reduce atonic vowels to [ɨ], schwa is disallowed by the constraint militating against empty root nodes, here informally referred to as *ə ('A vocalic root dominates a vocalic place node', see van Oostendorp, 1995: 138). As raising to [ɨ] entails a violation of IDENT[–high], the ranking of *ə *vs.* IDENT[–high] determines which vowel, [ɨ] or [ə] will surface as optimal in a given dialect. This is illustrated in Tableau (3) by a hypothetical evaluation of the vowel /o/. Note that the candidates (3a) and (3b) fare equally well on the constraint $*\text{-}\Delta_{\omega}\geq\{i,u\}$. The ranking *IDENT[–high] >> *ə chooses schwa in candidate (3a), while the reverse ranking, *ə >> IDENT[–high], would give preference to [ɨ].

(3) *Extreme reduction*

/o/	$*\text{-}\Delta_{\omega}\geq\{i,u\}$	IDENT[–high]	*ə
⇒ a. ə			*
b. ɨ		*!	
c. o	*!		

Tableau (4) below shows how the interaction of constraints generates reduction to [ə] in the standard Russian word *volos* [ˈvoləs] 'hair', nom. sg. (*cf.* the nom. pl. dim. form *volosiki* [vaˈlosʲɪkʲɪ]). Candidates (4a) and (4b) fare equally well on the constraint $*\text{-}\Delta_{\omega}\geq\{i,u\}$. The decision in made by the

[52] In dissimilative [a]-reduction, the quality of the reduced vowel in the pretonic position depends on the quality of the stressed vowel. Dissimilative reduction is discussed in detail in Chapters 5 and 6.

[53] Vajtovič (1968: 115) reports that very often a vowel of an intermediate quality between [ɨ] and [ə] is heard in Belarusian dialects.

constraint IDENT[–high] because the reduction to a featureless schwa comes at no cost, while reduction to any other vowel violates faithfulness.

(4) *Extreme reduction: standard Russian*

/ˈvolos/	$*\text{-}\Delta_{\omega}\geq\{i,u\}$	IDENT[–high]	*ə
⇒ a. ˈvoləs			*
b. ˈvolɨs		*!	
c. ˈvolos	*!		
d. ˈvolas	*!		

Interestingly, high vowels are resistant to reduction and only non-high vowels are neutralized to schwa in dialects with dissimilative reduction. Pretonic /o/ and /a/ are reduced to [ə] after non-palatalized consonants whereas underlying /ɨ/ surfaces as [ɨ]. The nonreduction of high vowels follows from the constraint set established above, as shown in Tableau (5) below. IDENT[–high] is mute with respect to an input containing a high vowel and, consequently, candidate (5b) with a non-reduced [ɨ] harmonically binds a candidate with a schwa (5a).

(5) *Non-reduction of high vowels*

/ɨ/	$*\text{-}\Delta_{\omega}\geq\{i,u\}$	IDENT[–high]	*ə
a. ə			*!
⇒ b. ɨ			
c. o	*!		

To summarize, extreme reduction takes effect because prosodically recessive positions are required to contain low-sonority vowels. In the next section, I turn to the reduction pattern attested in positions in which, for a number of reasons, extreme reduction fails to apply.

4.3. Blocking of extreme reduction

Traditional descriptions of Russian report blocking of the extreme reduction in absolute phrase-initial position, for example, [agaˈrot] *[əgaˈrot] 'garden', [akruˈʒat^j] *[əkruˈʒat^j] 'surround'. In addition, reduction to schwa does not occur in hiatus positions in which /o/ or /a/ is preceded by /e/ or followed by another /o/ or /a/, for instance, [n^{j}ɪadnaˈkratnɨj̯] 'frequent', [naabaˈrot] 'conversely' (see section 2.3 in Chapter 2 for details; the discussion and analysis presented in this section is based on Mołczanow, 2015).

Schwa is excluded from word-initial position in many languages, for instance French (Anderson, 1982), Dutch (Booij, 1995), or German (Wiese, 1996). The phonotactic restrictions on the distribution of schwa have been usually attributed to its structure. Van Oostendorp (1995: 123) suggests that schwa lacks melodic content, and, thus, the gaps in the distribution of [ə] can be accounted for by assuming that an empty vowel cannot occur in a syllable with an empty onset. This idea is formalized in terms of OT by means of the following constraint (van Oostendorp, 1995):

(6) CONTOUR: If the head of a syllable is empty, its onset may not be empty.

In Russian, reduction to a schwa is blocked both phrase-initially as well as in word-medial positions, which can be modelled by granting CONTOUR the status of an undominated constraint. While extreme reduction does not take place phrase-initially, it applies regularly in vowel-initial words which occur inside a phonological phrase, as in /vsko'pal ogo'rodɨ/ [fska'pal əga'rodɨ] 'he dug gardens', *cf.* /ogo'rod/ [aga'rot] 'garden'. However, the failure of extreme reduction to be blocked in phrase-internal positions does not constitute counterevidence for the operation of CONTOUR. Knjazev (2006: 36–42) offers ample evidence demonstrating that there is resyllabification across word boundaries in Russian. Therefore, a sequence of a consonant and a vowel flanking two adjacent words is monosyllabic, as in [fska.'pa.lə. ga.'ro. dɨ]. In this scenario, CONTOUR does not block extreme reduction because schwa is preceded by an onset which is filled with a melodic material.[54] When a word-initial vowel occurs after another vowel, as in /mo'i ogo'rodɨ/ [ma'i aga'rodɨ] 'my gardens', reduction to schwa is prevented because the reduced vowel is not preceded by a tautosyllabic consonant.

Schwa can be preceded by another vowel in word-internal positions in loan words, for example, [vʲɪəlan't͡ʃʲelʲ] 'violoncello', [pʲi'rʲiət] 'period'.[55] However, traditional descriptions vary as to the quality of the reduced vowel. Kalenčuk and Kasatkina (2013: 76–78) record two pronunciations, [ɪa] and [ɪə], for the sequences /io/, /ia/, for example, [dʲɪaga'nalʲ]/[dʲɪəga'nalʲ] 'diagonal'; and [ɨə] for /ɨa/, e.g. [nət͡sɨənalʲi'zat͡sɨ̯jə] 'nationalisation'. Shapiro (1968: 24) transcribes /io/ as [ɪa] in the word [vʲɪalan't͡ʃʲelʲ] 'violoncello'. According to Avanesov (1984: 109–110), hiatus sequences consisting of a high vowel followed by a nonhigh vowel are tautosyllabic as they tend to be pronounced as centring diphthongs. Avanesov (1984:110) transcribes them as [ⁱə], [ⁱə], [ᵘa], for instance, [nət͡sⁱənalʲi'zat͡sɨ̯jə]. A schwa which is a part of a

[54] CONTOUR has to operate at the level of a phrase, after the resyllabification at word boundaries takes effect; otherwise, it would block reduction in vowel-initial words occurring in phrase medial positions.

[55] Vowel reduction is suspended in borrowings which are perceived as foreign words, whereas borrowings which cease to be felt as foreign undergo vowel reduction (Jones and Ward, 1923/1969; Shapiro, 1968).

diphthong [ˈə], [ˈə] does not occur in an onsetless syllable, and, consequently, is not within the purview of CONTOUR.

As mentioned in section 2.3, reduction does not take place in hiatus sequences. Whereas reduction regularly applies when the second member in hiatus is a high vowel, as in [nəiˈzusʲtʲ] 'by heart', [nəuˈgat] 'by guesswork', reduction to schwa is blocked in the first position in hiatus involving vowels /o/ and /a/, so instead of the expected [əa], the underlying /aa/, /oo/, /ao/ and /oa/ reduce to [aa]. Some examples from section 2.3 are repeated below.

(7) /oo/ → [aa]/ [vaapˈʃ:e] *[vəapˈʃ:e]'generally'
/ao/ → [aa]/ [naabaˈrot] *[nəabaˈrot] 'conversely'

The blocking of the extreme reduction in hiatus positions can be assumed to constitute a case of coarticulation, where the first vowel assimilates to the height feature of the following low vowel. In OT terms, assimilation is compelled by the following markedness constraint:

(8) ALIGN-L([+low], Word): For the feature [+low] associated to a segment in a word, that feature has an association to the leftmost segment of a word.

This constraint belongs to the family of alignment constraints used to derive harmony in OT (Kirchner, 1993; harmonic processes and the ways to model them are further discussed in Chapter 6, section 6.2). As shown by the evaluation of the unstressed string /naa/ in [naabaˈrot] in Tableau (9), candidate (9b) loses because it does not comply with ALIGN-L([+low], Word).

(9) *Blocking of extreme reduction in hiatus positions*

/naa/	ALIGN-L([+low], Word)	CONTOUR	$*\text{-}\Delta_{\omega}\geq\{i,u\}$
⇒ a. na.a			**
b. nə.a	*!		*

Assimilation to the following vowel in hiatus is blocked when the reduced vowel is followed by a high vowel (10a) or when the first vowel is front (10b).

(10) a. [əu] [pəuˈka] 'spider' (gen. sg.)[56]
b. [ɪa] [nʲɪakuˈratnɨj] *[nʲaakuˈratnɨj] 'untidy'

Assimilation in hiatus with high vowels, as in (10a) is blocked by the faithfulness constraints requiring the identity of the height features. The evaluation

[56] In casual speech, the vowel [ə] may optionally assimilate to the following [u]: *pauka* [pəuˈka] ~ [pʊuˈka] 'spider' (gen. sg.) (Paufošima, 1980).

of the unstressed sequence /au/ is displayed in Tableau (11). On the one hand, progressive assimilation (candidate (11d) is prevented by a high-ranked IDENT-V[+high].[57] On the other hand, regressive assimilation is ruled out by the low-ranked $*\text{-}\Delta_{\omega}\geq\{i,u\}$, which plays a decisive role in choosing between candidates (11a) and (11c). Notably, candidate (11c) is the optimal output in casual speech (see fn. 56). This can be formalized by assuming that the constraint ALIGN-L([Feature], Word) requiring spreading of all vocalic features is high-ranked in informal register in Russian.

(11) *Extreme reduction in hiatus positions*

/au/	IDENT-V[+high]	ALIGN-L([+low], Word)	$*\text{-}\Delta_{\omega}\geq\{i,u\}$
⇒ a. ə.u			*
b. a.u			**!
c. ʊ.u			**!
d. a.a	*!		**

The blockage of assimilation in (10b) is analysed in Tableau (12), which shows the evaluation of the initial sequence of the word *neakkuratnyj* [nʲɪaku'ratnɨj̯] 'untidy'. The faithful mapping (candidate 12b) and the assimilated sequence [a.a] in candidate (12c) lose due to the undominated AGREE[+high] ('A consonant and a following vowel agree in height'). [58]

(12) *[i]-reduction in hiatus positions*

/nʲea/	AGREE [+high]	IDENT-V [-back]	ALIGN-L ([+low], Word)	$*\text{-}\Delta_{\omega}\geq\{i,u\}$
⇒ a. nʲɪ.a			*	*
b. nʲe.a	*		*!	**
c. nʲa.a	*	*!		**

The final point to be addressed concerns the quality of a reduced vowel in onset-initial positions. Here, /o/ and /a/ neutralize in favour of the low vowel [a], which is identical to the outcome of moderate reduction taking place in immediately pretonic positions. However, the lowering to [a] in onsetless atonic syllables cannot be attributed to the interaction with a High tone, because the High tone is only associated with vowels which occur in tonic and immediately pretonic positions. As demonstrated in section 4.2 earlier

[57] It will be demonstrated in section 5.3 that this faithfulness constraint is responsible for blocking the reduction of high vowels in general.

[58] This constraint is further discussed in section 7.2.2 in Chapter 7.

in this chapter, there is a pressure to reduce sonority in unstressed syllables in Russian, which is formally expressed by the constraint $*\text{-}\Delta_{\omega}\geq\{i,u\}$. This constraint assures that only high vowels and schwa are allowed to occur in atonic positions. While schwa is excluded from atonic onsetless syllables by the high-ranked CONTOUR, both [o] and [a] fail on $*\text{-}\Delta_{\omega}\geq\{i,u\}$ (see the evaluation of the initial vowel in the word *ogorod* [aga'rot] 'garden' in Tableau (14)). I assume that the tie between [a] and [o] is resolved by the constraint $*\Delta_{\sigma}\leq\{e,o\}$, which prefers high-sonority syllable heads (adapted from de Lacy, 2006: 288).

(13) $*\Delta_{\sigma}\leq\{e,o\}$: Assign a violation mark for every head of a syllable that contains a segment with sonority less than or equal to {e,o}.

(14) *Phrase-initial blocking of extreme reduction*

/o/	CONTOUR	$*\text{-}\Delta_{\omega}\geq\{i,u\}$	$*\Delta_{\sigma}\leq\{e,o\}$	IDENT-V[−high]
⇒ a. a		*		
b. o		*	*!	
c. ə	*!		*	
d. u		*	*!	*

In order not to block the reduction to schwa in atonic positions which are not within the purview of CONTOUR, $*\text{-}\Delta_{\omega}\geq\{i,u\}$ must dominate the constraint $*\Delta_{\sigma}\leq\{e,o\}$ forcing high-sonority nuclei.[59]

To conclude, extreme reduction is blocked phrase-initially and in hiatus sequences consisting of non-high vowels. In the present analysis, these two contexts are subsumed under a broader rubric of an onsetless syllable. The high-ranked CONTOUR disallows schwa to occur in a syllable without a filled onset. However, no reduction to schwa is observed in vowel-initial words in phrase-internal positions. It has been argued that this data does not constitute counterevidence because schwa does not occur in onsetless syllables in these contexts. Furthermore, the blockage of extreme reduction does not result in a faithful mapping between the input and the output. Instead, the onset-initial /o/ lowers to [a], which makes this process similar to reduction found in immediately pretonic positions. Despite the surface parallelism, I suggest that vowel lowering in immediately pretonic syllables and in atonic onsetless syllables are produced by two different mechanisms. In the former case, the neutralization to a low vowel [a] has been motivated by its association with the High tone, while in the latter, the reduction is forced by a prosodic well-formedness constraint $*\Delta_{\sigma}\leq\{e,o\}$ requiring sonority maximization in syllabic heads.

---

[59] This analysis is parallel to de Lacy's (2006) account of Catalan.

4.4. Previous approaches to Russian vowel reduction

As been mentioned above, vowel reduction has been extensively studied within most phonological theories, and, most recently, within the framework of Optimality Theory (van Oostendorp, 1995; Alderete, 1995; Crosswhite, 2001; de Lacy, 2006; Iosad, 2012; among many others). The models of vowel reduction in Russian usually address two facts. The first fact has to do with different types of reduction occurring in unstressed syllables: extreme reduction in atonic contexts and moderate reduction in immediately pretonic positions. The second fact is related to the quality of the reduced vowels in palatalized and non-palatalized contexts. In this section, I show how these issues have been dealt with in some of the previous models of vowel reduction.

The first fact, concerning the asymmetry between immediately pretonic and atonic positions, has been either marginalized or not addressed at all in the previous accounts of vowel reduction. In some models, extreme reduction is denied a phonological status and is claimed to be a phonetic effect of reduced duration (Barnes, 2006, 2007; Iosad, 2012). On this view, the outcomes of extreme and moderate reductions are distinct due to differences in the phonetic realization of the same vowel in durationally impoverished contexts. Another approach to extreme reduction states that syllables showing extreme reduction are extrametrical (Crosswhite, 2001). That is, they are not incorporated into the foot, but linked directly to the phonological word (PW) node. This structural distinction (footed *vs.* stray syllables) relates to position's ability to undergo reduction in that moderate reduction affects vowels in a foot-dependent position, while unfooted vowels undergo extreme reduction. Furthermore, Crosswhite hypothesizes that reduced vowels occurring in stray syllables are nonmoraic. This approach raises an objection, as it is not clear how moraless vowels could function as syllable peaks. In autosegmental phonology (Goldsmith, 1976, 1990), the structure wherein a vocalic melody is not linked to a mora has been reserved for glides. To distinguish nonmoraic vocalic segments from consonants, which are inherently moraless, and from glides, which lose their moras in the process of gliding, Crosswhite re-introduces the SPE feature [±syllabic]. This, however, forfeits the basic insight of autosegmental phonology that syllabicity is predictable and, therefore, need not be encoded in the underlying representation.

The second fact mentioned above, concerning distinct vowel inventories found in different prosodic and segmental contexts, has been at the centre of attention of many researchers working on the subject of vowel reduction. Crosswhite (2001) suggests that reduction to peripheral vowels in immediately pretonic positions is perceptually-driven, whereas centralization in atonic syllables is articulatory-driven. Reduction in pretonic syllables serves to enhance contrast: peripheral vowels are more salient and, hence, easier to perceive in prosodically weak positions. In turn, reduction in atonic contexts is analysed as prominence reduction and is assumed to result from a production-based target undershoot.

In contrast, non-functional accounts view vowel reduction as a process not grounded in phonetics. A proposal in terms of a substance-free phonology by Iosad (2012) builds an analysis of Russian vowel reduction based on a representational model. In this approach, [a]-reduction consists in a loss of a privative feature [closed] and an addition of the feature [open]. By referring to just one feature, it has an advantage over accounts using feature conjunction. Nevertheless, the analysis prohibiting the feature [closed] in prosodically weak positions is a restatement of a descriptive generalization about the non-occurrence of mid vowels in unstressed syllables. Moreover, it can equally well generate the opposite system, in which *u* reduces to *o*, and it does not provide an explanation why mid vowels, and not high or low vowels, are targets of reduction.

This problem does not arise in the markedness-based approach, in which the reduction of /o/, /e/ to [a], [i] is taken to reflect the fact that mid vowels are typologically more marked than high and low vowels (Maddieson, 1984). Within the paradigm of Optimality Theory, this is analysed employing the constraint *Mɪᴅ ('No mid vowels') (e.g., Alderete, 1995; Mołczanow, 2007). However, the change of /o/ to [a] is attested in systems which also exhibit the raising of /a/ to [e] after palatalized consonants (as discussed in section 7.2.1, Chapter 7). In effect, models explicitly banning mid vowels from prosodically weak positions are bound to stipulate that mid back vowels but not mid front vowels are subject to a constraint against unstressed mid vowels in East Slavic dialects with [a]-reduction and [e]-reduction.

An attractive alternative to markedness approaches is offered by the element-based theory (e.g., Harris, 1994, 2005), in which the avoidance of unstressed mid vowels is modelled in terms of the reduction in segmental complexity. In this approach, the corner vowels *a, i, u* are represented with the single resonance elements A, I, and U, whereas the melodic make-up of the mid vowels ɔ and ɛ is characterized with the two expressions, {U,A} and {I,A}. Vowel reduction then consists in the elimination of one (or all) of the elements. For instance, the change of *o* to *a* is viewed as the loss of the element {U}, and the reduction to schwa, which is a common process cross-linguistically, is analysed as the loss of all the resonance elements.

However, all the models banning mid vowels from prosodically weak positions (whether based on contrast enhancement, markedness, or element complexity) fail in cases where mid vowels are not the targets but the outcomes of reduction. A pattern in which unstressed /a/ and /o/ are neutralized into [e] after palatalized consonants and into [o] after non-palatalized consonants is attested in a number of East Slavic dialects, including northern Russian dialects, south-western dialects, and northern Ukrainian dialects (Nazarova, 1961; Vajtovič, 1968; Jakobson, 1971; Al'muxamedova and Kul'šaripova, 1980; Kasatkin, 2005; Požarickaja, 2005; Bethin, 2012). Some examples from the northern Russian dialects are provided below; the data come from Kasatkin (2005: 41), Požarickaja (2005: 46), and Al'muxamedova and Kul'šaripova (1980: 17–18).

(15) *Northern Russian dialects with [o]-reduction and [e]-reduction*
a. *Pretonic [e] after* palatalized *consonants*
[rʲeˈdɨ] 'row' (nom. pl.) *cf.* [ˈrʲat] id. (nom. sg.)
[nʲeˈsu] 'carry' (1st pers. pres. sg.) [ˈnʲos] id. (3rd pers. past masc.)
[pʲeˈtak] 'five-rouble note' [ˈpʲatʲ] 'five'
b. *Pretonic [o] after non-palatalized consonants*
[stoˈrʲik] 'old man' (nom. pl.) *cf.* [ˈstar] 'old' (short form)
[soˈdɨ] 'garden' (nom. pl.) [ˈsat] id. (nom. sg.)
[stoˈlɨ] 'table' (nom. pl.) [ˈstol] id. (nom. sg.)

Systems exhibiting [e]-reduction and [o]-reduction, as in (15) above, are problematic from the perspective of both the markedness-based and the element-based models banning mid vowels from prosodically weak positions. First, raising to the mid vowels creates more marked segments, thus defying the main assumption of the markedness-based approaches, in which vowel reduction is equated with the reduction in markedness. Second, the existence of such patterns demonstrates that not all cases of neutralization lead to the decrease in the segmental complexity, as assumed in the element-based theory. It was mentioned earlier in this section that [a] is represented with the element 'A', while [o] is defined by the combination of the elements 'A' and 'U', so the change from *a* to *o* increases segment's complexity. Similarly, the raising from *a* to *e* is implemented through the addition of the element 'I', rendering the outcome of reduction more complex than its unreduced counterpart.

As regards [e]-reduction, it might be objected that the neutralization of non-high vowels into [e] in (15a) does not constitute reduction as such, but is due solely to the palatalization of the preceding consonant. In terms of the Element Theory, this can be achieved through the spreading of the element I, which is independently present in palatalized consonants. The same result can be obtained using the OT constraint Cʲ/[+front] ('In unstressed syllables, a palatalized consonant must be followed by a [+front] vowel', Crosswhite, 2001: 77), or PAL ('A consonant and a following vowel agree in backness', Rubach, 2003: 216). A special status of [e]-raising as an independent process is supported by the fact that it is often attested in the absence of [o]-raising (i.e., in the dialects which preserve the full set of vowels in unstressed positions after non-palatalized consonants).[60] Yet, as shown by the data in (15) above, there exist systems in which [e]-raising is accompanied by [o]-raising, the latter change taking place after non-palatalized consonants. As the secondary articulation of velarization is represented with the particle @ in the Element Theory (*cf.* Harris, 1994: 119), its spreading cannot be responsible for the switch of *a* {A} to *o* {AU}. The same problem arises in the feature-based theories, which define velarization either with the feature [+back], as in the Halle–Sagey model (Sagey, 1986; Halle, 1992), or with the privative feature [dorsal], as in the Clements–Hume model of feature geometry (Clements, 1985; Clements and Hume, 1995) or the Parallel Structures Model (Morén, 2003).[61] As both *a* and *o* are specified for the feature [+back] in the Halle–Sagey model, and for [dorsal] in the Clements–Hume model, the addition of neither [+back] nor [dorsal] can derive the raising of /a/ to [o]. Therefore, while [e]-raising can be analysed in terms of the coarticulation with the preceding consonant, this explanation is not available in the case of the raising of /a/ to [o].[62] The present model analyses raising of the low vowel /a/ in terms of prominence reduction. It is assumed that High tone is not active in the dialects not exhibiting [a]-reduction in the immediately pretonic position. Consequently, such dialects are predicted either to lack phonological reduction altogether or to exhibit one-degree reduction. As discussed earlier in this chapter, phonological reduction in positions not affected by the lexical tone is analysed, after de Lacy (2006), by means of the constraint families regulating the sonority level of prosodic heads and non-heads. On this view, vowel raising is driven by the constraint $*\text{-}\Delta_{\omega}\geq\{a\}$, which prohibits highly sonorous low vowels in prosodically recessive positions. This analysis explains the asymmetry in the distribution of [e]-reduction and [o]-reduction: if a given dialect raises /a/ after non-palatalized consonants, it also raises it after palatalized consonants, but not the other way round. That is, the high-ranked $*\text{-}\Delta_{\omega}\geq\{a\}$ drives both [e]-raising and [o]-raising, whereas PAL only triggers the raising

[60] Interestingly, the opposite pattern, with [o]-raising but no [e]-raising, is rare (*cf.* Bethin, 2012a: 3).

[61] The Parallel Structures Model (Morén, 2003) has been employed in the Iosad's (2012) analysis of Russian vowel reduction.

[62] Bethin (2012a) suggests a phonetically-based explanation, in which both [e]-raising and [o]-raising are argued to be motivated by the extended onset-nucleus transitions and the close transitions from a vowel into a following consonant.

of /a/ to [e] after palatalized consonants. It is predicted then that a system with a high-ranked $*\text{-}\Delta_{\omega}{\geq}\{a\}$ will raise /a/ both after palatalized and non-palatalized consonants (to [o] and [e], respectively), while a system with a high-ranked PAL will only exhibit [e]-raising.

4.5. Summary

This chapter has presented an analysis of vowel reduction taking place in positions not immediately preceding tonic syllables. This pattern of reduction is generated by the requirement to decrease vocalic sonority in prosodically recessive positions, where /o/ and /a/ neutralize to [ə]. Additionally, the blocking of extreme reduction in phrase-initial and hiatus positions has been attributed to the prohibition against onsetless syllables headed by the featureless vowel schwa. The next chapter will demonstrate that vowels in immediately pretonic positions do not reduce to schwa due to the High tone, which forces the lowering of /o/ to [a].

Chapter 5

Tone-driven reduction

5.1. Introduction

The goal of this chapter is to develop an analysis of vowel neutralization attested in immediately pretonic position. I argue that [a]-reduction is directly connected with the presence of High tone and demonstrate that the constraints which directly relate High tone to sonority levels account for vowel neutralizations occurring in immediately pretonic positions in various reduction systems both in standard Russian as well as in various dialects .

The chapter is structured as follows. Background information motivating the tonal analysis is provided in section 5.2. Then, the OT model of the non-dissimilative reduction attested in standard Russian is presented in section 5.3. Section 5.4 looks at dissimilative patterns of reduction, arguing that the subtle differences between different types of dissimilative reduction can be modelled based on minimal variations in the rankings of the members of the *H≤V family and HEAD=H, the constraint requiring stressed syllable to be associated with H. Next, section 5.5 brings in data from pretonic length dialects, which, though similar in terms of foot structure to the dissimilative patterns discussed earlier, are argued to be generated by an additional mechanism. Section 5.6 discusses the factorial typology, demonstrating how the constraints permutations (FT=BIN, ALIGN-L(H, FT), HEAD=H, *H≤V, and constraints on sonority of prosodic heads and non-heads) generate further reduction systems. Finally, section 5.7 presents an interim conclusion.

5.2. Background

It is noteworthy that two seemingly disparate processes are found in the same position in East Slavic. That is, the so-called moderate reduction in Contemporary Standard Russian occurs in the position in which some East Slavic dialects exhibit lengthening (Vojtovič, 1972a; Belaja, 1974; Bethin,

2006). This is illustrated in (1) with different pronunciations of the word *nosit'* 'to carry'.

(1) /no'sʲitʲ/ *nosit'* 'to carry'

a. [na'sʲitʲ]: reduction	*Standard Russian*
b. [no:'sʲitʲ]: lengthening	*Belarusian dialect of Malyja Aŭciuki*
c. [na:'sʲitʲ]: reduction *and* lengthening	*Ukrainian Upper Snov Basin dialects*

The mid vowel /o/ is lowered to [a] in the immediately pretonic syllable in standard Russian (1a), and lengthened in the pretonic position in the Belarusian dialect of Malyja Aŭciuki (1b). Interestingly, immediately pretonic vowels undergo both reduction and lengthening in Ukrainian Upper Snov Basin dialects (1c).

Bethin (2006) argues that pretonic lengthening in East Slavic is caused by a rising tone which is associated with the immediately pretonic syllable. Instrumental measurements as well as impressionistic descriptions confirm the presence of the LHL contour in this context at least in some dialects (Bethin, 2006).

Tone has played an important role in the development of Slavic, and its presence is manifest in the present-day Slavic languages (Jakobson, 1929, 1931, *et seq.*; Inkelas and Zec, 1988; Halle, 1997; Bethin, 1998, 2006; Dubina, 2012; and others). Contrastive tone is employed in the dialects of Serbian and Croatian (Lehiste and Ivić, 1986) and in Slovenian (Becker and Jurgec, 2017). In addition to East Slavic dialects (Bethin, 2006), non-contrastive tone has been postulated for standard Russian (Halle, 1997) and Belarusian (Dubina, 2012).

Bethin (2006) suggests that the lengthening of pretonic vowels found in East Slavic dialects is due to the underlying tonal contour LHL. Furthermore, she relates intrinsic vowel duration to sonority and the ability to carry High tone in dissimilative East Slavic dialects, with High tone preferring more sonorous vowels to vowels with lower sonority (Bethin, 2006: 144–146). The distribution of High tone in dissimilative dialects is shown in (2), reproduced from Bethin (2006: 145).

(2) *Tonal contour in the dissimilative dialects*

H L		HL
CV_1'CV_2	~	CV_1'CV_2
V_1= non-high V_2= high		V_1= high V_2= non-high

Dubina (2012) extends this analysis to standard Belarusian and suggests that the increased prominence of the immediately pretonic syllable results from a process of Anticipatory H-spreading (p. 187).

(3) *Anticipatory H-spreading (Dubina, 2012)*

H

ɣaladranačkaj

'tramp' (fem., dim., instr. sg.)

According to Dubina (2012), the lowering of mid vowels to [a] occurring in immediately pretonic syllables of Belarusian increases the intrinsic duration, which, in turn, promotes the production of the pitch contour.

Anticipatory H-spreading postulated for Belarusian mirrors the analysis of Inkelas and Zec (1988), who suggest that pitch contrasts attested in the Neo-Štokavian dialects of Serbian and Croatian are due to the leftward spreading of the lexically specified High tone, as shown in (4a) and (4b) below.

(4) *Neo-Štokavian leftward tone spreading*

a. Short Rising	b. Long Rising
H	H
paprika	raazlika
'pepper'	'difference'

It should be borne in mind that, despite the postulated structural similarity, there is an important difference between Neo-Štokavian and Belarusian, because the tonal contour in Neo-Štokavian is contrastive and manifested through F_0 properties. In Belarusian, in turn, tone is employed as a phonological construct not translatable into phonetic pitch.

Similarly to the analysis of Belarusian proposed by Dubina (2012), I assume that H tone is present in the phonological system of standard Russian and the dialects exhibiting pretonic neutralizations. I further suggest that in systems with both non-dissimilative and dissimilative [a]-reduction, immediately pretonic vowels lower because they are linked to High tone.

5.3. Non-dissimilative reduction

As we have seen in Chapter 1, some languages display an interaction between tone and segmental structure. For example, high tones do not co-occur with high vowels in a number of Japanese dialects (Haraguchi, 1984), High tone is predictable in Ngizim, in which it is associated with the low vowel [a] in some grammatical categories (Schuh, 1971), and the interaction of tone with ATR has been reported in Slovenian (Becker and Jurgec, 2017), to mention just a few examples (see section 1.3 in Chapter 1 for further discussion of cases of tone–vowel interaction). I have suggested that the interaction between tone and segmental quality can be modelled in OT employing the constraints formed by conflating the sonority scale with tonal prominence scale.

The markedness constraints relating High tone with sonority which are relevant to the analysis of vowel reduction are repeated in (5).

(5) *H/ɨ: Assign a violation mark for every high central vowel associated with a High tone.
*H/ɨ;ə: Assign a violation mark for every high or mid central vowel associated with a High tone.
*H/ɨ;ə;i,u: Assign a violation mark for every central or high peripheral vowel associated with a High tone.
*H/ɨ;ə;i,u;e,o: Assign a violation mark for every central, high, or mid-high peripheral vowel associated with a High tone.
*H/ɨ;ə;i,u;e,o;ɛ,ɔ: Assign a violation mark for every central or non-low peripheral vowel associated with a High tone.
*H/ɨ;ə;i,u;e,o;ɛ,ɔ;a: Assign a violation mark for every vowel associated with a High tone.

Let us recall from Chapter 3 (section 3.5) that the pretonic vowel is associated with H tone in standard Russian, in which the tone-bearing syllable is parsed into the weak position of a disyllabic iamb as follows.

(6) H
σ(σ'σ)σ

The constraints generating this metrical structure include FtForm=Iamb and Ft=Bin, which are responsible for the binary iambic forms, and HdFt = H and Align-L(H, Ft), insuring that the output contains H tone aligned with the left edge of the foot (the constraints are motivated in section 3.5, see also Tableau 11 in section 3.5 showing the evaluation of the candidate set using these constraints). These constraints work in tandem with the *H≤V family of constraints formulated in (5) above in inducing the lowering of the vowel associated with H tone.

The illustration is provided in Tableau (7) showing the evaluation of the word /vo'da/ [va'da] 'water', nom. sg. (*cf.* acc. sg. form *vodu* ['vodʊ]). For compactness, the range of candidates is limited to those that are relevant to the analysis of pretonic reduction.

(7) *[a] – reduction*

/vo'da/	ALIGN-L (H, FT)	HDFT = H	FT = BIN	*H/≤a	*H/≤ə	*H/≤e,o	HD = H	IDENT [-low]	IDENT [+round]
H ⇒ a. (va'da)				*			*	*	*
H b. (vo'da)				*		*!	*		
H c. (və'da)				*	*!	*	*		
H d. (vo'da)	*!			*					
H e vo('da)			*!	*					
f. (vo'da)		*!					*		

The candidate (7a) wins over a more faithful candidate (7b) because it lowers the immediately pretonic mid vowel and thus avoids violating the markedness constraint *H/≤e,o. Candidate (7d) eschews violation of *H/≤e,o by associating High tone to the right-hand syllable in the foot, which results in a fatal violation of ALIGN-L(H, FT). The comparison of candidates (7d) with the winner (7a) provides an argument for the ranking ALIGN-L(H, FT) >> *H/≤a. Reduction to schwa in candidate (7c) is not an option due to the violations of a host of markedness constraints (*H/≤ə, *H/≤e,o, and *H/≤a). Unlike the optimal output (7a), candidate (7e) does not violate faithfulness constraints; but it parses the stressed syllable into a unary foot and thus is excluded by FT=BIN. The most faithful contender (7f) loses due to its fatal violation of HDFT = H.

The vowels in the stressed syllables do not lower under the pressure of tone. It has been long known that certain positions, including stressed syllables, resist phonological change (Trubetzkoy, 1939). In OT, this observation has been incorporated into the positional faithfulness approach, stating that faithfulness constraints are stronger in some positions (Beckman, 1997; Casali, 1997). In the case at hand, stressed syllables are the privileged position where markedness considerations are overridden by the following requirement to preserve feature identity:

(8) IDENT-V[feature]$_{\mathrm{HDFT}}$: In stressed syllables, a given value of the feature on a vowel in the input must be preserved on the corresponding vowel in the output.

The evaluation of the word /'kot/ ['kot] 'cat' is illustrated in Tableau (9).

(9) *Preservation of vocalic contrast in stressed syllables*

/ˈkot/	IDENT-V [feature]$_{HDFT}$	*H/≤e,o	*H/≤a	IDENT [-low]	IDENT [+round]
H ⇒ a. (ˈkot)		*	*		
H b. (ˈkat)	*!		*	*	*

Let us observe that high vowels should also lower under the constraint scheme suggested (5). However, they do not undergo reduction either in systems with non-dissimilative reduction, as in standard Russian, or in the dialects with different types of dissimilative reduction. Notably, high vowels also do not lengthen in East Slavic dialects, in which lengthening of the immediately pretonic vowels is conditioned by a tonal contour (Bethin, 2006). Experimental phonetic studies have demonstrated that high vowels are produced with higher fundamental frequencies than low vowels (Lehiste and Peterson, 1961; Mohr, 1971; Hombert *et al.*, 1979). So it might be the case that higher intrinsic pitch renders high vowels good carriers of High tone. However, it is not clear whether this fact is responsible for the absence of reduction and lengthening of high vowels. I assume that the reduction of high vowels is blocked by a high-ranked faithfulness constraint IDENT-V[+high] mandating that correspondent vowels in the input and the output are [+high].

As shown in (10) by the evaluation of the word /duˈʃa/ [duˈʃa] 'soul', nom. sg. (*cf.* nom. pl. form *dušy* [ˈduʃɨ]), the faithful candidate (10a) wins despite the violation of the markedness constraints *H/≤i,u and *H/≤a because it preserves an underlying high vowel.

(10) *Non-reduction of high vowels*

/duˈʃa/	IDENT-V[+high]	*H/≤i,u	*H/≤a
H ⇒ a. (duˈʃa)		*	*
H b. (daˈʃa)	*!		*

Let us now consider the reduction of the unstressed vowel [e]. In native Russian words, this vowel can only occur after palatalized consonants.[63] In borrowings, however, the vowel [e] is found after non-palatalized consonants and

---

63 For the analysis of [e]-reduction after palatalized consonants, see Chapter 7.

in word-initial position, e.g. [ɛ'taʃ] 'floor', [sɛn'tɛnt͡sɨi̯ə] 'maxim'. According to the prescriptive norms, only fully assimilated borrowings undergo vowel reduction and the occurrence of reduced/unreduced vowels in loanwords is subject to much variation. For instance, the word /fo'nɛtʲika/ 'phonetics' can be pronounced either [fo'nɛtʲɪkə] or [fa'nɛtʲɪkə], where the immediately pretonic /o/ can optionally reduce to [a]. The present system of constraints predicts the same reduction pattern for the vowel [e] in immediately pretonic positions. However, unlike [o], [e] never reduces to [a] even in fully assimilated borrowings and native speakers find the pronunciations such as *[a'taʃ] and *[san'tɛnt͡sɨi̯ə] unacceptable (Crosswhite, 2001: 107). To account for the asymmetrical behaviour of the unstressed mid vowels in borrowings, I assume that the lowering of [e] is prevented by a high-ranked faithfulness constraint IDENT-V[-back]:

(11) IDENT-V[-back]: The feature [-back] on a vowel in the input must be preserved on the corresponding vowel in the output.

The ranking IDENT-V[-back] >> *H/≤ ɛ,ɔ ensures that [e] does not change into [a] under the pressure to maximize sonority of the immediately pretonic vowels. The evaluation of the word /ɛ'taʒ/ [ɛ'taʃ] 'floor' in (12) below illustrates the point.

(12) *Non-reduction of [e]*

/ɛ'taʒ/	IDENT-V[-back]	*H/≤ɛ,ɔ	*H/≤a
H ⇒ a. (ɛ'taʃ)		*	*
H b. (a'taʃ)	*!		*

The ranking which generates vowel neutralization in immediately pretonic positions is summarized in Figure 5.1. For compactness, the constraints on

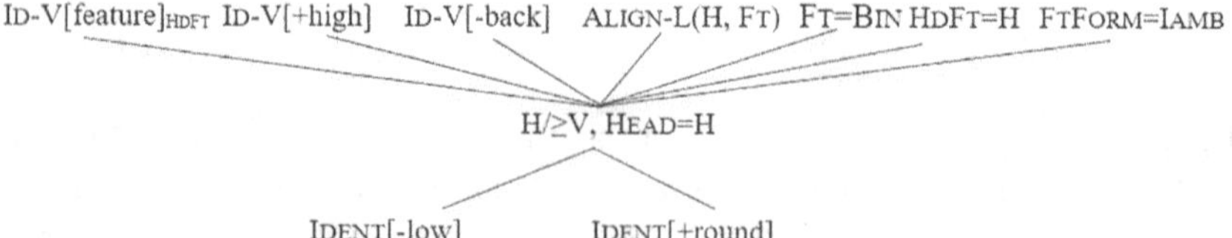

Figure 5.1: Pretonic reduction: Interim ranking.

the co-occurrence of the High tone with different vowels are collectively referred to as *H≤V.

As reflected by this ranking scheme, the lowering of mid vowels is driven by the family of constraints *H≤V, which dominate the faithfulness constraints IDENT[-low] and IDENT[+round]. Vowels in lexically accented syllables are immune to change due to the high-ranked ID-V[feature]$_{\text{HDFT}}$. In turn, high vowels and front vowels are excluded from lowering because *H/≤a is outranked by IDENT-V[+high] and ID-V[-back]. The ranking argument for ALIGN-L(H, FT) >> *H/≤V is based on the fact that the leftward spreading of the High tone takes place even though it produces a marked structure, as illustrated in Tableau (7) above. ALIGN-L(H, FT) outranks HEAD=H because H tone is linked to the pretonic syllable in systems with non-dissimilative reduction. HEAD=H is also dominated by FT=BIN, HDFT=H, and FTFORM=IAMB, the ranking arguments have been established in Chapter 3 (*cf.* Tableau (11) in section 3.5).

To conclude briefly, this section has developed an analysis of non-dissimilative vowel reduction. Based on the insight of Bethin (2006), I assumed that tone can directly interact with vowel quality due to the family of markedness constraints *H≤V, which are derived by combining the sonority scale with the tonal prominence scale. Whereas vocalic sonority is decreased in prosodically recessive positions, in which /o/ and /a/ neutralize to [ə] (analysed in Chapter 4), vowels in immediately pretonic positions do not reduce to schwa due to the High tone, which forces the lowering of /o/ to [a].

In the ensuing sections, I turn to more complex patterns of dissimilative reduction attested in different East Slavic dialects. It is demonstrated that these systems are generated by minimal rerankings of constraints generating non-dissimilative vowel reduction in standard Russian.

5.4. Dissimilative reduction

5.4.1. Preliminaries

I have suggested in the previous section that [a]-reduction found in the pretonic position in standard Russian is tone-driven. The structural well-formedness constraint ALIGN-L(H, FT) ranked above HEAD=H ensures that High tone is associated with the pretonic syllables, while the *H≤V family of constraints require vowels associated with High tone to lower. Lowering to [a] maximizes vocalic duration, rendering the vowel a better carrier of High tone. The constraint ranking established for standard Russian is provided in (13) below.

(13) *Non-dissimilative reduction*

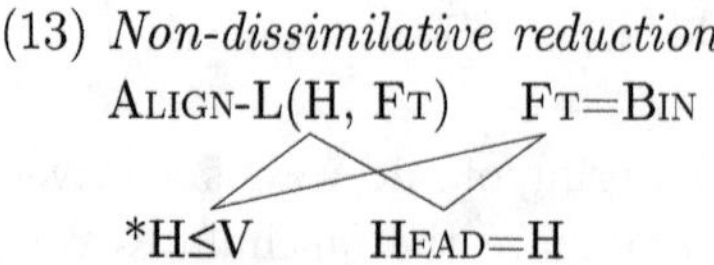

It will be demonstrated in the remainder of this chapter that minimal ranking permutations between (i) Ft=Bin and Align-L(H, Ft) and (ii) Head=H and the members of the *H≤V family of constraints generate vowel reduction systems attested in different East Slavic dialects. Specifically, the demotion of Ft=Bin constraints generates systems in which H tone is not bound to the stressed syllable. Such a system can improve on markedness by placing High tone on the vowel either in the tonic or the pretonic syllable, depending on which vowel makes a better docking site for High tone. The constraint ranking generating these patterns is provided below.

(14) *Dissimilative reduction: general scheme*

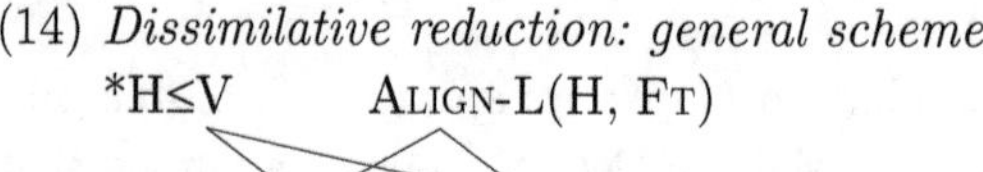

5.4.2. Analysis

Let us recall that systems with dissimilative reduction exhibit neutralization patterns in which the quality of the vowel in pretonic position depends on the quality of the vowel in the stressed syllable (see section 2.5 in Chapter 2 for descriptive generalizations). The low vowel [a] appears in the pretonic syllable if the vowel in the tonic syllable is high, whereas [ə] is found before a low vowel in the tonic syllable. Stressed mid vowels do not exhibit a uniform behaviour in that, depending on the dialect, they trigger either reduction to [a] or to [ə]. This is illustrated in (15), the patterns of dissimilative vowel reduction are schematically represented in (16), repeated from section 2.5, Chapter 2.

(15) [a] before high vowels in the tonic syllable (Žizdra, Obojan', Don)
[tra'vɨ] 'grass' (gen. sg.)
[ə] *before low vowels in the tonic syllable (Žizdra, Obojan', Don)*
[trə'va] 'grass' (nom. sg.)
[a] *before mid vowels in the tonic syllable (Žizdra)*
[tra'vʲɛ] 'grass' (dat. sg.)
[ə] *before mid vowels in the tonic syllable (Don)*
[trə'vʲɛ] 'grass' (dat. sg.)
[a] *before high mid vowels,* [ə] *before low mid vowels (Obojan')*
[sa'voi̯] 'owl' (instr. sg.)
[kə'nʲɔm] 'horse' (instr. sg.)

(16) *Types of dissimilative vowel reduction*

a. Žizdra

pretonic	tonic
a	i ɨ u
	ɛ ɔ
ə	a

b. Don

pretonic	tonic
a	i ɨ u
ə	ɛ ɔ
	a

c. Obojan'

pretonic	tonic
a	i ɨ u
	e o
ə	ɛ ɔ
	a

I assume that the differences in behaviour of the pretonic vowel in the three systems arise from the ranking permutations between HEAD=H and the constraints regulating the association of H with vowels of different sonority profiles. HEAD=H, interleaved between the members of the *H≤V family of constraints, determines the sonority thresholds at which a vowel still qualifies as a carrier of High tone (see ranking scheme in (17) below). In Žizdra (17a), HEAD=H is ranked below *H≤V, which ensures that High tone is preserved only on the low vowel [a] in the stressed syllable. High tone moves to the pretonic position if vowels in the tonic syllables are non-low. As unstressed vowels are not protected by positional faithfulness constraints, they can lower to [a] to accommodate H tone. In Obojan' (17b), HEAD=H is placed higher in the constraint hierarchy, producing a system with high mid vowels triggering [a]-reduction and low mid vowels triggering reduction to [ə]. HEAD=H is situated yet higher in Don (17c), where all non-high vowels are allowed to carry High tone.

(17) *Dissimilative patterns: partial rankings*

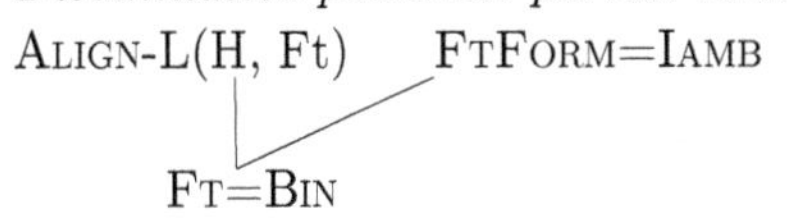

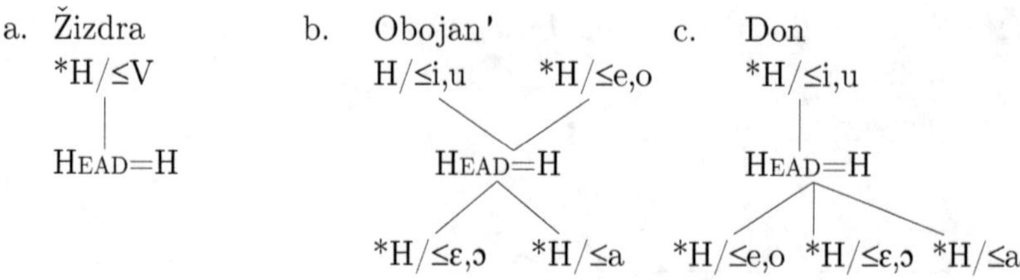

To illustrate how these rankings generate dissimilative reduction patterns, let us first consider the contexts before high and low vowels in the stressed syllables. Let us recall that high vowels trigger [a]-reduction, and low vowels trigger [ə]-reduction in all dissimilative dialects. This is achieved due to the ranking of Head=H below *H/≤i,u. In addition, candidate evaluations show the constraint on foot size Ft=Bin and constraint Align-L(H, Ft) regulating the association of H with foot edge. As established previously (*cf.* section 3.6.2 above), Align-L(H, Ft) dominates Ft=Bin in systems with dissimilative reduction. The evaluation of the words /vɔ'da/ [və'da] 'water' (nom. sg.) and /vɔ'dɨ/ [və'dɨ] 'id.' (gen. sg.). shown in the tableaux in (18) serves to illustrate the point.

(18) *Dissimilative reduction before low and high vowels (all types of dissimilative reduction)*

i. /vo'da/	*H/≤i,u	*H/≤a	Head=H	Align-L(H, Ft)	Ft=Bin
H ⇒ a. və('da)		*			*
H b. (va'da)		*	*!		
H c. (və'da)		*		*!	
ii. /vo'dɨ/	*H/≤i,u	*H/≤a	Head=H	Align-L(H, Ft)	Ft=Bin
H ⇒ a. (va'dɨ)		*	*		
H b. və('dɨ)	*	*!			*

In (18i), the constraint Head=H chooses candidate (18ia) in which High tone docks on the stressed vowel [a]. In (18ii), the high vowel [ɨ] in the stressed syllable is not sonorous enough to host H tone, so the tone docks onto the immediately preceding syllable, as in candidate (18iia).

The outcome of reduction before stressed mid vowels is determined by the ranking of Head=H with respect to *H/≤e,o and *H/≤ɛ,ɔ (see the ranking scheme in (17) above). The tableaux in (19) show the evaluation of the words /sɔ'vʲɔnɨʃ/ [sa'vʲɔnɨʃ] 'baby owl' and /sɔ'voj/ [sə'voj] 'owl' (instr. sg.) in the three patterns of dissimilative reduction. For compactness, only relevant constraints are shown (cf. Tableau 18 in section 3.6.2, Chapter 3, and Tableau in (18) above).

(19) *Dissimilative [a]-reduction before mid vowels*

i. Žizdra

/sɔ'vʲɔnɨʃ/	*H/≤e,o	*H/≤ɛ,ɔ	*H/≤a	Head=H
H ⇒ a. (sa'vʲɔ)nɨʃ			*	*
H b. sə('vʲɔ)nɨʃ		*	*!	

ii. *Don*

/sɔ'voj/	Head=H	*H/≤e,o	*H/≤ɛ,ɔ	*H/≤a
H a. (sa'voj)	*!			*
H ⇒ b. (sə'voj)		*	*	*

iii. *Obojan'*

/sɔ'vjɔnɨʃ/	*H/≤e,o	Head=H	*H/≤ɛ,ɔ	*H/≤a
H a. (sa'vʲɔ)nɨʃ		*!		*
H ⇒ b. sə('vʲɔ)nɨʃ			*	*
/sɔ'voj/	*H/≤e,o	Head=H	*H/≤ɛ,ɔ	*H/≤a
H ⇒ a. (sa'voj)		*		*
H b. sə('voj)	*!		*	*

As shown above, the ranking of Head=H beneath both *H/≤e,o and *H/≤ɛ,ɔ, places H tone on the pretonic syllable, as in Žizdra (see candidate (19ia). The opposite ranking generates the Don pattern, in which H tone is realized on the stressed syllable and pretonic vowels are subject to extreme reduction (19ii). The third option, with Head=H interleaved between *H/≤e,o and *H/≤ɛ,ɔ, is instantiated by the Obojan' pattern (19iii). Here, H tone can be linked to the half-open vowels [e] and [o], but not to the mid vowels [ɛ] and [ɔ]. As a result, pretonic vowels undergo [a]-reduction before [e] and [o], and extreme reduction before [ɛ] and [ɔ].

As mentioned earlier in this chapter, parallel dissimilation patterns are attested after palatalized consonants. The main difference between the two contexts (non-palatalized *vs.* palatalized consonants) lies in the quality of the reduced vowel: schwa is found after non-palatalized consonants, while [i] or [e] after palatalized consonants, e.g. [trəˈva] 'grass' (nom. sg.) *vs.* [tʲiˈlʲat] or [tʲeˈlʲat] 'calf' (gen. pl.). Front vowels appear after palatalized consonants due to the markedness constraint Pal ('A consonant and a following vowel agree in backness', Rubach, 2003: 216)[64], and the further raising to [i] is motivated by Agree[+high] ('A consonant and a following vowel agree in height', Mołczanow, 2007: 206).[65] The choice of either [e] or [i] in a given dialect is made by the relative ranking of Agree[+high] *vis-à-vis* Ident[–high]: the former constraint opts for [i], while the latter gives preference to the output [e]. The point is illustrated by the evaluation of the words /sʲɛˈlɔm/ [sʲiˈlɔm] 'village' (instr. sg.) in the Obojan' type of dissimilative [ja]-reduction.

(20) *Dissimilative [ja]-reduction: Obojan'*

/sʲɛˈl+ɔm/	*H/≤e,o	Head=H	*H/≤ɛ,ɔ	*H/≤a	Pal	Agree [+high]	Ident [–high]
⇒ a. sʲi(ˈlɔm) (H on ɔ)			*	*			*
b. (sʲaˈlɔm) (H on a)		*!		*	*	*	
c. sʲɛ(ˈlɔm) (H on ɔ)			*	*		*!	
d. sʲə(ˈlɔm) (H on ɔ)			*	*	*!		

Candidate (20a) wins because it satisfies both Pal and Agree [+high], at the cost of violating a lower-ranked Ident[–high]. Candidate (20c) comes out as optimal in Zadon, where Ident[–high] outranks Agree [+high].

In some dialects, [e] and [i] occur in free variation (Djačenko, 2013: 341). Standard Optimality Theory deals with variation by forfeiting the principle of a total ordering of constraints, as first defined by Prince and Smolensky (1993/2004), and assuming that some constraints may be unranked with respect to one another (Kiparsky, 1993; Anttila, 1997, *et seq.*).[66] When two constraints are crucially unranked, either ranking is randomly chosen in the process of the input-output mapping. In order to model the

---

64 Pal is called Pal-*æ* in Rubach (2003). This is a generic constraint subsuming all front vowels. Rubach (2003) distinguishes further constraints, referring to palatalisation in the context of *j*, *i*, and ɛ.

65 See Chapter 7 below for further discussion.

66 There is a considerable body of literature on the OT modelling of variation; for a comprehensive overview, see Bermúdez-Otero (2007) and Coetzee and Pater (2011).

variation between [e] and [i], AGREE[+high] has to be unranked with respect to IDENT[–high]. In this setting, pretonic [i] surfaces if AGREE[+high] dominates IDENT[–high], while pretonic [e] appears under the opposite ranking of the two constraints.

The next section discusses East Slavic dialects with pretonic length, which in many respects resemble the dissimilative reduction systems analysed in this section. The main point of similarity consists in the interaction of tone and foot structure, which results in the same prosodic parsing in the two types of systems. Pretonic length dialects are different from the dissimilative systems discussed so far in that they exhibit lengthening which may or may not be accompanied by reduction of the vowel in pretonic position. The ensuing sections argue that, in addition to the constraints proposed for the dissimilative dialects, HEAD=H and *H/≤a, another mechanism is needed to generate pretonic length systems.

5.5. Pretonic length dialects

5.5.1. Basic generalizations and previous studies

As mentioned earlier in Chapter 2, some East Slavic dialects exhibit an unusual type of prosodic structure with pretonic vowels exceeding in duration the following tonic vowels (Vojtovič, 1972a; Belaja, 1974; Bethin, 2006). In the south-eastern Belarusian dialects and in the north-eastern Ukrainian dialects, the non-high pretonic vowel is lengthened if the vowel in the tonic syllable is high or high mid, as illustrated in (21). In the Upper Snov Basin dialects, increased duration is accompanied by the neutralization of non-high vowels (21b).

(21) a. *South-Eastern Belarusian dialect of Aŭciuki*[67]

[sʲɛːˈstru]	'sister' (acc. sg.)
[ɣɔːˈdow]	'year' (gen. pl.)
[brɨɣaːˈdziram]	'crew chief' (dat. sg.)
[sʲɛˈstra]	'sister' (nom. sg.)
[skaˈzɔw]	'he said'
[bɨˈkʲi]	'bull' (nom. pl.)

[67] Data come from Vojtovič (1972a) and Borise (2015).

b. *Upper Snov Basin Ukrainian dialects*[68]

[xa:ˈdʲilʲi]	'they went'
[ka:ˈʒu]	'I say'
[pʲɛ:ˈsku]	'sand' (dat. sg.)
[kaˈta]	'cat' (gen. sg.)
[ʋaˈza]	'cart' (gen. sg.)
[pamaˈlɔla]	'she ground up'

The presence of pretonic lengthening has been confirmed by instrumental studies. Belaja (1974) reports on the measurements of the duration of the pretonic [a] in the Upper Snov Basin dialects, where the duration of [a] exceeds in duration the following stressed high vowel. The examples provided in Belaja (1974: 26) show that the difference between the tonic and the pretonic vowels ranges from 100 ms to 160 ms (e.g. in [va:ˈzɨ] 'cart' (nom. pl.), [a] = 240 ms and [ɨ] = 100 ms). For comparison, the pretonic vowel [a] is 190 ms shorter than the following stressed [a] in the word [kaˈtʲaka] 'cat' (expr.).[69] Belaja's results are consistent with the findings of a recent acoustic study conducted by Borise (2015) in the area where the Aŭciuki pattern has been attested in the past century.[70] The measurements of the vocalic duration in the pretonic and tonic positions reveal statistically significant differences in the duration of pretonic vowels. Non-high pretonic vowels are on average 28 ms longer than the high vowels in the tonic positions and 60 ms shorter than the following non-high tonic vowels (Borise, 2015: 5).[71]

Bethin (2006) suggests that pretonic lengthening is triggered by phonological tone. It is not clear whether the tone is expressed as pitch in these dialects, as the descriptions of F_0 patterns of these dialects are inconclusive. A 'singsong' rising-falling or a rising-falling-rising pitch has been reported to occur in the Upper Snov Basin dialects (Belaja, 1974: 29). Based on the instrumental measurements, Belaja (1974) asserts that while pretonic [a] is associated with high fundamental frequency, high front vowels [i] and [ɨ] carry no tonal prominence. At the same time, pretonic [a] has lower F_0 than

---

68 Examples are taken from Belaja (1974) and Bethin (2006).

69 Belaja (1974) provides raw measurements for individual items, recorded in carrier sentences produced with different intonation patterns (declarative, interrogative, exclamative, listing).

70 Compare the descriptions in Kryvicki (1959) and Vojtovič (1972a).

71 The data was collected from three female speakers (aged 61, 80, 83). The analysis is based on the 75 tokens with pretonic vowels occurring in the contexts warranting pretonic lengthening (a low and a mid-low pretonic vowel and a high tonic vowel) and 25 tokens with two non-high vowels in the pretonic and tonic positions.

the following stressed high back [u] and the diphthongs [ie] and [uo]. This result is unexpected given that both back and front high vowels as well as high mid diphthongs induce lengthening of the vowel in the preceding syllable. In sum, the results of the Belaja's study do not fully support the generalization that pretonic lengthening is accompanied by the heightened F_0 values.

In the older sources, the long pretonic vowels are reported to be pronounced with a rising-falling pitch in the Belarusian dialect of Aŭciuki (Vojtovič, 1972a: 22). In a recent acoustic study of the Aŭciuki dialect, Borise (2015) found no significant difference between the F_0 maxima of the vowels in the tonic and pretonic positions. Borise (2015) takes these facts to indicate that pretonic syllables lack a rising-falling pitch contour, and concludes that pretonic prominence in this dialect cannot be analysed in terms of phonological tone. Instead, she suggests that the increased duration of the pretonic syllable serves to manifest stress, whose domain extends to two syllables (tonic and pretonic).

However, the absence of distinctive pitch contrasts in pretonic length dialects does not imply that tone is not part of a phonological system of these dialects. Perception studies on the relationship between tones and tone-bearing units have amply demonstrated that segments with F_0 excursions are perceived as longer than otherwise identical segments produced with a level F_0 (Cumming, 2011; Lehiste, 1976; Lehnert-LeHouillier, 2007; Yu, 2010). Interestingly, Yu (2010) notes that the oppositions between rising and falling tones can develop into systems with contrastive vowel length. In the Weert dialect of Dutch, for instance, distinctions in vocalic duration correspond to tonal contrasts in the neighbouring dialect of Baexem (Heijmans, 2003). As shown in Tableau (22), reproduced from Heijmans (2003: 15), Weert long vowels correspond to the falling-rising pattern (Accent II) in Baexem, whereas short vowels correspond to a falling pitch contour (Accent I).

(22) *Average vowel durations in Weert and Baexem (in milliseconds) (Heijmans, 2003)*

Weert		*Baexem*		*gloss*
kni:n	220	kni:n^{II}	186	rabbit
knin	143	kni:n^{I}	177	rabbits
stɛin	273	ʃtɛin^{II}	254	stone
stæjn	192	ʃtɛin^{I}	219	stones

Given that dynamic F_0 increases perceived duration, the complex tonal contour of Accent II may have been reinterpreted as prolonged vocalic duration in the Weert dialect.[72] A parallel mechanism may be responsible for the evolution of pretonic length in East Slavic dialects, where the subjective increase in length provoked by the pitch contour has been reanalysed as an independent durational phenomenon. That is, listeners probably misinterpreted the perceived lengthening effect of the contour tone as the actual duration of the tone-bearing units. In effect, pretonic lengthening took on the role previously assigned to a pitch contour. Increased duration, then, is functionally analogous to a pitch rise in that both express an underlying H tone.[73]

It has been argued in this book that vocalic lowering ([a]-reduction) attested in various East Slavic dialects is also driven by H tone which interacts directly with vocalic quality. However, though both [a]-reduction and lengthening are triggered by the presence of H tone, the two phenomena stem from phonetically distinct mechanisms. Whereas lengthening is perceptually-driven, [a]-reduction is best explained in articulatory terms. There is a substantial body of evidence showing that rising tones are better expressed on longer vowels (Ohala and Ewan, 1973; Gandour, 1977; Zhang, 2002, 2004). Since low vowels are intrinsically longer, they make better carriers of tone than mid or high vowels. So, on the one hand, listeners perceive increased duration of vowels associated with a pitch excursion, and, in response, lengthen pretonic vowels. On the other hand, speakers lower the vowels so that they can better accommodate the tonal contour. Bethin (2006) explains the interaction of tone with both vocalic quantity and quality in terms of articulatory adaptations to the requirements of the rising pitch contour (*cf.* Bethin, 2006: 139). However, as demonstrated in the remainder of this section, the recognition of an additional perceptually-based mechanism allows for a better understanding of a number of processes taking place in the East Slavic dialects.

The East Slavic dialects described in the literature exhibit either lengthening or lowering of the pretonic vowels. The former is widespread in the Aŭciuki and Vladimir-Volga Basin dialects[74], while the latter occurs in the

---

[72] This and related phenomena are discussed in Yu (2010). For further discussion of the listener-based sound change, see Ohala (1981, *et seq.*), Blevins and Garrett (2004), Hansson (2008), and the work cited therein.

[73] This interpretation is consistent with the listener-based theory of sound change (Ohala, 1981, *et seq.*).

[74] See Bethin (2006: 128–132) for further description of the Vladimir-Volga Basin dialects.

dialects with [a]-reduction. It is noteworthy that the two processes co-occur in the Upper Snov Basin dialects. If pretonic lengthening and vowel lowering are generated by the same articulatory mechanism, whose primary purpose is to maximize vocalic duration, it is unclear why some systems employ them simultaneously. The co-existence of the two processes in the Upper Snov Basin dialects is straightforwardly accounted for on the view that lowering is an articulatory adaptation while lengthening is a perceptual response to tone.

Furthermore, the Belarusian dialect of Aŭciuki discussed above has an optional process of [a]-reduction, which only occurs in contexts not warranting pretonic lengthening. This is illustrated by the data in (23), taken from Vojtovič (1972a: 22).[75] Note that this dialect distinguishes between lax and tense mid vowels [o] and [ɔ] in the outputs.

(23) *Aŭciuki pretonic reduction and lengthening*

Nom.	[ˈstol]	[ˈkonʲ]	[raˈsa] ~ [rɔˈsa]	[ʋɔːˈlɨ]
Gen.	[staˈla] ~ [stɔˈla]	[kaˈnʲa] ~ [kɔˈnʲa]	[rɔːˈsɨ]	[ʋɔˈlɔw]
Dat.	[stɔːˈlu]	[kɔːˈnʲu]	[rɔːˈsʲe]	[ʋɔˈlɔm] ~ [ʋaˈlam]
Acc.	[ˈstol]	[ˈkonʲ]	[rɔːˈsu]	[ʋɔːˈlɨ] ~ [ʋɔˈlɔw]
Instr.	[staˈlɔm]	[kaˈnʲɔm] ~ [kɔˈnʲɔm]	[raˈsɔi̯u]	[ʋaˈlamʲi]
Loc.	[stɔːˈlʲe]	[kɔːˈnʲu]	[rɔːˈsʲe]	[ʋaˈlax] ~ [ʋɔˈlɔx]
	‘table’	‘horse’	‘dew’	‘oxen’

In stems with the underlying vowel /o/, the [ɔ] ~ [a] variation is attested before the endings beginning with non-high vowels, e.g. [kaˈnʲa] ~ [kɔˈnʲa] ‘horse’ (gen. sg.).[76,77] In some cases, only the reduced variant is attested, as in [staˈlɔm] ‘table’ (instr. sg.). Most importantly, no variation is possible before stressed high or mid high vowels, where only the lengthened mid vowel [ɔː] appears, e.g. [kɔːˈnʲu] id. (dat. sg.). The absence of a variant with a long [a], as in *[kaːˈnʲu], is surprising in view of the fact that the underlying [a] is regularly lengthened in words such as [traːˈʋu] ‘grass’ (acc. sg.), *cf.* [traˈʋɔi̯u] id. (instr. sg.). Also, as [a] has intrinsically greater duration, one might expect variation between [ɔː] ~ [a] in the pretonic length contexts. However, the form *[kaˈnʲu] is not attested. The fact that [a]-reduction is blocked in words

---

[75] These data come from Vojtovič's (1972a) fieldwork conducted in the Aŭciuki dialect area. Vojtovič asked schoolchildren and adult speakers to inflect some nouns and verbs, as well as elicited these forms by asking prompting questions.

[76] The Aŭciuki dialect has an eight-vowel system [i-ɨ-u-e-o-ɛ-ɔ-a] under stress. In unstressed syllables, the vowels [e] and [o] reduce to [ɛ] and [ɔ], respectively.

[77] There is usually no variation before the stressed [ɔ]: the pretonic vowel is realized as an unreduced [ɔ] in this context due to the harmony for the feature [+round], which is characteristic of the southeastern Belarusian dialectal area (Vajtovič, 1968; Vojtovič, 1972a).

such as [kɔːˈnʲu] shows that it is not driven by the same force as lengthening. That is, if lengthening is used to render the vowel a better host of H tone, then one would not expect it to conflict with lowering, which serves essentially the same purpose. These patterns are analysed in section 5.5.2.2.

To conclude, the tone-driven processes attested in East Slavic dialects, pretonic vowel neutralization and lengthening, are motivated by two phonetically distinct mechanisms. Specifically, while vowel neutralization is best accounted for in articulatory terms, pretonic lengthening is rooted in perception. Next section formalizes this generalization in terms of an optimality-theoretic analysis.

5.5.2. Aŭciuki: an OT analysis

5.5.2.1. Tone-induced lengthening

It should be noted that, unlike the articulatory-based lowering, the perceptually-based lengthening is non-teleological in nature, and, thus, not readily amenable to analysis in terms of the output-oriented Optimality Theory. The listener-based adjustment of vowel length can be indirectly modelled in terms of a constraint forcing lengthening of the vowels which are associated with a tonal contour (Zhang, 2002; Gordon, 2006). Bethin (2006) argues that immediately pretonic syllables are linked to the LH contour in the East Slavic dialects exhibiting pretonic length. The constraint LH=LONG, adopted from Gordon (2006: 105), induces lengthening in systems in which the LH contour is present in output representation (formulated in (24a) below). In contrast to the neutralization systems analysed so far in this chapter, pretonic length dialects are characterized by the presence of a tonal contour, whose location either on the tonic or on the pretonic syllable is determined by the quality of the stressed vowel (*cf.* Bethin, 2006: 139). I suggest formalizing this generalization in terms of an OT constraint HDFT = LH (defined in 24b), requiring output head feet to be associated with a contour tone. This constraint resembles the constraint HDFT = H ('Assign a violation mark for every head foot not associated with H tone in the output', formulated in (8) in section 3.5, Chapter 3). Let us recall that HDFT = H plays a key role in the analysis of both non-dissimilative and dissimilative reduction patterns, ensuring that either pretonic or tonic syllable carries H tone in the output. Similarly, HDFT = LH enforces the insertion of tonal contours in the outputs in pretonic length dialects.

(24) a. LH=LONG: A contour tone is licensed by a rime with two syllabic timing slots.

b. HDFT = LH: Assign a violation mark for every head foot not associated with a contour tone in the output.

LH=Long works in concert with the members of the *H≤V family of constraints to generate the Aŭciuki pattern discussed above (illustrated in (21) and (23)). *H≤V ensures that H tone is associated with the pretonic vowel when the vowel under stress is high, and LH=Long causes lengthening of the high-toned vowel. Given free rein, *H≤V would cause lengthened mid vowels to lower. However, it was pointed out above that mid vowels in pretonic length contexts are exempt from [a]-reduction (see examples in (23) above). This is modelled using the faithfulness constraint Ident[-low]. Ranked above *H≤V, Ident[-low] blocks the lowering of mid vowels. The ranking of constraints generating pretonic lengthening is presented in Tableau (25), which shows the evaluation of the word /sto'lu/ [stɔ:'lu] 'table' (dat. sg.).[78]

(25) *Aŭciuki pretonic lengthening*

/sto'lu/	HdFt = LH	LH = Long	Ident [-low]	*H/≤i,u	Head = H	*H/≤ε,ɔ	*H/≤a
LH ⇒ a. (stɔ:'lu)					*	*	*
HL b. stɔ('lu)		*!		*		*	*
LH c. (stɔ'lu)		*!			*	*	*
LH d. (sta:'lu)			*!		*		*
e. (stɔ'lu)	*!				*		

It has been mentioned above that Aŭciuki lengthens pretonic vowels if the vowel under stress is high or mid high. Like the Obojan' pattern of dissimilation, Aŭciuki disallows high and mid high vowels to host High tone, which is analysed by ranking Head=H just above *H/≤ε,ɔ. The comparison of candidates (25a) and (25b) shows that the latter loses because it links H to the high vowel [u] in the stressed syllable. The optimal candidate (25a) avoids the violation of a high-ranked *H/≤i,u by associating H tone with a more sonorous segment in pretonic position. Candidate (25c) does not lengthen pretonic [ɔ], and, hence, is excluded by LH=Long. Finally, the least marked candidate (25d) is eliminated due to the fatal violation of the faithfulness constraint Ident[-low].

[78] Let us note that the underlyingly tense vowel /o/ surfaces as the lax [ɔ]. This issue is addressed later in this section.

5.5.2.2. Neutralization as markedness reduction

Turning now to the contexts which do not license pretonic lengthening, let us observe that here vowels show a variation between [a] and [ɔ], e.g. [sta'la] ~ [stɔ'la] 'table' (gen. sg.). Also, similarly to pretonic length contexts, the underlying distinction /o/ – /ɔ/ is neutralized in unstressed positions in favour of the lax vowel [ɔ].[79] It is important to note that the lowering of /o/ to [ɔ] or [a] is not motivated by tone in these cases. Mid vowels are prohibited from unstressed positions in many languages, e.g., Basque (Hualde, 1991), Bulgarian (Lehiste and Popov, 1970), Catalan (Recasens, 1991). Crosswhite (2001) interprets the reduction of mid vowels to peripheral segments [a], [i], [u] as a contrast-enhancing process which creates a maximally dispersed vowel system [i-u-a]. On this view, mid vowels are eliminated by the constraint License-Nonperipheral/Stress 'Nonperipheral vowels are licensed only in stressed positions' (Crosswhite, 2001: 24). While successfully dealing with the cases of [a]-reduction, as in ['stol] 'table' – [sta'lɔm] 'id.' (instr. sg.), this constraint obviously cannot generate the Aŭciuki *o/ɔ* neutralization, e.g. in ['konʲ] 'horse' (nom. sg.) – [kɔ'nʲa] 'id.' (gen. sg.) – [kɔː'nʲu] 'id.' (dat. sg). To account for a similar lax/tense neutralization attested in Slovene, Crosswhite introduces an additional constraint banning the feature [ATR] from unstressed (monomoraic) positions (Lic-[ATR]/μμ 'Feature specifications for [ATR] may only occur in association with bimoraicity).[80] Assuming that Aŭciuki stressed vowels are bimoraic, and that [o]/[ɔ] opposition is accountable for in terms of the [ATR] distinction, the constraint Lic-[ATR]/μμ can generate the reduction of /o/ to [ɔ] in [kɔ'nʲa]. However, this analysis fails in cases such as [kɔː'nʲu], where the deletion of the feature [ATR] befalls a long vowel.

The Aŭciuki data can be successfully dealt with in terms of an alternative model suggested by de Lacy (2006), who argues that mid vowels reduce to [a] not to optimize perceptual contrast, but to enhance prominence. This generalization is captured by a family of markedness constraints which prohibit low-sonority vowels in syllable heads (de Lacy, 2006; these constraints are introduced in section 1.2.1 in Chapter 1). The constraints relevant for the present discussions are $*\Delta_{\sigma}\leq\{e,o\}$('Assign a violation mark for every head of a syllable that contains a segment with sonority less than or equal to {e,o}') and $*\Delta_{\sigma}\leq\{\varepsilon,ɔ\}$ ('Assign a violation mark for every head of a

---

[79] Likewise, the unstressed front mid vowel /e/ is reduced to [ɛ], e.g. [dzʲet] 'grandfather' – [dzʲɛ'dɨ] id. (nom. pl.) (Vojtovič, 1972a: 23).

[80] In Slovene, the tense/lax opposition is only maintained in long stressed vowels (Bidwell, 1969, cited in Crosswhite, 2001: 31).

syllable that contains a segment with sonority less than or equal to {ɛ,ɔ}'). These markedness constraints, when unchecked by faithfulness, eliminate mid vowels. In Aŭciuki, both reduction to [ɔ] and to [a] can be generated by high-ranked $*\Delta_\sigma \leq$ {e,o} and $*\Delta_\sigma \leq$ {ɛ,ɔ} serving to increase the sonority of syllable heads. The switch from /o/ to [ɔ] is driven by $*\Delta_\sigma \leq$ {e,o}. A further, optional, change from [ɔ] to [a] is induced by $*\Delta_\sigma \leq$ {ɛ,ɔ}. Thus, this model provides a uniform account for the Aŭciuki reduction patterns.

It was pointed out earlier that the variation between [ɔ] and [a] is attested in positions not warranting pretonic lengthening, as in [sta'la] ~ [stɔ'la] 'table' (gen. sg.). Standard Optimality Theory deals with optionality by forfeiting the principle of a total ordering of constraints, as first defined by Prince and Smolensky (1993/2004), and assuming that some constraints may be unranked with respect to one another (Kiparsky, 1993; Reynolds, 1994; Anttila, 1997; *et seq.*). When two constraints are crucially unranked, either ranking is randomly chosen in the process of the input-output mapping. In order to model variation between [ɔ] and [a] attested in Aŭciuki, $*\Delta_\sigma \leq$ {ɛ,ɔ} has to be unranked with respect to IDENT[low]. In this setting, pretonic [a] surfaces if $*\Delta_\sigma \leq$ {ɛ,ɔ} dominates IDENT[-low] (shown in (26i) below), while pretonic [ɔ] appears under the opposite ranking of the two constraints (26ii).

(26) *Aŭciuki pretonic reduction*

i. [a]-reduction: $*\Delta_\sigma \leq$ {ɛ,ɔ} >> IDENT[-low]

/sto'la/	$*\Delta_\sigma \leq$ {e,o}	$*\Delta_\sigma \leq$ {ɛ,ɔ}	IDENT[-low]
a. stɔ('la)		*!	
⇒ b. sta('la)			*
c. sto('la)	*!	*	
d. stɔ:('la)		*!	

ii. [ɔ]-reduction: IDENT[-low] >> $*\Delta_\sigma \leq$ {ɛ,ɔ}

/sto'la/	IDENT[-low]	$*\Delta_\sigma \leq$ {e,o}	$*\Delta_\sigma \leq$ {ɛ,ɔ}
⇒ a. stɔ('la)			*
b. sta('la)	*!		
c. sto('la)		*	*!

This analysis predicts that all unfooted unstressed syllables should show variation, in either undergoing neutralization to [a] under the pressure of the markedness constraint $*\Delta_\sigma \leq$ {ɛ,ɔ} (as in 26i), or not neutralizing unstressed non-high vowels, as in (26ii). Systematic descriptions of the vowel qualities in unstressed positions other than pretonic are lacking for Aŭciuki. Let us note, however, that Aŭciuki is a dialect of Belarusian, and standard Belarusian reduces mid vowels /ε/ and /ɔ/ to [a] in all unstressed positions (Czekman and Smułkowa, 1988). Borise (2015: 3–4) points out that Aŭciuki is spoken in a dialectal area which 'lies on the boundary between vowel neutralising and non-vowel neutralising dialects, and has rather irregular vowel neutralisation.' These fact are accounted for in the present model, which predicts that either of the rankings of the constraints *Δ_σ≤{ε,ɔ} and Ident[-low] can be randomly chosen, generating either [a]-reduction or no reduction in all unstressed positions.

This model also predicts that, similarly to words such as [ka'nʲɔm] ~ [kɔ'nʲɔm], lengthened vowels should also be subject to variation in the pretonic length contexts. Yet, the long vowel [ɔ:] does not undergo lowering, and *[ka:'nʲu] is not an attested variant of [kɔ:'nʲu] 'horse' (dat. sg.). I assume that the constraint *Δ_σ≤{ε,ɔ} driving [a]-reduction of short vowels does not induce the same change in long vowels because the forms [kɔ:'nʲu] and [ka'nʲɔm] are structurally different. Just like the dissimilative reduction patterns discussed in section 5.4, Aŭciuki parses pretonic syllables into an iambic foot if the stressed vowel is high (i.e., pretonic length contexts), and leaves pretonic syllables unfooted if the stressed vowel is non-high, as shown in (27) below.[81]

(27)
HL — a. [ka('nʲɔm)]
LH — b. [(kɔ:'nʲu)]

I suggest that the identity of vowels in footed syllables is protected by the positional faithfulness constraint Ident[-low]$_{\text{HdFt}}$. Positions which have been standardly assumed to be resistant to neutralization include stressed syllables and root-initial syllables (Beckman, 1997). However, faithfulness to head feet has also been postulated in the literature. Alderete (1995) analyses the two-degree reduction in Russian by assuming that contrast is retained in the binary iambic foot due to the constraint Head(F)-Ident(F). The idea that prosodic heads serve as the privileged domain protected by positional faithfulness constraints is further exploited in Yip (1999), who refers to footed material in her analysis of tonal reduction in Wenzhou. In a similar vein, the constraint Ident[-low]$_{\text{HdFt}}$ target segments which are parsed into the iambic foot in the output; the formal definition of the constraint is provided in (28) below (based on Alderete, 1995: 14).

[81] These structures are in line with Bethin's (2006: 139) suggestion that in pretonic length dialects, High tone is associated with the pretonic syllable if the stressed vowel is high, and to the tonic syllable if it contains a non-high vowel.

(28) IDENT[-low]$_{\text{HDFT}}$: Correspondent segments in head feet agree in value for feature [-low]. If head foot contains ß, and aRß, then α and ß agree in the value of [-low].

The structural difference depicted in (27) allows us to explain the distinct behaviour of pretonic vowels in (27a) and (27b). Specifically, [a]-reduction in the former is driven by the constraint *Δ_{σ}≤{ε,ɔ} ('Assign a violation mark for every head of a syllable that contains a segment with sonority less than or equal to {ε,ɔ}'), which dominates the generic faithfulness constraint IDENT[-low]. The effect of *Δ_{σ}≤{ε,ɔ} is overridden in (27b), where the identity of the pretonic vowel is protected by a high-ranked IDENT[-low]$_{\text{HDFT}}$.

Let us note that the parsing of the word [ka'nʲɔm] 'horse' (instr. sg.) shown in (27a) produces a monosyllabic foot, which is disallowed by FT=BIN. In order to generate the structure in (27a), FT=BIN has to be outranked by ALIGN-L(H, FT), as in the dissimilative reduction patterns in Žizdra, Obojan', and Don analysed in section 5.4 above. To recapitulate, the partial rankings responsible for the Aŭciuki pretonic reduction are as follows.

(29) *Aŭciuki: partial rankings*
a. ALIGN-L(H, Ft) >> FT=BIN
b. IDENT[-low]$_{\text{HDFT}}$ >> *Δ_{σ}≤{ε,ɔ} >> IDENT[-low]

The ranking in (29a) ensures that H tone is always aligned with the left edge of the foot, irrespective of whether H docks on the tonic or the pretonic syllable, whereas the ranking in (29b) eliminates mid vowels from prosodically weak (unfooted) positions. The interaction of constraints generating the output forms of the words /sto'la/ [sta'la] 'table' (gen. sg.) and /sto'lu/ [stɔ:'lu] id. (dat. sg.) is illustrated in Tableaux (30).

(30) *Aŭciuki pretonic reduction*

i. /sto'la/	LH = LONG	*H/≤i,u	HEAD = H	ALIGN-L (H, FT)	FT = BIN	IDENT [-low]$_{\text{HDFT}}$	*Δ_{σ}≤{ε,ɔ}	IDENT [-low]
HL ⇒ a. sta('la)					*			*
LH b. (stɔ:'la)			*!				*	
HL c. stɔ('la)					*		*!	
HL d. (stɔ'la)				*!			*	
LH e. (stɔ'la)	*!		*				*	

ii. /sto'lu/	LH = LONG	*H/≤i,u	HEAD = H	ALIGN-L (H, FT)	FT = BIN	IDENT [−low]$_{HDFT}$	$*\Delta_\sigma \leq \{\varepsilon, ɔ\}$	IDENT [−low]
LH ⇒ a. (stɔ̆:'lu)			*				**	
HL b. stɔ('lu)		*!			*		**	
LH c. (sta:'lu)			*			*!	*	*
LH d. (stɔ̆'lu)	*!		*				**	

This analysis allows us to explain a phenomenon related to stress perception in Aŭciuki. Namely, it has been often remarked in the fieldwork descriptions that stress seems to shift leftward in words with a long pretonic syllable (Kryvicki, 1959; Belaja, 1974; Borise, 2015). This auditory impression has been reported both by researchers, as well as native speakers (Belaja, 1974: 29). Yet, it is not the case that stress has moved from its etymological position one syllable to the left in words showing pretonic length. Borise (2015) reports that native speakers point to the etymologically correct position when explicitly asked to assign stress.[82] More importantly, vowels in etymologically stressed syllables never undergo vowel reduction, which indicates that they do occur in the metrically dominant position. So, on the one hand, both native speakers and non-native listeners perceive the leftward stress shift in words with pretonic length. On the other hand, native speakers' intuitions and the lack of vowel reduction indicate that stress remains in its original position. This ambiguous relationship between pretonic length and stress is accounted for in the present model, which assumes that the foot boundary shifts leftwards when H tone is expressed on the pretonic syllable (shown in 27b) above). The originally stressed syllable still occupies the head position within the foot, but the left boundary of the foot, associated with foot head in (27a), is aligned with the left edge of the pretonic syllable in (27b). On this view, the indeterminate status of the pretonic syllable with respect to stress can be assumed to arise from the exceptional footing of syllables in pretonic length contexts.

---

82 An anonymous reviewer points out that such judgements cannot be taken as reliable indication of the location of accent as they may be affected by other factors, such as the knowledge of the standard.

5.6. Typology

I have argued that the constraints responsible for the metrical parsing and the interaction between vowel quality and prosody in East Slavic include FT-FORM=IAMB, ALIGN-L(H, FT), FT=BIN, HEAD=H, and *H≤V. The constraint on foot form FTFORM=IAMB is high-ranked in most East Slavic dialects.[83] This foot form can be argued for both on theory external and theory-internal grounds. Empirical evidence for iambic footing in standard Russian has been provided based on evidence from language games (see section 3.3). On the theoretic side, there are no clear indications pointing to this foot type in East Slavic, which would be comparable to the evidence for trochaic footing in Germanic languages, in which many phonological processes are clearly foot-based.[84] However, reference to iambic foot structure in the model proposed in this book remarkably simplifies the analysis of complex reduction patterns attested in East Slavic.

It has been demonstrated that the difference between three dissimilative reduction patterns (Žizdra, Obojan', Don) arises due to distinct rankings between HEAD=H and the members of the *H≤V family of constraints.

(31) *Dissimilative reduction patterns*

a. *H/≤i,u, *H/≤e,o, *H/≤ɛ,ɔ, *H/≤a >> **HEAD=H** (Žizdra)

b. *H/≤i,u, *H/≤e,o >> **HEAD=H** >> *H/≤ɛ,ɔ, *H/≤a (Obojan')

c. *H/≤i,u >> **HEAD=H** >>*H/≤e,o, *H/≤ɛ,ɔ, *H/≤a (Don)

The ranking shown in (31a) for Žizdra is also operative in non-dissimilative reduction systems, including standard Russian. The difference between the two patterns (dissimilative *vs.* non-dissimilative reduction) arises due to differences in foot structure. The former admits unary feet, while the latter system requires binary footing, as illustrated in (32).[85]

---

83 An exception is constituted by hybrid metrical systems discussed in section 3.5, which admit both iambs and trochees. As noted previously, such systems are rare.

84 The role of foot as a prosodic constituent in Slavic is further discussed in Mołczanow and Łukaszewicz (2021).

85 There exists one type of dissimilative systems, referred to as assimilative-dissimilative reduction, in which binary feet are constructed at the expense of violating ALIGN-L(H, FT). Assimilative-dissimilative patterns were mentioned in section 3.6.2, analysis is provided in section 6.3 in Chapter 6 below.

(32) a. *Dissimilative systems: foot structure*

H | σ σ('σ) σ [–high]   H | σ (σ'σ) σ [+high]

b. *Non-dissimilative systems: foot structure*

H | σ (σ'σ) σ

The differences in foot structure shown in (32) are modelled by locating the constraint FT=BIN either at the top (33a) or at the bottom (33b) of the constraint hierarchy.

(33) a. **FT=BIN** >> *H/≤V >> HEAD=H (Non-dissimilative reduction)
b. *H/≤V >> HEAD=H >> **FT=BIN** (Dissimilative reduction)

In the non-dissimilative and dissimilative dialects discussed so far, the key role is played by the constraint ALIGN-L(H, FT). In non-dissimilative patterns (34a), ALIGN-L(H, FT) ensures that H tone is associated with the pretonic syllable, whereas in dissimilative systems (34b), ALIGN-L(H, FT), which is ranked above FT=BIN, determines whether the resulting foot is unary or binary.

(34) a. **ALIGN-L(H, FT)**, FT=BIN >> *H/≤V >> HEAD=H (Non-dissimilative reduction)
b. *H/≤V >> HEAD=H, **ALIGN-L(H, FT)** >> FT=BIN (Dissimilative reduction)

It will be demonstrated in Chapter 6 below that the opposite ranking of the constraints ALIGN-L(H, FT) and FT=BIN is present in dialects with assimilative-dissimilative reduction:

(35) *H/≤V >> HEAD=H, FT=BIN >> **ALIGN-L(H, FT)** (Assimilative-dissimilative reduction)

In this setting, the difference in the quantity and the quality of the pretonic vowels in [tra:'vɨ] 'grass' (gen. sg.), [tra'va] 'grass' (nom. sg.) and [ləp'tʲɛi̯] 'bast shoe' (gen. pl.) arises due to distinct metrical structures, as illustrated in (36) below (see section 6.2 for an analysis; *cf.* also section 3.6.2, example 17b).

(36) *Foot structure in dialects with assimilative-dissimilative reduction*

H | (tra:'vɨ)   H | (tra'va)   H | ləp('tʲɛi̯)

The same ranking of constraints, FT=BIN >> ALIGN-L(H, FT), combined with a high-ranked HEAD=H, produces a system with disyllabic iambic feet always comprising pretonic and the following tonic vowels, with H always linked to the lexically stressed syllable. Such systems are schematically shown in (37).

(37) *Systems without tone-induced reduction: foot structure*

H
σ (σˈσ) σ

The vocalic patterns of unstressed syllables in this setting is predicted not to be affected by H tone, so any reduction occurring in syllables not associated with H tone is attributable to the interplay of the prominence-reducing constraints in prosodic non-heads and prominence enhancing constraints in prosodic heads (see Chapter 4).

We have seen in the analysis of Aŭciuki that the reduction of /ɔ/ to [a] in the pretonic syllable has been generated by the following constraint ranking, repeated from (29) in section 5.5.2.

(38) *Aŭciuki: partial rankings*
   a. ALIGN-L(H, FT) >> FT=BIN
   b. IDENT[-low]$_{HDFT}$ >> *Δ_σ≤{ɛ,ɔ} >> IDENT[-low]

When combined with the reduction pattern generated by the constraints in (38b), the ranking FT=BIN >> ALIGNL(H, FT) produces a system exhibiting [a]-reduction in all unstressed syllables except for the pretonic position. This ranking is shown in (39) below.

(39) *Incomplete okan'e dialects*
   FT=BIN >> ALIGN-L(H, FT)
   IDENT[-low]$_{HDFT}$ >> *Δ_σ≤{ɛ,ɔ} >> IDENT[-low]

Such a pattern is attested in the central Russian dialects with the so-called incomplete *okan'e*, in which unstressed vowels reduce to [a], whereas pretonic vowels retain their quality, e.g. /bɔrɔˈdatɨj/ [barɔˈdatɨj̯] 'beardy' (*cf.* Kasatkin, 2005: 53). I assume that in these systems, as in the majority of East Slavic dialects, FTFORM=IAMB is a high-ranked constraint. Tableau in (40) displays the ranking.

(40) *Incomplete okan'e*

/bɔrɔ'datɨi̯/	FtForm = Iamb	Ft = Bin	Align-L (H, Ft)	Ident [low]$_{\text{HdFt}}$	*Δ$_\sigma$≤{ε,ɔ}	Ident [–low]
H ⇒ a. ba(rɔ'da)tɨi̯			*		**	*
H b. bara('da)tɨi̯		*!			*	**
H c. bɔ(rɔ'da)tɨi̯			*		***!	
H d. ba(ra'da) tɨi̯			*	*!	*	**
H e. (barɔ)'(datɨi̯)	**!				**	*

The winning candidate (40a), unlike its contender in (40b), eschews the violation of Ft=Bin by parsing the lexically accented syllable together with the immediately preceding syllable into a right-headed foot. The faithful candidates (40c) violates *Δ$_\sigma$≤{ε,ɔ} three times because it contains two mid vowels and one high vowel. The constraint *Δ$_\sigma$≤{ε,ɔ} is violated only once in candidate (40d), which turns two unstressed vowels into [a], but by doing so incurs a fatal violation of the faithfulness constraint Ident[-low]$_{\text{HdFt}}$. Candidate (40a) comes out as optimal because it keeps the vowel in the pretonic (footed) syllable intact, only reducing the unfooted vowel in the initial syllable. This move allows to achieve a decrease in markedness at a minimal cost of violating the low-ranked Ident[-low]. Trochaic footing in (40e) is penalized by the high-ranked FtForm=Iamb.

Besides [a], another vowel commonly attested in prosodically weak position is [ə]. I have previously assumed that reduction to [ə] constitutes prominence reduction in prosodically recessive positions, driven by the constraint *-Δ$_\omega$≥{i,u} ('Assign a violation mark for every non-head of a word that contains a segment with sonority greater or equal to {i,u}', de Lacy (2006), see Chapter 4 for further discussion). If *-Δ$_\omega$≥{i,u} and not *Δ$_\sigma$≤{ε,ɔ} occupies a dominant position in the constraint hierarchy, as shown in (41) below, then all unstressed vowels reduce to low-sonority vowels, such as [ə]. This type of reduction is attested in the regional dialects spoken in the eastern and western Russia (Knjazev, 2000: 87).

(41) *Regional Russian*

Ft=Bin >> Align-L(H, Ft)
*-Δ$_\omega$≥{i,u} >> Ident[-low], Ident[-low]$_{\text{HdFt}}$

The interaction of constraints generating reduction to [ə] in regional Russian is shown in Tableau (42).

(42) *Regional Russian*

/bɔrɔ'da/	$*\text{-}\Delta_{\omega}\geq$\{i,u\}	$*\Delta_{\sigma}\leq$\{ɛ,ɔ\}	IDENT[-low]$_{\text{HDFT}}$	IDENT[-low]
H ⇒ a. bə(rə'da)		**!	*	**
H b. ba(ra'da)	**!		*	**

The ranking of $*\Delta_{\sigma}\leq$\{ɛ,ɔ\} and $*\text{-}\Delta_{\omega}\geq$\{i,u\} below the faithfulness constraints generates a pattern without phonological reduction. Lack of phonological neutralization in unstressed positions is a distinctive trait of most northern Russian dialects (Kuznecov, 1960; Avanesov, 1974), Southern Belarusian dialects (Vajtovič, 1968), as well as of standard Ukrainian (Ziłyński, 1932; Toc'ka, 1973).

Finally, let us recall from section 5.3 that while the *H≤V constraints drive the lowering of the vowel in pretonic positions, the featural identity of vowels in stressed syllables is protected by the high-ranked positional faithfulness constraints, *cf.* Tableau (9). The architecture of OT predicts the existence of a system with a reverse ranking, where positional faithfulness constraints are dominated by the markedness constraints of the *H≤V family. However, there are no dialects which would lower the stressed vowel under the pressure of *H≤V. This gap can be explained by the lexical nature and the high functional load of East Slavic stress. As stress is often the only means of differentiating between words or different forms of the same word, the identity of stressed vowels needs to remain intact in order to preserve lexical contrasts.

5.7. Interim conclusion

This chapter has looked at the pretonic alternations which are conditioned by the quality of the vowel in the stressed syllable. It has been argued that these alternations are explicable in terms of phonological tone, which can be correlated with both segmental and suprasegmental properties. On the segmental level, H tone triggers lowering of pretonic vowels in dialects with dissimilative reduction. On the suprasegmental level, tone is associated with increased vocalic duration in pretonic length dialects.

There is a long-standing debate in the literature concerning the origin of dissimilative and non-dissimilative reduction, with numerous attempts made to determine which of the two processes emerged first in East Slavic. Beginning with Šaxmatov (1915), most Russian dialectologists (Durnovo, 1917; Avanesov, 1952; Gorškova and Xaburgaev, 1981; and others) considered dissimilative [a]-reduction to arise first, with non-dissimilative reduction constituting a further development consisting in the spread of [a] to all pretonic positions, irrespective of the quality of the vowel in the tonic syllable. Conversely, Kurylo (1928), van Wijk (1934/1935), Vaillant (1950), Čekmonas (1987) present a view that non-dissimilative [a]-reduction is an earlier development, which formed the basis for dissimilative reduction. In Vojtovič (1972a, 1972b), as well as in more recent studies of Kasatkin (1999) and Savinov (2013b), dissimilative reduction is assumed to represent a rhythmically-conditioned realization of non-dissimilative [a]-reduction. That is, it is argued that dialects with dissimilative reduction are characterized by an alternation of short and long syllables, and the phonetic realization of the low vowel [a] reflects the temporal differences between metrically strong and weak positions.[86] However, this account is problematic because, first, the alternation of strong and weak syllables constitutes the most widespread pattern cross-linguistically, whereas the dissimilation patterns attested in East Slavic dialects are typologically isolated. Second, attributing the cause of the vocalic alternations to the rhythmic structure does not explain why most dialects with dissimilative reduction limit the alternation to the disyllabic domain of the tonic and the immediately adjacent syllable.

In the present model, vocalic changes in quality and quantity are triggered by High tone, whose position is determined by the stressed syllable, so the absence of dissimilation in positions removed from main stress by more than one syllable is the expected result. At the same time, this analysis does not preclude the existence of systems in which tonally-driven alternations co-occur with quantitative and qualitative changes resulting from the metrical footing. Such patterns are attested in dialects which contrast full and reduced vowels in the structures 1-2-3 and 2-1-3, e.g. [gəspaˈda] 'gentlemen', [pədaˈʒdi] 'wait' (imp.) *vs.* [basʲiˈkɔm] 'barefoot', [galuˈbʲei̯] 'dove' (gen. pl.) (see Avanesov and Orlova, 1965: 67).

Furthermore, the chicken-and-egg question as to which type of reduction (dissimilative or non-dissimilative) is 'primary' ontologically does not arise in the optimality-theoretic model, where both patterns are generated by means of the same set of constraints (HEAD=H, ALIGN-L(H, FT), and the members of the *H≤V family). Specifically, non-dissimilative [a]-reduction is the result of the ranking ALIGN-L(H, FT), FT=BIN >> *H≤V, HEAD=H, whereas dissimilative patterns, including pretonic length systems, are generated by a different arrangement of these constraints: ALIGN-L(H, FT),

---

[86] A similar idea underlies a recent model of vowel reduction in standard Russian developed by Iosad (2012).

*H/≤V >> HEAD=H, FT=BIN. Both rankings are equally possible, so it is a matter of chance which one will be picked up by a given system. Moreover, it is predicted that the sound change can go in both directions: the promotion of HEAD=H above all members of the *H/≤V constraint family results in a switch from dissimilative to non-dissimilative reduction, whereas the demotion of HEAD=H leads to the emergence of various dissimilation patterns. In sum, H tone is the most important factor initiating both dissimilative and non-dissimilative reduction, with the two patterns instantiating different types of the interaction of tone with metric and segmental structure.

Let us note that the key idea of the present analysis is that tone interacts directly with vowel quality without the mediation of phonetic pitch. Vowel lowering, which is initiated by the High tone, serves to increase the duration and sonority of the tone-bearing unit. Nevertheless, the question arises whether there are other prosodic differences between words in which H is aligned with pretonic vowels and words in which H is linked to the tonic vowels. Specifically, it is possible that the vowels associated with High tone could display the heightened values of F_0. There are indications in the literature pointing to the differences in pitch between words containing different vowel qualities in the tonic syllable, but detailed instrumental measurements of the dialects in question are rare, and the descriptions are scarce and are mostly based on impressionistic evidence.[87] However, the absence of reliable acoustic measurements confirming the presence of rising pitch contours on the pretonic syllables does not undermine the present model, because the posited phonological High tone serves a diacritic purpose which is not expected to be realized as pitch contrast phonetically.

Finally, let us note that previous accounts have analysed dissimilative vowel reduction either as dissimilation in quality (Halle, 1965; Davis, 1970; Nelson, 1974; Suzuki, 1998) or in quantity (Broch, 1916; Kurylo, 1928; Vojtovič, 1972a; Belaja, 1974; Timberlake, 1993; Crosswhite, 2000, 2001; Kasatkina, 2005). Analyses attributing dissimilative reduction to the influence of the quality of the following stressed vowels have originated within the generative tradition. The common feature of these accounts is that they establish a direct link between the quality of the pretonic and tonic vowels. Beginning with Broch (1916), many researchers have viewed dissimilative patterns in terms of quantitative dissimilation (Kurylo, 1928; Vojtovič, 1972a; Belaja, 1974; Timberlake, 1993; Crosswhite, 2000, 2001; Kasatkina, 2005). Within Optimality Theory, this idea is formalized by Crosswhite

87 See Bethin (2006) for an overview of the available literature on F_0 in the East Slavic dialects.

(2000, 2001), who proposes that the pretonic vowel is non-moraic when followed by the long (bimoraic) vowel [a], and monomoraic when followed by non-low (monomoraic) vowels, schematically CV'Ca$_{\mu\mu}$ *vs.* CV$_{\mu}$'Cu$_{\mu}$. Different dissimilative patterns are generated by positing limitations on which vowels can be bimoraic in a given dialect. In this analysis, a three-way length contrast in vowels is also used as a diacritic because the abstract distinction in vocalic duration (zero mora *vs.* one mora *vs.* two moras) does not express a lexical contrast and is employed to identify the locations of different types of neutralizations.

In the next chapter, I look at several other patterns of dissimilative reduction where the quality of the pretonic vowel is determined by the vowel under stress. These systems exhibit a complex interplay between tone-driven neutralizations with harmony in backness and height.

Chapter 6

Harmonic systems

6.1. Introduction

The previous chapter considered reduction patterns in which the quality of the pretonic vowel was determined by the sonority level of the vowel under stress (referred to as dissimilative patterns). In addition, several other patterns of reduction are reported in the literature. Among these, four types (called Ščigry, Sudža, Mosal'sk, and Dmitrov) are described under the heading 'other dissimilative reduction patterns', and five further types (Novoselki, Kidusovo, Orexovo, Kultuki, and Bel'sk) are referred to as assimilative-dissimilative types of reduction (*cf.* Avanesov, 1974; Kasatkin, 2005; among others).[88] These patterns share one common trait: in addition to dissimilation, as in dissimilative patterns discussed in Chapter 5, they exhibit some kind of feature harmony between the vowel in pretonic position and the following stressed vowel. I argue in this chapter that these additional types arise as a result of the harmonic processes affecting vowels in pretonic positions. That is, they combine the constraint rankings of one of the dissimilative patterns with assimilation in backness and/or height.

Systems showing backness harmony are quite common, e.g. Tuvan (Anderson and Harrison, 1999), Turkish (Clements and Sezer, 1982), Hungarian (Vago, 1973), and Finnish (Kiparsky, 1973). Languages with height harmony have also been reported in the literature, but, while the harmony for the feature [high] has been attested, e.g., in Kera (Pearce, 2013), the harmony in [low] is rare cross-linguistically (see Rose and Walker, 2011 for disscussion). One example comes from the Bantu languages, where high vowels are lowered to [e] and [o] if the first vowel of the stem is non-high (Clements, 1991;

[88] Descriptions of the reduction patterns analysed in this chapter are provided in section 2.6 and section 2.7 in Chapter 2.

Hulst and Weijer, 1995). However, as the low vowel /a/ does not act as a trigger of the [low] harmony, it is a matter of debate whether the lowering operating in the Bantu languages involves the spread of the feature [low]. The present chapter describes several vocalic systems attested in the southern Russian dialects in which the vowels in pretonic syllables harmonize with the low vowel [a] in the tonic syllable. The East Slavic data described in this chapter enriches the typology of harmonic systems by bringing in uncontroversial cases of vowel harmony which can be straightforwardly interpreted as the assimilation of the feature [low].

The structure of this chapter is as follows. First, section 6.2 analyses patterns which show harmony in backness (referred to as compound dissimilative reduction). Next, section 6.3 discusses systems exhibiting assimilation of the feature [low] (called assimilative-dissimilative reduction patterns). I demonstrate that the ranking of constraints established for dissimilative patterns also generates compound dissimilative and assimilative-dissimilative systems, with one additional constraint, Align-L([back], Ft) shaping the compound dissimilative reduction pattern (section 6.2), and the constraint Align-L([low], Ft) (section 6.3) operating in assimilative-dissimilative systems (section 6.3). Both constraints apply within the foot domain, which is argued to represent a salient prosodic position constituting the domain of application of positional faithfulness and markedness constraints in East Slavic. Section 6.4 presents interim conclusions.

6.2. Backness harmony (compound dissimilative patterns)

This section develops an analysis of the dissimilative patterns traditionally called Ščigry, Sudža, Mosal'sk, and Dmitrov; these patterns, described in section 2.6 in Chapter 2, are referred to as compound dissimilative reduction in this book.

Let us recall that in the dissimilative systems analysed in Chapter 5, [a] occurs before non-high vowels in Žizdra, before high vowels in Don, and before high and high mid vowels in Obojan'. Likewise, the patterns of reduction attested in Ščigry, Sudža, Mosal'sk, and Dmitrov use [a] before high vowels and [i] before back vowels. The difference between these patterns and the dissimilative systems of Žizdra, Don, and Obojan' consists in the quality of pretonic vowels before front mid vowels in stressed syllables: [i] appears instead of [a] before etymological /ɛ/ in Ščigry, before etymological /e/ in Mosal'sk, and before etymological /ɛ/ and /e/ in Sudža and Dmitrov. Examples illustrating the reduction before mid vowels in compound dissimilative systems and schematic representations are provided below, repeated from (22) and (23) in section 2.6 in Chapter 2.

(1) *Compound dissimilative reduction*

Ščigry	*Dmitrov*	*Sudža*	*Mosal'sk*	*Gloss*
a. Before etymological /o/ in the tonic syllable				
[s^{j}aˈlo]	[s^{j}aˈlo]	[s^{j}aˈlɔ]	[s^{j}aˈlɔ]	'village' (nom. sg.)
b. Before etymological /ɔ/ in the tonic syllable				
[s^{j}aˈlɔm]	[s^{j}iˈlɔm]	[s^{j}aˈlɔm]	[s^{j}aˈlɔm]	'village' (instr. sg.)
c. Before etymological /e/ in the tonic syllable				
[s^{j}aˈl^{j}e]	[s^{j}iˈl^{j}e]	[s^{j}iˈl^{j}ɛ]	[s^{j}iˈl^{j}ɛ]	'village' (loc. sg.)
d. Before etymological /ɛ/ in the tonic syllable				
[n^{j}iˈs^{j}ɔm]	[n^{j}iˈs^{j}ɔm]	[n^{j}iˈs^{j}ɔm]	[n^{j}aˈs^{j}ɔm]	'carry' (1st pl. pres.)

(2) *Types of compound dissimilative reduction*

a. Ščigry

pretonic	tonic		
a	i	ɨ	u
	e		o
i	ɛ, ɔ (> ɛ)		ɔ
			a

b. Dmitrov

pretonic	tonic		
a	i ɨ		u
	e		o
i	ɛ		ɔ
			a

c. Sudža

pretonic	tonic		
a	i	ɨ	u
i	ɛ, ɔ (> ɛ)		ɔ
			a

d. Mosal'sk

pretonic	tonic		
a	i ɨ		u
i	ɛ		ɔ
			a

It can be observed that compound dissimilative patterns employ the same mechanism as dissimilative patterns in the context of high and low tonic vowels: [a] is attested in the pretonic syllable if the stressed syllable contains high vowels and [i] occurs before a stressed low vowel. The distinction between the two systems (dissimilative and compound dissimilative) is seen before mid vowels. The vowel [a] is found before both back mid vowels [o] and [ɔ] in Ščigry and Sudža/Mosal'sk, which makes this type of dissimilation similar to the one found in Žizdra. In Dmitrov, only half-open [ɔ] induces reduction to [i], while half-close [o] is preceded by [a], as in the Obojan' type of dissimilation. The difference between Sudža and Mosal'sk lies in their treatment of the stressed [ɔ] after soft consonants, which come from the etymological /ɛ/. In Mosal'sk, [a] is found before both the underlying and derived /ɔ/, while in Sudža and Ščigry, [a] is pronounced before the underlying /ɔ/, and [i] is pronounced before [ɔ] which comes from /ɛ/. Based on the similarities between the systems of dissimilative and compound dissimilative reduction, I propose that compound dissimilative patterns constitute a combination of dissimilative reduction with assimilation in backness between vowels in two neighbouring syllables. It has often been noted in the literature that both standard Russian as well as many East Slavic dialects exhibit various patterns of vowel harmony (Paufošima, 1981; Paufošima, 1983; Kasatkina, 1996a). Kasatkina (1996a) demonstrates that Russian dialects show different degrees of assimilation in height both between tonic and pretonic syllables, as well as in positions not immediately preceding tonic syllables. Furthermore, Kasatkin (1999) argues that in the northern dialects of Russian, the alternations ɛ – *i* and *a* – ɛ in stressed syllables in words such as *be̲lyj* [ɛ] 'white' – *bi̲lenkij* [i] id. (dim.), *gla̲nu* [a] 'look' (1st pers. sg. pres.) – *gle̲net* [ɛ] id. (3rd pers. sg. future), which are traditionally assumed to be triggered by the following palatalized consonant, are in fact conditioned by the front vowel in the adjacent syllable. The argument is based, among others, on the fact that these alternations are attested in dialects which do not exhibit a contrast between palatalized and non-palatalized consonants (*cf.* Kasatkin, 1999: 398ff.). I assume that a similar mechanism is at work in compound dissimilative reduction patterns, where pretonic non-high vowels neutralize into [i] instead of the expected [a] if the following stressed syllable contains a front vowel.

Long-distance feature assimilations are widely attested cross-linguistically, and vowels in stressed syllables often act as triggers of harmony. For instance, pretonic vowels assimilate in height to a stressed high vowel in Servigliano Italian (Walker, 2005). The fact that unstressed vowels are more likely to harmonize with the adjacent vowel has been taken to indicate that these harmony patterns have an articulatory basis (Majors, 1998; see Rose and Walker (2011) for further discussion). The present data is compatible with the theoretical options which are employed in the optimality-theoretic literature to enforce vowel harmony. These include feature agreement (e.g., Lombardi, 1999; Baković, 2000) and feature spreading/alignment (e.g., Kirchner, 1993; Pulleyblank, 1996; Walker, 2000; Padgett, 2002).[89] Padgett (2002) points out that alignment incorporates directionality in the statement of constraints. A feature alignment approach is adopted in the current analysis, which models vowel harmony in the compound dissimilative neutralization patterns in terms of the alignment of the feature [back]. To ensure that vowels in other unstressed positions are not targeted by [back] harmony, I assume that the alignment constraint formulated in (3) below operates within the domain of the domain of the foot. The motivation for the foot as a salient prosodic domain is provided in section 3.4.

---

[89] See McCarthy (2011) and Rose and Walker (2011) for a review and criticism of different OT approaches to vowel harmony.

(3) ALIGN-L([back], FT): For any feature [back] associated to a segment in a foot, that feature has an association to the leftmost syllable of a foot.

The compound dissimilative reduction patterns attested in East Slavic combine assimilation in the feature [back] with patterns of dissimilative reduction. The type of dissimilation in Ščigry, Sudža, and Mosal'sk is analogous to the one found in Žizdra, while Dmitrov is similar to the Obojan' pattern. Therefore, it can be assumed that the ranking of HEAD=H with respect to the members of the *H≤V family of constraints in these dialects is the same as the ones established for Žizdra and Obojan' (see (17) in section 5.4.2, Chapter 5). The innovation of compound dissimilative reduction patterns consists in promoting ALIGN-L([back], FT) to such a position in the constraint hierarchy where it can override the pressure exerted by *H≤V. (See the ranking scheme in (4) below.) To be able to induce fronting (and subsequent raising), ALIGN-L([back], FT) has to be ranked above the constraint demanding that stressed vowels carry High tone (HEAD=H). In addition, ALIGN-L([back], FT) must dominate at least one of the members of the *H≤V family to ensure that it is more important to agree in the feature [back] with the following vowel than to realize High tone on a more sonorous vowel. There are two locations in the constraint hierarchy at which ALIGN-L([back], FT) can be ranked above HEAD=H in the Žizdra pattern (shown in (4a) and (4c) below), and one place to rank it above both HEAD=H and one of the *H≤V constraints in the Obojan' pattern (4b). As demonstrated in (4), all these options are exploited by the dialects with compound dissimilative reduction patterns.[90]

[90] Let us note that ALIGN-L([back], FT) does not combine with the Don pattern. In this type of dissimilation, the only possibility to rank ALIGN-L([back], FT) above HEAD=H and above one of the *H/≥V constraints dominating HEAD=H would be to place it above *H/i,u. This would produce an unattested system in which [i] appears before front mid and high vowels, as well as before the low vowel [a]. The pretonic vowel [a], in turn, would surface only before the back vowels [ɨ] and [u]. However, such a pattern would be arbitrary as it shows neither dissimilation (because [i] is found before both low and high vowels) nor the assimilation in backness (because [i] can be followed by both front and back vowels).

(4) *Compound dissimilative patterns: partial rankings*

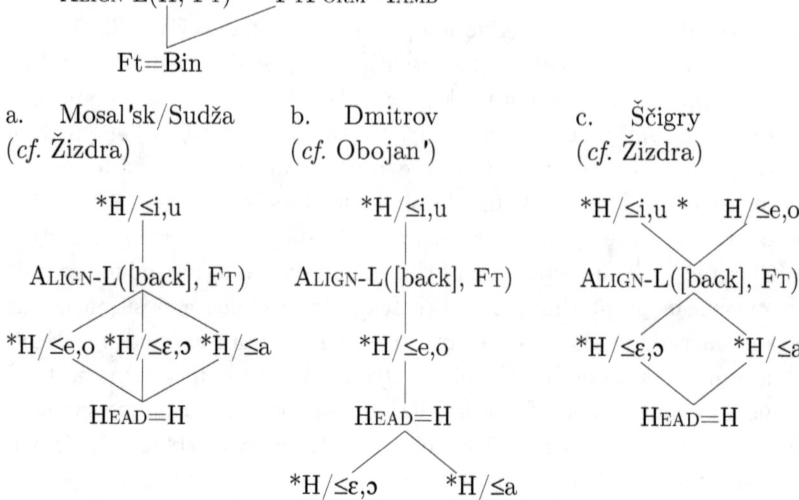

The tableaux in (5) illustrate how the constraint system provided in (4) generates reduction in Mosal'sk. In addition, the tableaux display the constraints on foot form (FT=BIN and FTFORM=IAMB) and the constraint ALIGN-L(H, FT) regulating the association of H with foot edge. As established previously (*cf.* section 3.6.2 above), ALIGN-L(H, FT) dominates FT=BIN in systems with dissimilative reduction. The words /sʲɛˈl+itʲ/ [sʲaˈlʲitʲ] 'to settle', /sʲɛˈl+ɛnʲij̯/ [sʲiˈlʲɛnʲɪj̯] 'settlement' (gen. pl.), /sʲɛˈl+ɔm/ [sʲaˈlɔm] 'village' (instr. sg.), and /sʲɛˈl+a/ [sʲiˈla] id. (gen. sg.) serve as diagnostic forms. Only a subset of possible output candidates is shown for compactness.

(5) *Dissimilative [ja]-reduction: Mosal'sk*

i. /sʲɛˈl+itʲ/	*H/≤i,u	ALIGN-L ([back], FT)	*H/≤ɛ,ɔ	*H/≤a	HEAD = H	FTFORM = IAMB	ALIGN-L (H, FT)	FT = BIN
H ⇒ a. (sʲaˈlʲitʲ)		*		*	*			
H b. sʲi(ˈlʲitʲ)	*!		*	*				*

ii. /sʲɛˈl+ɛnʲij̯/	*H/≤i,u	ALIGN-L([back], FT)	*H/≤ɛ,ɔ	*H/≤a	HEAD = H	FTFORM = IAMB	ALIGN-L (H, FT)	FT = BIN
H ⇒ a. sʲi(ˈlʲɛ)nʲɪj̯			*	*				*
H b. (sʲaˈlʲɛ)nʲɪj̯		*!		*	*			
H c. sʲi(ˈlʲɛnʲɪj̯)			*	*		*!		

iii. /sʲɛ'l+ɔm/	*H/≤i,u	ALIGN-L([back], FT)	*H/≤ɛ,ɔ	*H/≤a	HEAD = H	FTFORM = IAMB	ALIGN-L (H, FT)	FT = BIN
a. sʲi('lɔm) (H on ɔ)			*!	*				*
⇒ b. (sʲa'lɔm) (H on a)				*	*			

iv. /sʲɛ'l+a/	*H/≤i,u	ALIGN-L([back], FT)	*H/≤ɛ,ɔ	*H/≤a	HEAD = H	FTFORM = IAMB	ALIGN-L (H, FT)	FT = BIN
⇒ a. sʲi('la) (H on a)				*				*
b. (sʲa'la) (H on first a)				*	*!			
c. (sʲi'la) (H on i)		*!		*			*	

The optimal outputs in (5i) and (5iv) are chosen by the ranking *H/≤V >> HEAD=H: lowering to [a] takes place in (5i) because the high-ranked *H/≤i,u prohibits the association between H and the high vowel in the tonic syllable; in (5iv), the stressed vowel is low, so *H/≤i,u is mute and the choice between (5iva) and (5iva) is made based on a lower-ranked HEAD=H. Thus, the evaluation of the forms in (5i) and (5iv) is parallel to the dissimilative pattern attested in Žizdra (cf. Tableaux (18) and (19) in section 5.4).

The comparison of the evaluation in (5ii) and (5iii) shows that both /sʲɛ'l+ɛnʲi̯/ in (5ii) and /sʲɛ'l+ɔm/ in (5iii) contain mid vowels in the tonic syllable. In (5ii), the optimal form [sʲi'lʲɛnʲɪi̯] (5iia) wins over the candidate form [sʲa'lʲɛnʲɪi̯] shown in (5iib), because the latter fatally violates ALIGN-L([back], FT). The outcome of the evaluation is different in (5iii), in which the vowel in the stressed syllable is mid back. In contrast to (5ii), ALIGN-L([back], FT) is satisfied in [sʲa'lɔm] (5iii) because the stressed back vowel [ɔ] is preceded by the back vowel [a] in this output form.

Additionally, let us observe that the form [sʲi('lʲɛnʲɪi̯)] in (5iic) parses the penultimate and the final syllable into a binary trochaic foot in compliance with FT=BIN and ALIGN-L(H, FT) (*cf.* a unary foot in the winner [sʲi('lʲɛ) nʲɪi̯] in (5iia)). However, contender (5iic) with the trochaic parse is excluded by the ranking FTFORM=IAMB >> FT=BIN. Finally, note that another strategy to satisfy the requirement of foot binarity is to foot the pretonic and the tonic syllable into a disyllabic iamb, as in the winning candidate in (5ia). However, as demonstrated by the comparison of (5ia) with (5ivc), such a parse is only possible in this system if the pretonic syllable hosts H tone. In this respect, dissimilative and compound dissimilative varieties differ from non-dissimilative and assimilative-dissimilative dialects (analysed in sections 5.3 and 6.3), which, due to a low ranking of ALIGN-L(H, FT), parse pretonic and tonic syllables into a disyllabic iamb irrespective of the location of H within the foot. The significance of foot structure in the analysis presented above is evident in (5iv), in which the footing [sʲi(ˈla)] allows the optimal candidate (5iva) to eschew a violation of a the high-ranked ALIGN-L([back], FT).

Turning now to the Dmitrov pattern, its system parallels Mosal'sk in ranking ALIGN-L([back], FT) immediately below *H/≤i,u. This ranking ensures that pretonic vowels assimilate in the feature [back] to the following mid front vowels but not to the high front vowels. Unlike Mosal'sk, Dmitrov distinguishes between high mid and low mid back vowels, which induce distinct reduction patterns in the pretonic syllable: [a] surfaces before [o] and [i] before [ɔ] in the stressed syllable (see Tableau (6) below). This is achieved by ranking HEAD=H above *H/≤ɛ,ɔ and below *H/≤e,o, as in the dissimilative pattern in Obojan' (cf. the analysis in (19iii) in section 5.4 in Chapter 5). As can be seen in (6), the input vowel /ɛ/ maps onto the output [a] in (6i) due to the highranked *H/≤e,o, which gives preference to the form [sʲaˈlo] (6ia). *H/≤e,o is mute in (6ii), so the optimal output [sʲiˈl ɔm] is chosen by HEAD=H. Candidate (6iic) is excluded because it incurs a fatal violation of ALIGN-L([back], FT). Let us note that the winner (6iia), though segmentally identical to (6iiac), does not violate ALIGN-L([back], FT) because [a] and [ɔ] are not parsed into one foot in this candidate.

(6) *Dissimilative [ja]-reduction: Dmitrov*

i. /sʲɛˈl+o/	ALIGN-L ([back], FT)	*H/≤e,o	HEAD = H	*H/≤ɛ,ɔ	*H/≤a	ALIGN-L (H, FT)	FT = BIN
⇒ a. (sʲaˈlo) (H on a)			*		*		
b. sʲi(ˈlo) (H on o)		*!		*	*		*
ii. /sʲɛˈl+ɔm/	**ALIGN-L ([back], FT)**	***H/≤e,o**	**HEAD = H**	***H/≤ɛ,ɔ**	***H/≤a**	**ALIGN-L (H, FT)**	**FT = BIN**
⇒ a. sʲi(ˈlɔm) (H on ɔ)				*	*		*
b. (sʲaˈlɔm) (H on a)			*!		*		
c. (sʲiˈlɔm) (H on ɔ)	*!			*	*	*	

To summarize briefly, the assimilation in backness in Dmitrov, Sudža, and Mosal'sk is induced by front mid vowels but not by the front high vowel [i]. These patterns have been analysed by sandwiching ALIGN-L([back], FT) between *H/≤i,u and *H/≤e,o, which ensures that only mid vowels act as triggers of assimilation in these dialects.

A one-step demotion of the constraint ALIGN-L([back], FT) produces a different pattern of reduction, attested in Ščigry (see the ranking scheme in (4c) and the evaluation in (7) below). Note that symbol '☹' denotes the intended winner, and symbol '⇐' indicates the output which is erroneously chosen as optimal.

(7) *Dissimilative [ja]-reduction: Ščigry*

i. /sʲɛ'l+e/	*H/≤e,o	ALIGN-L([back], FT)	*H/≤ɛ,ɔ	*H/≤a	HEAD=H
H ☹ a. (sʲa'lʲe)		*!		*	*
H b. sʲi('lʲe)	*!		*	*	
H ⇐ c. (sʲɛ'lʲe)			*	*	*
ii. /sʲɛ'l+ɛnʲiɪ̯/	*H/≤e,o	ALIGN-L([back], FT)	*H/≤ɛ,ɔ	*H/≤a	HEAD=H
H ⇒ a. sʲi('lʲɛnʲ)ɪɪ̯			*	*	
H b. (sʲa'lʲɛnʲ)ɪɪ̯		*!		*	*
iii. /sʲɛ'l+ɔm/	*H/≤e,o	ALIGN-L([back], FT)	*H/≤ɛ,ɔ	*H/≤a	HEAD=H
H ⇒ a. (sʲa'lɔm)				*	*
H b. sʲi('lɔm)			*!	*	
iv. /sʲɛ'l+a/	*H/≤e,o	ALIGN-L([back], FT)	*H/≤ɛ,ɔ	*H/≤a	HEAD=H
H ⇒ a. sʲi('la)				*	
H b. (sʲa'la)				*	*!

As shown in the tableaux above, the two input forms (7ii) and (7iii) containing stressed half-open vowels trigger two different reduction patterns: [sʲi'lʲɛnʲɪɪ̯] and [sʲa'lɔm]. The [i]-reduction in the former is driven by the constraint ALIGN-L([back], FT). The constraint system established so far ensures that High tone is shifted leftwards whenever the vowel in the stressed syllable is non-low. A pretonic vowel linked to High tone lowers to [a] because High tone is better expressed on the more sonorous low segments. However, the vowel [a] is back, so [a]-reduction creates a marked structure in forms with a front vowel in the tonic syllable. In the case of the tonic [ɛ] (as in (7ii) above), ALIGN-L([back], FT) ranked above *H/≤ɛ,ɔ prevents High tone from moving to the pretonic syllable. As ALIGN-L([back], FT) is ranked below *H/≤e,o, High tone shifts to the pretonic vowel when the stressed syllable contains [e] (candidates (7ia) and (7ic). The comparison of candidates (7ia) and (7ic) demonstrates that the ranking ALIGN-L([back], FT) >> *H/≤ɛ,ɔ prefers candidate (7ic) because, unlike the intended winner (7b), it complies with ALIGN-L([back], FT).

Thus, the present analysis predicts that the pretonic vowel should surface as [ɛ] before front high and/or high mid vowels, and as [a] before the corresponding back vowels. This prediction applies to Ščigry, which distinguishes between the underlying vowels /e/ and /ɛ/, but not to Mosal'sk, Dmitrov, and Sudža. These patterns lack the underlying /e/ because they neither preserve the surface contrast between [e] and [ɛ] nor exhibit differences in reduction patterns depending on the etymological origin of [ɛ] (i.e., [ɛ] > /e/ and [ɛ] > /ɛ/). Interestingly, traditional grammars report that a pretonic vowel preceded by a palatalized consonant can be realized phonetically by a range of sounds (Durnovo, 1917; Avanesov, 1974; Kasatkin, 1999; Kalenčuk and Kasatkina, 2013). On the one hand, Durnovo (1917) and Avanesov (1974) classify pretonic vowels into *a* and *non-a*: the former appears before high vowels and the latter before low vowels in the following stressed syllable. Non-*a* is reported to be realized by sounds placed on a continuum between [ɛ] and [i]. Kasatkin (1999, 2005), on the other hand, demonstrates that *a* can surface as a sound whose quality ranges from [a] to [ɛ], and argues that it is more appropriate to classify pretonic vowels into *i* and non-*i*, the latter represented by the variants [a] and [ɛ]. The OT model of dissimilative reduction developed in this book is consistent with Kasatkin's (1999b, 2005) classification of pretonic vowels into *i* and non-*i*. However, the present analysis predicts that the choice between [a] and [ɛ] in the Ščigry pattern should not be random: [a] should occur before back vowels, and [ɛ] should be used before front vowels in the tonic syllable. Impressionistic descriptions available in the literature are not sufficient and further instrumental studies are needed to validate this assumption. However, the data from dialects with the Obojan' pattern of [a]-reduction provide support to the analysis predicting that the variation between [a] and [ɛ] is conditioned by the vowel in the following syllable. Kasatkina and Ščigel' (1995) report that pretonic /a/ and /o/ are realized as the front vowel [æ] before [ɛ] in the next syllable, for example /o'tʲɛt͡s/ [æ'tʲɛt͡s] 'father' (Kasatkina and Ščigel', 1995; Savinov, 2013a). Therefore, it is likely that a similar coarticulation effect occurs in Ščigry, where /a/ is fronted to [ɛ] or [æ] in the context of the following front vowel.

It was mentioned above that the Sudža pattern is minimally different from Mosal'sk in the way it treats the stressed vowel [ɔ] which originally comes from /ɛ/. In Mosal'sk, [a] is attested before both underlying and derived [ɔ], while in Sudža, [a] is found before the underlying /ɔ/, while [i] occurs before [ɔ] which is historically derived from /ɛ/. The same pattern of pretonic reduction before the vowel [ɔ] is found in Ščigry. As shown in

(8) below, the system of constraints established so far predicts that words like /sʲɛ'lʲɔd+k+a/ 'herring' should surface with the pretonic [a] in dialects which rank HEAD=H below *H/≤ɛ,ɔ and, therefore, disallow the vowels [ɛ] and [ɔ] to carry High tone.

(8) i. *Mosal'sk*

/sʲɛ'lʲɔd+k+a/	ALIGN-L([back], FT)	*H/≤e,o	*H/≤ɛ,ɔ	*H/≤a	HEAD=H
H a. sʲi('lʲɔt)kə			*	*!	
H ⇒ b. (sʲa'lʲɔt)kə				*	*

ii. *Sudža/Ščigry*

/sʲɛ'lʲɔd+k+a/	*H/≤e,o	ALIGN-L([back], FT)	*H/≤ɛ,ɔ	*H/≤a	HEAD=H
H ☹ a. sʲi('lʲɔt)kə			*	*!	
H ⇐ b. (sʲa'lʲɔt)kə				*	*

The constraint *H/≤ɛ,ɔ outranks HEAD=H in Sudža, Mosal'sk, and Ščigry.[91] However, only Mosal'sk reduces a pretonic vowel to [a], e.g. [sʲa'lʲɔtkə], while Sudža and Ščigry have [i] in this position, e.g. [sʲi'lʲɔtka]. One way to generate the correct output for Sudža and Ščigry would be to re-rank HEAD=H above *H/≤ɛ,ɔ. This, however, would produce a completely different type of dissimilation (the Obojan' type), incorrectly generating reduction to [i] before non-palatalized consonants, *[sʲi'lɔm] instead of *[sʲa'lɔm].

Alternatively, it can be assumed that [i]-reduction is not triggered by the front vowel in the stressed syllable but by the following palatalized consonant. This generalization lies at the core of the OT analysis of dissimilative [ja]-reduction suggested by Crosswhite (2001), who generates the change to [i] by means of the markedness constraint Cʲ_Cʲ/[+front] ('A vowel may not occur between two palatalized consonants unless it is [+front]', Crosswhite, 2001: 93). In Sudža and Ščigry, high-ranked Cʲ_Cʲ/[+front] correctly generates [i]-reduction both before the front mid vowel [ɛ], as in [sʲi'lʲɛ], as well as before the back vowel [ɔ], e.g. [sʲi'lʲɔtka]. However, this analysis is problematic for several reasons.

First, the model deriving [i]-reduction by means of the constraint Cʲ_Cʲ/[+front] fails to account for the Mosal'sk pattern of reduction, which is similar to Sudža, except for the lack of [i]-reduction before the stressed [o] preceded by a palatalized consonant in words such as [sʲa'lʲɔtka]. Cʲ_Cʲ/

91 In Dmitrov, the vowels [ɛ] and [ɔ] preserve the high tone due to the ranking HEAD=H >> *H/≤ɛ,ɔ, which correctly derives pretonic reduction to [i] in this dialect.

[+front] incorrectly triggers [i]-reduction in such cases: *[s^{j}i'l^{j}ɔtka]. Crosswhite (2001) acknowledges this problem and, based on the comment of Avanesov and Bromlej (1986: 103) that the Mosal'sk pattern is rarely attested, suggests that this pattern 'results from morphological re-interpretation of the dissimilative pattern, or from dialect mixing' (Crosswhite, 2001: 70).[92] For this reason, the Mosal'sk pattern is excluded from the analysis (*cf.* Crosswhite, 2001: 97). However, Avanesov and Bromlej (1986) only describe the Russian dialects, whereas the Mosal'sk type is widespread in the East Slavic dialects spoken in Belarus (Vajtovič, 1968: 58ff.). Therefore, the exclusion of the Mosal'sk pattern on the grounds of its rare attestation is not warranted.

Another unwelcome consequence of Crosswhite's analysis is that the constraint C^j_C^j /[+front] does not generate correct outputs in forms with a palatalized consonant followed by a high mid back vowel [o] in the stressed syllable. In Sudža, for instance, C^j_C^j/[+front] produces the forms [C^{j}iC^{j}e], [C^{j}iC^{j}ɛ], [C^{j}iC^{j}ɔ] and [C^{j}iC^{j}o], the first three of which are attested. The fourth one, [C^{j}iC^{j}o], is predicted to be possible but unattested because [o] 'does not occur after C^j' (Crosswhite, 2001: 69). Though true in a historical sense, this generalization is not valid synchronically, as [o] appears in the place of the etymological [ɛ] after palatalized consonants due to analogy in a number of words (Avanesov, 1974: 217ff.). For instance, *dete* [ɛ] 'child' has changed into *detjo* [o] by analogy to words such as *selo* [o] 'village', preserving palatalization of the consonant [t^j]. Avanesov (1974: 217) reports that in systems with archaic types of dissimilation, such as Obojan' and Dmitrov, the non-etymological [o] occurring after palatalized consonants functions similarly to the etymological one in that it fails to induce [i]-reduction, for instance [pl^{j}a't͡ʃ^{j}om] 'shoulder' (instr. sg.), [b^{j}a'l^{j}jo] 'linen' (nom. sg.) (see also Zaxarova, 1959). These forms are contrasted with words such as [pl^{j}i't͡ʃ^{j}e] 'shoulder' (dat. sg.), [b^{j}i'l^{j}je] 'linen' (dat. sg.), in which [e], the front counterpart of [o], triggers [i]-reduction in the pretonic syllable. In Crosswhite's model, both [pl^{j}a't͡ʃ^{j}om] and [pl^{j}i't͡ʃ^{j}e] come within the purview of C^j_C^j/[+front], which incorrectly derives [i]-reduction in *[pl^{j}i't͡ʃ^{j}om]. The Sudža pattern is more complicated in that it does not distinguish between [o] and [ɔ] phonetically – both are pronounced [ɔ]. However, the two vowels are distinct

---

92 The description of the Mosal'sk pattern provided by Crosswhite (2001: 70) incorrectly suggests that pretonic vowels reduce to [i] before the non-palatalized consonant followed by the stressed vowel [ɔ]: [s^{j}i'lɔm] 'village' (instr. sg.). This is, clearly, not what one would expect if the [i]-reduction was triggered by the palatalized consonant. However, the descriptive sources uniformly report that pretonic vowels neutralize in [a] in this context, as in [s^{j}a'lɔm] 'village' (instr. sg.) (*cf.* Avanesov & Orlova, 1965: 51; Kasatkin, 2005: 45; and others).

phonologically as they trigger two different reduction patterns: [ɔ] (>o) induces [a]-reduction and [ɔ] (>ɔ) triggers [i]-reduction, *cf.* [vʲiˈdʲɔm] *vs.* [mʲidʲvʲaˈdʲɔm] (Avanesov, 1974: 218). The constraint Cʲ_Cʲ /[+front] does not distinguish between the two contexts, incorrectly generating [i]-reduction in *[mʲidʲvʲiˈdʲɔm].

Next, the analysis locating the trigger of dissimilative [ja]-reduction solely in the palatalized consonant makes wrong predictions for words with the pretonic vowel followed by consonantal clusters. First, this model generates an incorrect reduction pattern in pretonic positions before a cluster of a palatalized consonant followed by a non-palatalized consonant. In the Dmitrov type of dissimilation (repeated in (9) below), [i]-reduction occurs before the stressed high mid front vowel [e] but not before its back correspondent [o].

(9) *Dmitrov reduction pattern*

pretonic	tonic		
a	i	ɨ	u
	e		o
i	ɛ		ɔ
			a

According to Crosswhite (2001: 98), Cʲ_Cʲ/[+front] is assumed to be mute when the pretonic vowel is followed by the stressed [o], because [o] does not occur after palatalized consonants. However, there are words in which stressed [o] is preceded by a cluster of a palatalized plus a non-palatalized consonant, e.g. /sʲelʲˈt͡so/ [sʲalʲˈt͡so] 'a small village'. If [i]-reduction is triggered by Cʲ_Cʲ/[+front], this word should be pronounced *[sʲilʲˈt͡so], on a par with /sʲeˈlʲe/ [sʲiˈlʲe] 'village' (dat. sg.). This prediction is not borne out: words such as [sʲalʲˈt͡so] exhibit reduction to [a] in Dmitrov (Zaxarova, 1959; Kasatkin, 2005: 45).[93]

In addition, a cluster of a non-palatalized consonant followed by a palatalized one is also not within the purview of the constraint Cʲ_Cʲ/[+front]. So it is predicted that pretonic vowels preceding the cluster CCʲ should not be subject to [i]-reduction. Contrary to this prediction, pretonic vowels reduce to [i] in these contexts, as shown by the pronunciation of the word [svʲiˈtlʲɛt͡sʲ] 'to grow lighter' in Mosal'sk (Vajtovič, 1968: 60). In [zʲaˈmlʲɔj̯] 'earth' (instr. sg.), the same cluster [mlʲ] is preceded by [a]. These examples

[93] The word /sʲelʲˈtso/ is pronounced [sʲalʲˈt͡so] in all dialects with dissimilative [ja]-reduction with the exception of Don. In Don, all stressed mid vowels can carry High tone, so the raising to [i] in words such as [sʲilʲˈt͡so] is triggered by PAL (after non-palatalized consonants, pretonic vowels reduce to schwa in this dialect, *cf.* /salʲˈt͡so/ 'lard', dim. [səlʲˈt͡so]).

show clearly that [i]-reduction is not motivated by the following palatalized consonant.[94]

Finally, the analysis assuming that dissimilative reduction is triggered by a palatalized consonant cannot account for patterns attested in the southern Russian dialects with a seven-vowel system. The type of vocalism distinguishing high mid and low mid vowels is attested in present-day archaic dialects, such as Obojan', Zadon and Novoselki (Savinov, 2013a: 318–319). These dialects palatalize consonants before the high mid vowel [e] but not before the low mid [ɛ], e.g. [vʲera] 'faith', [vɛrx] 'top' (Kasatkin, 1999: 393, 2005: 75; Djačenko, 2013: 343–344). In dialects with the Novoselki type of reduction (discussed in detail in section 3.1 below), [i] is used before the tonic [ɛ], and [a] before the tonic [e]. The analysis deriving [i]-reduction by means of the constraint Cʲ_Cʲ/[+front] (*cf.* Crosswhite, 2001: 97) predicts an opposite scenario, in which *Cʲe* but not *Cɛ* sequences induce vowel fronting in the preceding syllable.

Let us recall that the model developed in this chapter views [i]-reduction as a result of assimilation in backness between two adjacent vowels. In OT terms, this generalization is expressed by the constraint ALIGN-L([back], FT) (defined in (3) earlier in this section). The table in (10) compares the predictions of the models employing Cʲ_Cʲ/[+front] and ALIGN-L([back], FT).

(10) *Comparison of Cʲ_Cʲ/[+front] and ALIGN-L([back], FT)*

Patterns	Context	Example	Cʲ_Cʲ/[+front]	ALIGN-L([back], FT)
a. Sudža/Ščigry	CʲiCʲɔ	[sʲi'lʲɔtkə]	✓	*[sʲa'lʲɔtkə]
	CʲaCʲɔ	[mʲidʲvʲa'dʲɔm]	*[mʲidʲvʲi'dʲɔm]	✓
b. Obojan'	CʲaCʲo	[plʲa't͡ʃʲom]	*[plʲi't͡ʃʲom]	✓
c. Dmitrov	CʲaCʲCo	[sʲalʲ't͡so]	*[sʲilʲ't͡so]	✓
d. Mosal'sk	CʲaCʲɔ	[sʲa'lʲɔtkə]	*[sʲi'lʲɔtkə]	✓
e. Mosal'sk	CʲiCCʲɛ	[svʲi'tlʲɛt͡sʲ]	*[svʲa'tlʲɛt͡sʲ]	✓

The comparison of the two models shows that ALIGN-L([back], FT) cannot deal with the Sudža pattern (10a), whereas Cj_Cj/[+front] produces incorrect outputs in Sudža (10a), Obojan' (10b), Dmitrov (10c), and Mosal'sk (10d,e). In sum, the constraint Cʲ_Cʲ/[+front] is problematic because it overgenerates [i]-reduction before palatalized consonants in (10a-d) and

[94] To support her analysis, Crosswhite (2001: 71) cites Nelson (1974: 166), who adduces data taken from the fieldwork notes of Russian dialectologists showing that [a] was recorded several times instead of [i] in words with a consonant cluster preceding the stressed vowel, e.g. [tʲa'mnʲɛtʲ], [svʲa'tlʲɛtʲ], [vvʲa'drʲɛ]. However, as these notes are based on one dialect with the Mosal'sk reduction pattern, it cannot be taken as a decisive argument for employing the constraint Cʲ_Cʲ/[+front].

incorrectly blocks [i]-reduction before non-palatalized consonants in (10e). To conclude, the analysis employing the constraint Cj_Cj/[+front] must be rejected because it cannot adequately account for the reduction patterns attested in East Slavic dialects with dissimilative [ja]reduction.

The alternative analysis employing ALIGN-L([back], FT) fails in cases where [i]-reduction occurs before the vowel [ɔ] preceded by a palatalized consonant. It was shown in (8) above that it cannot generate the pattern of reduction attested in Sudža and Ščigry because ALIGN-L([back], FT) is mute in the case of inputs in which the tonic and pretonic vowels are not parsed into the same foot. Let us observe that the back vowel [ɔ] in the position after palatalized consonants is the outcome of a process changing *e* to *o* in stressed syllables before a non-palatalized consonant. In many cases, stressed [ɔ] before the non-palatalized consonant alternates with [ɛ] followed by a palatalized consonant, e.g. [vʲi'sʲɔlɨi̯] ‘joyful’ – [vʲi'sʲɛlʲjə] ‘joy’. It was mentioned above that only [ɔ] which is derived from /ɛ/ induces [i]-reduction in the preceding syllable, as in [vʲi'sʲɔlɨi̯] ‘joyful’, [vʲi'dʲɔm] ‘lead’ (1st pers. pl. pres.). In contrast, the vowel [ɔ] in words such as [mʲidʲvʲa'dʲɔm] ‘bear’ (instr. sg.), [plʲa't͡ʃʲɔ] ‘shoulder’, [zʲa'mlʲɔi̯] ‘earth’ (instr. sg.) is preceded by [a] in the pretonic syllable. Historically, this [ɔ] also comes from [ɛ] which has changed into [o] in some endings by grammatical analogy to existing forms containing [ɛ] (Avanesov, 1974: 218). However, the contrast [vʲi'dʲɔm] – [mʲidʲvʲa'dʲɔm] demonstrates that the former [ɔ] patterns together with front vowels inducing [i]-reduction, whereas the latter [ɔ] functions as a back vowel not triggering [i]-reduction in the preceding syllable. Based on these observations, it can be legitimately concluded that [ɔ] is represented as /ɛ/ in the underlying representation in dialects with dissimilative [ja]-reduction. The vowel /ɛ/ affects the preceding vowel in words such as /vʲe'dʲɛm/ [vʲi'dʲɔm] by inducing the change to [i], just as in /sʲɛ'l+ɛnʲii̯/ [sʲi'lʲɛnʲɪi̯] ‘settlement’ (gen. pl.), in which /ɛ/ in the stressed syllable does not undergo the change to [ɔ] as it is followed by a palatalized consonant. On the surface, the underlying /ɛ/ is realized as [ɔ] in /vʲe'dʲɛm/ [vʲi'dʲɔm] before the non-palatalized consonant, resulting in non-surface-true forms such as [vʲi'dʲɔm]. The interaction between the two processes (i.e., backness harmony and [ɛ]-retraction) is opaque, because backness harmony applies prior to [ɛ]-retraction (ɛ → ɔ/ Cʲ_C); in turn, [ɛ]-retraction creates potential inputs to backness harmony. This type of opacity, called counterfeeding in generative literature, is not compatible with the standard OT concept of parallel evaluation, which assumes that inputs are mapped onto the outputs directly, without intermediate stages.

Since its inception, OT research has accumulated a massive body of evidence proving the inadequacy of parallel evaluation in dealing with opacity. Several attempts have been made to resolve this issue without forfeiting the principle of strict parallelism;[95] however, all of them have proven unsatisfactory for various reasons.[96] The opacity problem does not arise in the serial version of OT (Inkelas and Orgun, 1995; Kiparsky, 1997, 2000; Rubach, 1997, *et seq.*; Bermúdez-Otero, 1999, 2003; Ito and Mester, 2001, 2003). The principal difference between standard OT and serial OT (called Stratal OT, Derivational OT, or LP/OT) is that the latter admits intermediate levels of derivation, each of which contains a separate constraint ranking. The evaluation of candidates proceeds in stages, with the output at level_{n} constituting the input at level_{n+1}.

Slavic languages with their complex morphological structure provide a strong argument for the derivational levels in phonology. Rubach (1997, *et seq.*) demonstrates that the assumption of a serial evaluation of the candidate forms allows for a more insightful analysis of numerous opaque processes in various Slavic languages, including palatalization, glide insertion, yer vocalization, or syllabification. The data from Sudža and Ščigry discussed above furnishes further motivation for level distinction. In serial OT, the interaction of the processes producing opaque forms such as [vʲiˈdʲɔm] *vs.* [mʲidʲvʲaˈdʲɔm] is straightforwardly accounted for in assuming that backness harmony is a level 1 process and [ɛ]-retraction is a level 2 process.

Given that the retraction of /ɛ/ to [ɔ] is triggered by the immediately following non-palatalized consonants, this process can be analysed in terms of backness assimilation between a consonant and a following vowel.[97] The constraint expressing this generalization is stated in (11a) below. The change

---

[95] The auxiliary theories include sympathy theory (McCarthy, 1999; McCarthy, 2003), output-output constraints (Kraska-Szlenk, 1995; Benua, 1997), targeted constraints (Wilson, 2001), lexically-indexed constraints (Pater, 2000), candidate chains (McCarthy, 2007), among others.

[96] See McCarthy (2007) for a discussion of different types of opacity, and for a review and a critical appraisal of the aproaches to opacity within OT.

[97] Retraction before non-palatalized consonants is widespread in both stressed and unstressed syllables in East Slavic. It is attested in the stressed syllable in Standard Russian and Belarusian, as well as in the majority of Russian and Belarusian dialects. Retraction in unstressed syllables (called *jokan'e* in traditional descriptions) is common in a number of Northern Russian dialects lacking [a]-reduction, e.g. [ˈpʲet͡ʃ] 'bake' (inf.) – [pʲoˈkut] id. (3rd pers. pl.) (Avanesov and Orlova, 1965; Kasatkin, 2005). Interestingly, the Northern Russian dialects showing retraction before non-palatalized consonants also exhibit fronting of *a* to *e* before palatalized consonants, e.g. [poˈtʲanut] 'pull' (3rd pers. pl. future) – [poˈtʲenʲeʃ] id. (2rd pers. sg. future) – [potʲaˈnu] id. (1st pers. sg. future) – [potʲeˈnʲi] id. (imp.) (Kuznecov, 1960: 147; Kasatkin, 2005: 42). Therefore, vowels and the following consonants appear to agree for both values of the feature [±back]. It is an open question whether both retraction and fronting can be derived by means of one general constraint demanding backness agreement in the *VC* sequences. As this issue is outside the scope of the present study, its resolution is left for future research.

of the underlying feature [-back] in the stressed syllable is prohibited by the positional faithfulness constraint formulated in (11b).

(11) a. AGREE-VC[+back]$_{\text{HD}\sigma}$: A consonant and a following vowel agree in the feature [+back] in the stressed syllables in the output.
b. IDENT-V[-back]$_{\text{HD}\sigma}$: The feature [-back] on a vowel in the input must be preserved on the corresponding vowel in the stressed syllables in the output.

At Level 1, AGREE-VC[+back]$_{\text{HD}\sigma}$ is inactive due to a higher ranked IDENT-V[-back]$_{\text{HD}\sigma}$. The output of Level 1 serves as the input to Level 2. At level 2, the change of ɛ to [ɔ] is possible because IDENT-V[-back]$_{\text{HD}\sigma}$ >> AGREE-VC[+back]$_{\text{HD}\sigma}$ is re-ranked as AGREE-VC[+back]$_{\text{HD}\sigma}$ >> IDENT-V[-back]$_{\text{HD}\sigma}$. The link of H to the tonic syllable is preserved at this level due to the constraint prohibiting the deletion of association lines, formulated below after Yip (2002: 83).

(12) *DISASSOCIATE: No removal of association lines.

The evaluation of the word *vedjom* [vʲiˈdʲɔm] at the two levels is shown in (13).

(13) Sudža/Ščigry: /vʲɛˈdʲɛm/ [vʲiˈdʲɔm] 'lead' (1st pers. pl. pres.)

i. Level 1

/vʲɛˈdʲɛm/	ALIGN-L ([back], FT)	IDENT-V [-back]$_{\text{HD}\sigma}$	AGREE-VC [+back]$_{\text{HD}\sigma}$	*H/≤ɛ,ɔ	*H/≤a
H ⇒ a. vʲi(ˈdʲɛm)			*	*	*
H b. (vʲaˈdʲɛm)	*!		*		*
H c. (vʲaˈdʲɔm)		*!			*

ii. Level 2

H vʲiˈ(dʲɛm)	ALIGN-L ([back], FT)	*DISASSOC	AGREE-VC [+back]$_{\text{HD}\sigma}$	IDENT-V [-back]$_{\text{HD}\sigma}$	*H/≤ɛ,ɔ	*H/≤a
H ⇒ a. vʲi(ˈdʲɔm)				*	*	*
H b. vʲi(ˈdʲɛm)			*!		*	*
H c. (vʲaˈdʲɔm)		*!		*		*

At Level 1, the high-ranked IDENT-V[-back]$_{\text{HD}\sigma}$ ensures that the input form /vʲɛˈdʲɛm/ is mapped onto the output [vʲiˈdʲɛm] in (13ia) instead of the expected *[vʲaˈdʲɔm] (cf. [mʲɪdvʲaˈdʲɔm]) shown in (13ic). Candidate (13ib), which, similarly to candidate (13ic), shifts tone to the pretonic syllable and thus lowers the pretonic vowel, is excluded by ALIGN-L([back], FT). At level

2, the winner (13iia) changes ε to [ɔ] to comply with AGREE-VC[+back]$_{\text{HD}\sigma}$, which is promoted to the echelon of high-ranked constraints at Level 2. Candidate (13iic) satisfies AGREE-VC[+back]$_{\text{HD}\sigma}$ by shifting H tone leftward and lowering the vowel in the pretonic syllable, but fatally violates *DISASSOCIATE.

In contrast to /vʲɛ'dʲɛm/ [vʲi'dʲɔm], [ɔ] in [mʲidʲvʲa'dʲɔm] comes from the underlying /ɔ/. The tableaux in (14) below show the evaluation of [mʲidʲvʲa'dʲɔm]. At level 1, ALIGN-L([back], FT) is vacuously satisfied because there is no front vowel in the stressed syllable to trigger the assimilation of the feature [back]. The choice between the candidates with [i]-reduction and [a]-reduction is made by the constraint *H/≤ε,ɔ disallowing the association of High tone with mid vowels. Similarly to ALIGN-L([back], FT), IDENT-V[-back]$_{\text{HD}\sigma}$ is inactive, so its ranking with respect to AGREE-VC[+back]$_{\text{HD}\sigma}$ is irrelevant for the evaluation of the candidates containing the vowel /ɔ/. The change in the location of H in candidate (14iib) is blocked by *DISASSOCIATE. Therefore, the optimal candidate at Level 1 (14ia) is also the winner at Level 2 (14iia).

(14) Sudža/Ščigry: /mʲɛdvʲɛ'dʲ+ɔm/ [mʲɪdvʲa'dʲɔm] 'bear' (instr. sg.)

i. Level 1

/mʲɛdvʲɛ'dʲ+ɔm/	ALIGN-L ([back], FT)	IDENT-V [-back]$_{\text{HD}\sigma}$	*H/≤ε,ɔ	*H/≤a	AGREE-VC [+back]$_{\text{HD}\sigma}$
H (on a) ⇒a. mʲɪd(vʲa'dʲɔm)				*	
H (on ɔ) b. mʲɪdvʲi('dʲɔm)			*	*!	

ii. Level 2

H (on a) mʲɪd(vʲa'dʲɔm)	ALIGN-L ([back], FT)	*DISASSOC	AGREE-VC [+back]$_{\text{HD}\sigma}$	IDENT-V [-back]$_{\text{HD}\sigma}$	*H/≤ε,ɔ	*H/≤a
⇒ a. H (on a) mʲɪd(vʲa'dʲɔm)						*
b. H (on ɔ) mʲɪdvʲi('dʲɔm)		*!			*	*

Summarizing briefly, this section has argued that compound dissimilative pretonic reduction constitutes a blend of tone-driven vocalic alternations, as in dissimilative reduction, with the assimilation in backness between the pretonic and the tonic syllables. It has been demonstrated that this analysis is superior to the model locating the trigger of pretonic reduction in the immediately following consonant.

Traditional descriptions emphasize the fact that compound dissimilative patterns of dissimilation after palatalized consonants are not paralleled by corresponding patterns in the context of the preceding non-palatalized consonants (*cf.* Požarickaja, 2005: 58; Djačenko, 2013: 337). In the present model, the absence of the comparable process after non-palatalized consonants can be attributed to the blocking effect of PAL (defined in (4) in section 7.2.1 in Chapter 7 below). That is, the assimilation of the feature [-back] would create a combination of a palatalized consonant and high front vowel, as in /no'gʲɛ/ *[ni'gʲɛ] 'leg' (dat. sg.) (*cf.* the correct form [nə'gʲɛ]). It is well known that *Ci* sequences disagreeing in backness are prohibited in the Slavic languages (see Rubach (2000, 2003) for further discussion). This restriction might account for the absence of the backness harmony if the vowel in the pretonic syllable is preceded by a non-palatalized consonant.

In the next section, I consider reduction types which combine dissimilative reduction and/or compound dissimilative reduction patterns with assimilation in height.

6.3. Height harmony (assimilative-dissimilative patterns)

Several other patterns of reduction, referred to as assimilative-dissimilative reduction, have been reported in the literature (see section 2.7 in Chapter 2 for a description and references). These dialects show reduction to [a] after palatalized consonants if the following tonic syllable contains high and low vowels. Before mid vowels, either [i] or [a] is attested, depending on a dialect. For ease of reference, relevant data is repeated in (15); assimilative-dissimilative reduction patterns are schematized in (16).

(15) i. *Reduction to [a] before high and low vowels in the tonic syllable (all dialects)*

[nʲa'su] 'carry' (1st pers. sg.)

[nʲa'sla] 'carry' (fem. past)

ii. *Reduction to [a]/[i] before* <u>mid</u> *vowels in the tonic syllable*

Stressed vowels	[e]	[ɛ]	[ɔ] (>ɛ)	[ɔ]	[o]	[e]
Novoselki	[sʲa'lʲe]	[sʲi'lʲɛnʲɪj]	[sʲi'lʲɔtkə]	[sʲa'lɔm]	[sʲa'lo]	[sʲa'lʲe]
Orexovo	[sʲa'lʲe]	[sʲi'lʲɛnʲɪj]	[sʲa'lʲɔtkə]	[sʲa'lɔm]	[sʲa'lo]	[sʲa'lʲe]
Kidusovo	[sʲi'lʲɛ]	[sʲi'lʲɛnʲɪj]	[sʲi'lʲɔtkə]	[sʲa'lɔm]	[sʲa'lɔ]	[sʲi'lʲɛ]
Kultuki	[sʲi'lʲɛ]	[sʲi'lʲɛnʲɪj]	[sʲa'lʲɔtkə]	[sʲa'lɔm]	[sʲa'lɔ]	[sʲi'lʲɛ]
Bel'sk	[sʲi'lʲɛ]	[sʲi'lʲɛnʲɪj]	[sʲi'lʲɔtkə]	[sʲi'lɔm]	[sʲi'lɔ]	[sʲi'lʲɛ]
	'village' (loc. sg.)	'settlement' (gen. pl.)	'herring'	'village' (instr. sg.)	'village' (nom. sg.)	'village' (loc. sg.)

(16) *Dissimilative patterns after palatalized consonants*

a. Novoselki

pretonic	tonic		
a	i	ɨ	u
	e		o
i	ɛ, ɔ (> ɛ)		ɔ
a			a

b. Orexovo

pretonic	tonic		
a	i	ɨ	u
	e		o
i	ɛ		ɔ, ɔ (> ɛ)
a			a

c. Kidusovo

pretonic	tonic		
a	i	ɨ	u
i	ɛ, ɔ (> ɛ)		ɔ
a			a

d. Kultuki

pretonic	tonic		
a	i	ɨ	u
i	ɛ		ɔ, ɔ (> ɛ)
a			a

e. Bel'sk

	tonic		
a	i	ɨ	u
i	ɛ		ɔ
a			a

Assimilative-dissimilative types of reduction have been also reported to occur in the context of non-palatalized consonants (Kasatkina and Ščigel', 1995). In these patterns, [ə] occurs before low mid vowels, and [a] before high, high mid, and low vowels, as illustrated in (17); the pattern is schematized in (18) below.

(17) [ləmˈtʲɛi̯] 'slice' (gen. pl.)
[traːˈvɨ] 'grass' (gen. sg.)
[saːˈvʲe] 'owl' (dat. sg.)
[traˈva] 'grass' (nom. sg.)

(18) *Assimilative-dissimilative reduction after non-palatalized consonants*

pretonic	tonic		
aː	i	ɨ	u
	e		o
ə	ɛ		ɔ
a		a	

Additionally, the vowel [a] is lengthened if the vowel in the stressed syllable is either high or high mid (e.g., [traːˈvɨ], [saːˈvʲe]), no increase in duration is observed before low vowels (e.g., [traˈva]). As noted earlier in Chapter 2 (section 2.7), this pattern instantiates the archaic Obojan'-like system of neutralization because it uses [ə] before low mid vowels, e.g. [ləmˈtʲɛi̯], but not before high mid vowels (e.g. [saːˈvʲe]).

The occurrence of [a] instead of [ə] or [i] before the low vowel [a] in the tonic syllable has been traditionally viewed as the assimilation in height (Avanesov, 1974; Kasatkin, 2005). Crosswhite (2000, 2001) proposes an alternative analysis which assumes that the identity of the reduced vowels ([a] *vs.* [i]) is determined by the nature of the following consonant. Specifically, she argues at length that the description relying on the quality of the stressed vowel is inadequate because it provides 'an (accidental) link between stressed vowel quality and consonant palatalization' (Crosswhite, 2000: 149). Instead, she suggests that a better characterization is achieved by differentiating between the two consonantal environments, as illustrated by the following description, reproduced from Crosswhite (2001: 68, 97) (Note: a shaded cell indicates that [o] does not occur in that context.)

(19) *Assimilative-dissimilative patterns (Crosswhite, 2001: 68, 97)*
i. *Kidusovo*

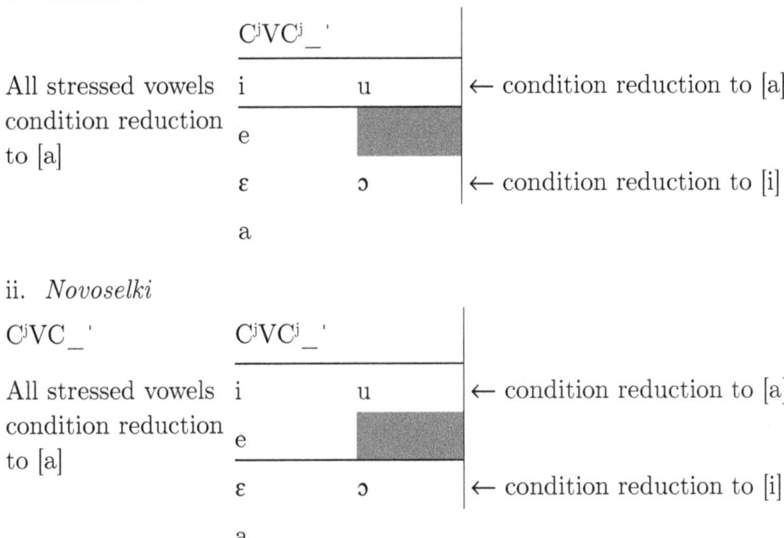

In this view, the reduction to [i] in Kidusovo and Novoselki is generated by means of the constraint $C^j\_C^j$ /[+front] ('A vowel may not occur between two palatalized consonants unless it is [+front]', Crosswhite, 2001: 93).[98]

However, the description in (19) is factually incorrect as it misrepresents the actual reduction patterns attested in Kidusovo and Novoselki by stating

[98] The reduction to [a] taking place before [i]/[u] in Kidusovo and before [i]/[u]/[e] in Novoselki is accounted for by locating $C^j\_C^j$ /[+front] at different places among the constraints of the *μμ/X family.

that [a] following a palatalized consonant conditions reduction to [i] in the preceding syllable. In fact, pretonic vowels reduce to [a] in this context, which is illustrated by the following examples, taken from Avanesov (1974: 157) and Kasatkin (2005: 46–47).

(20) [dʲaˈsʲatkə] 'ten' (nom. sg. fem.)
[zʲaˈtʲja] 'sons-in-law'
[strʲaˈlʲatʲ] 'shoot'
[ɣlʲaˈdʲatʲ] 'look' (3rd pers. pl.)

Hence, the analysis generating [i]-reduction in Kidusovo and Novoselki by means of Cʲ_Cʲ /[+front] is unacceptable because it fails to explain the presence of the low vowel [a] in the context of the following palatalized consonant.

Following traditional descriptions (e.g., Avanesov, 1974; Kasatkin, 2005), I assume that the use of [a] before the stressed low vowel in the assimilative-dissimilative patterns is best explained as assimilation in height. In terms of OT, this generalization is captured by the following foot bounded constraint.

(21) ALIGN-L([low], FT): For any feature [low] associated to a segment in a foot, that feature has an association to the leftmost syllable of a foot.

Similarly to the alignment constraint ALIGN-L([back], FT) (defined in (3) in section 6.2), ALIGN-L([low], FT) targets segments which are parsed in the head foot.

First, let us consider the assimilative-dissimilative [a]-reduction, schematically represented in (18) above. This pattern represents a combination of the Obojan'-type reduction with the assimilation in the feature [low]. Like in Obojan', the constraint HEAD=H interleaved between *H/≤e,o and *H/≤ɛ,ɔ ensures that pretonic non-high vowels merge in [a] if the vowel in the stressed syllable is either high or high mid. Let us recall that stressed low vowels in Obojan' trigger pretonic reduction to [ə]. In contrast, the assimilative-dissimilative type uses [ə] only before low mid vowels, while [a] appears before the low vowel [a] in the following syllable. I suggest modelling this neutralization (i.e., the assimilation of the pretonic syllable to the low vowel) employing the constraint ALIGN-L([low], FT), which complements the ranking of constrains established for the dissimilative pattern of Obojan'. The ranking generating assimilative-dissimilative reduction is shown in (22). The evidence for the ranking *H/≤e,o >> ALIGN-L([low], FT) is provided by the evaluation of the candidate set in (23i) and (23ii). A crucial difference between the assimilative-dissimilative pattern and the dissimilative/compound dissimilative systems discussed above consists in the ranking of constraints FT=BIN and ALIGN-L(H, FT), which are now re-ranked as Ft=Bin >> Align-L(H, Ft). This ranking ensures that disyllabic feet are constructed without reference to the location of High tone, so that the pretonic and the tonic syllable constitute a foot and, thus, are within the purview of Align-L([low], Ft) both when H is linked to the foot head, and when it lands on the syllable immediately preceding stressed position (cf. candidates (23iiic) and (23iiid) in Tableau 23).

(22) *Assimilative-dissimilative [a]-reduction: partial rankings*

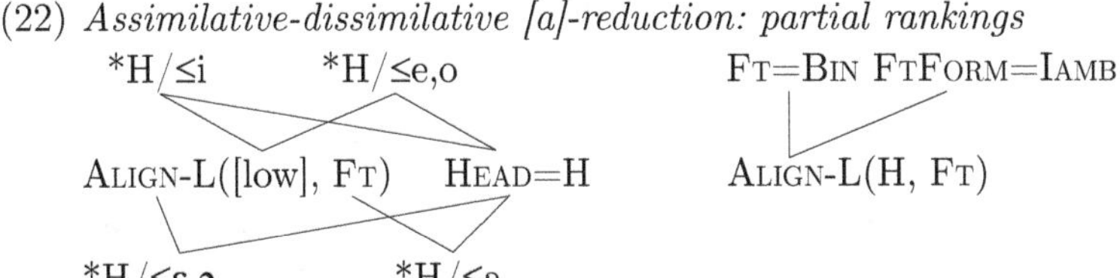

The evaluations shown in (23) illustrate how this constraint ranking chooses output forms for the words /soˈvu/ [saˈvu] 'owl' (acc. sg.), /soˈvʲe/ [saˈvʲe] id. (dat. sg.), /soˈva/ [saˈva] id. (nom. sg.) (*cf.* the gen. pl. form /ˈsov/ [ˈsof]), and /lapˈtʲɛi̯/ [ləpˈtʲɛi̯] 'bast shoe' (gen. pl.) (*cf.* the nom. pl. form /ˈlaptʲi/ [ˈlaptʲɪ]).

(23) *Assimilative-dissimilative [a]-reduction*

i. /soˈvu/	*H/≤i,u	*H/≤e,o	Align-L ([low], Ft)	Head = H	*H/≤ε,ɔ	*H/≤a	Ft = Bin	Align-L (H, Ft)
H ⇒ a. (saˈvu)			*	*		*		
H b. sə(ˈvu)	*!	*			*	*	*	

ii. /soˈvʲe/	*H/≤i,u	*H/≤e,o	Align-L ([low], Ft)	Head = H	*H/≤ε,ɔ	*H/≤a	Ft = Bin	Align-L (H, Ft)
H ⇒ a. (saˈvʲe)			*	*		*		
H b. sə(ˈvʲe)		*!			*	*	*	

iii. /lapˈtʲɛi̯/	*H/≤i,u	*H/≤e,o	Align-L ([low], Ft)	Head = H	*H/≤ε,ɔ	*H/≤a	Ft = Bin	Align-L (H, Ft)
H ⇒ a. (ləpˈtʲɛi̯)					*	*		*
H b. ləp(ˈtʲɛi̯)					*	*	*!	
H c. (lapˈtʲɛi̯)			*!	*		*		
H d. (lapˈtʲɛi̯)			*!		*	*		*

iv. /so'va/	*H/≤i,u	*H/≤e,o	ALIGN-L ([low], FT)	HEAD = H	*H/≤ɛ,ɔ	*H/≤a	FT = BIN	ALIGN-L (H, FT)
⇒ a. (sa'va) with H linked to 'va						*		*
b. (sa'va) with H linked to sa				*!		*		
c. (sə'va) with H linked to 'va			*!			*		*
d. sə('va) with H linked to 'va						*	*!	

Let us note that though the optimal outputs surface with the low vowel [a] in the pretonic syllable both in [sa'vu] (23i) and [sa'va] (23iv), the two vowels are structurally different in that only the former is linked to High tone. This analysis raises questions concerning the mapping of the phonological structure onto the phonetic form. Is there a difference in the timing of the pitch peak between the words with pretonic [a] linked to H tone, such as [sa'vu], and the words with pretonic [a] not associated with H, as in [sa'va]? Or, since phonological tone can be expressed by duration, are there quantitative differences between the two [a]'s? There are not many studies which would systematically investigate tonal properties of the East Slavic dialects (see discussion in Bethin, 2006: 139ff, and references therein), so, at present, it is not possible to answer the question concerning the alignment of the phonological tone with phonetic pitch in the dialects in question. As to the second question, there are indications in the literature pointing to the differences in duration of the two types of [a] (Belaja, 1974; Broch, 1916; Burova and Kasatkin, 1977; Kasatkina and Ščigel', 1996; Vojtovič, 1972a). Based on the analysis of the samples of spontaneous speech collected in the southern Russian dialectal area, Kasatkina and Ščigel' (1996: 237) report that '*a* is shortened before the stressed *a*, and lengthened before the stressed high vowels, that is *vădá – vādý*'.[99] Pretonic lengthening of [a] is also attested in the dissimilative-assimilative reduction pattern, as illustrated below.

(24) *Assimilative-dissimilative [a]-reduction*

a. [tra:'vɨ] 'grass' (gen. sg.)
   [sa:'vʲe] 'owl' (dat. sg.)

b. [tra'va] 'grass' (nom. sg.)
   [sa'va] 'owl' (nom. sg.)

c. [ləm'tʲɛi̯] 'slice' (gen. pl.)
   [nə'sɔk] 'sock' (nom. sg.)

---

[99] Translation is mine.

The differences in the duration of the pretonic [a] in (24a) and (24b) render support to the theoretical assumptions of the present model. In (24a), the pretonic syllable is the carrier of H tone, which is manifested by the increased length of the vowel [a]. In (24b), the pretonic syllable is not associated with High tone, so the pretonic [a], which is the result of the [low] assimilation, remains short. Structurally, it is similar to [ə] in (24c) because both vowels lack H tone and both occur in the dependent position in the binary iambic foot.

Returning to the assimilative-dissimilative [ja]-reduction patterns, let us first consider Bel'sk, which constitutes a combination of the Don-type reduction with the assimilation in the feature [low]. The ranking of constraints generating the Bel'sk pattern of dissimilation is shown below.

(25) *Assimilative-dissimilative patterns [ja]-reduction: interim rankings*

Bel'sk (*cf.* Don)

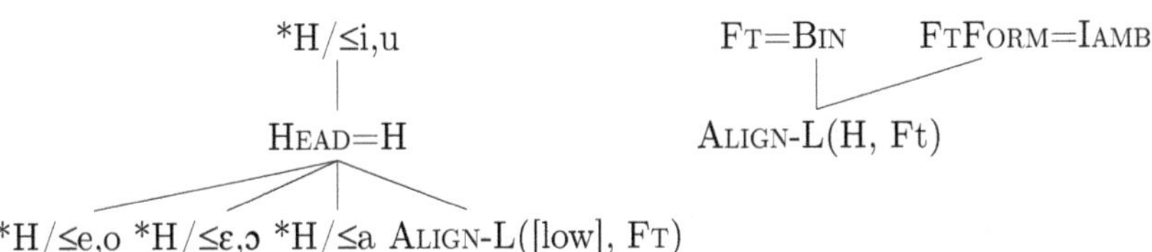

Tableau (26) provides the evaluation of the word /sʲɛ'la/ [sʲa'la] village (gen. sg.) in Bel'sk.

(26) *Dissimilation patterns after palatalized consonants: Bel'sk*

/sʲɛ'la/	HEAD = H	*H/≤ɛ,ɔ	*H/≤a	ALIGN-L ([low], FT)	FT = BIN	ALIGN-L (H, FT)
⇒ a. (sʲa'la) (H on la)			*			*
b. (sʲi'la) (H on la)			*	*!		*
c. sʲi('la) (H on la)			*		*!	
d. (sʲa'la) (H on sʲa)	*!		*			

As shown above, the assimilativedissimilative pattern of Bel'sk yields to the requirements of ALIGN-L([low], FT) and neutralizes non-high vowels in the low back vowel [a] (cf. candidate 26a). The constraint ALIGN-L([low], FT) excludes candidate (26b) in which the low vowel [a] is preceded by the high vowel [i]. Let us note that this constraint is not violated by candidate (26c), which is segmentally identical to candidate (26b) but has a different foot structure. The unary footing in (26c) is precluded by FT=BIN, which outranks ALIGN-L(H, FT) in systems with assimilative-dissimilative reduction.

Let us now consider the remaining assimilative-dissimilative patterns, Novoselki, Orexovo, Kidusovo, and Kultuki. I have suggested earlier in this chapter (section 6.2) that the compound dissimilative patterns attested in Ščigry, Sudža, and Mosal'sk, constitute a combination of the Žizdra dissimilation type with the assimilation in the feature [back]. Similarly, Dmitrov combines the Obojan' pattern with the assimilation in backness. In OT terms, this assimilation is analysed using the constraint ALIGN-L([back], FT), which ensures that front vowels in tonic positions are preceded by [i]. The reduction types attested in Novoselki, Orexovo, Kidusovo, and Kultuki (assimilative-dissimilative patterns) differ from compound dissimilative patterns in only one respect: they use [a] instead of [i] if the tonic syllable contains the low vowel [a]. As [a] is specified for the features [low] and [back], there are two ways to model this type of process: as assimilation in vowel height or as assimilation in backness. There is no empirical evidence favouring one of the analytical options. The analysis referring to the feature [back] appears attractive in view of the fact that the assimilation to [a] in assimilative-dissimilative patterns produces patterns in which a back vowel in the tonic syllable is always preceded by a back vowel in the pretonic syllable. However, theory-internal considerations speak against using the constraint ALIGN-L([back], FT) in the analysis of these dialects. First, the need for ALIGN-L([low], FT) is independently motivated by the patterns attested in the assimilative-dissimilative [ja]-reduction in Bel'sk and in systems with assimilative-dissimilative [a]-reduction. More importantly, the model employing ALIGN-L([back], FT) would generate unattested systems of [a]-reduction, in which non-high vowels merge into [i] if the following stressed vowel is front, and into [a] if the vowel in the stressed syllable is back. Therefore, I assume that assimilative-dissimilative patterns represent a combination of one of the compound dissimilative patterns showing assimilation in the feature [back] with assimilation in the feature [low]. This model aligns with the traditional descriptions of Novoselki as based on Ščigry, Kidusovo on Sudža, and Kultuki on Mosal'sk (Avanesov, 1974; Kasatkin, 2005). The ranking schemes generating the assimilative-dissimilative patterns are provided in (27).

(27) *Assimilative-dissimilative [ja]-reduction*

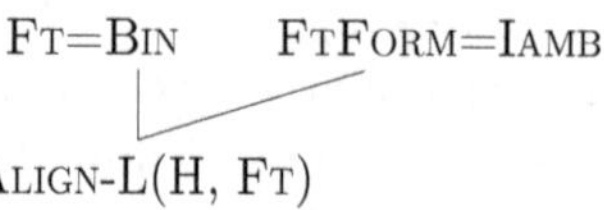

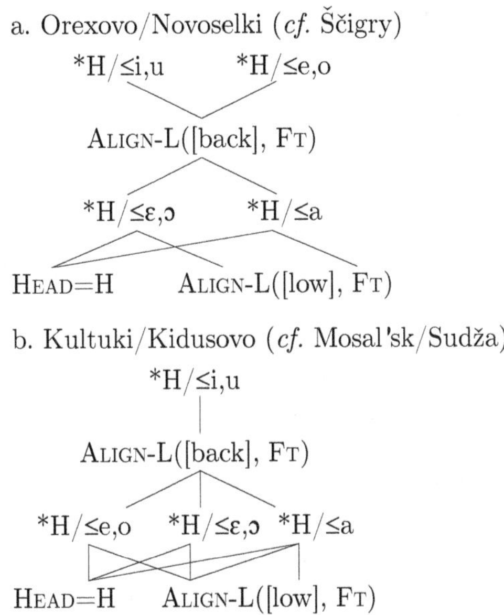

To illustrate how the rankings in (27) above generate correct outputs in Orexovo, let us consider the evaluation of the morphologically related words with [e], [ε], and [a] in the tonic syllable, shown in (28). In (28i), the dat. sg. form /sʲε'l+e/ [sʲa'lʲe] 'village' surfaces with pretonic [a] due to the high-ranked *H/≤e,o, which precludes the linking of High tone to a vowel with sonority equal to *e*. In contrast, the pretonic vowel is raised to [i] in (28ii) before the tonic [ε] due to the ranking ALIGN-L([back], FT) >> *H/≤ε,ɔ. This change ensures that the vowels in the two syllables agree in backness. The vowel [a] is chosen over [i] in the optimal output in (28iii) by ALIGN-L([back], FT).

(28) *Orexovo*

i. /sʲε'l+e/	*H/≤e,o	ALIGN-L([back], FT)	*H/≤ε,ɔ	*H/≤a	HEAD=H
⇒ a. (sʲa'lʲe) (H on a)		*		*	*
b. (sʲilʲe) (H on i)	*!		*	*	

ii. /sʲε'l+εnʲi̯/	*H/≤e,o	ALIGN-L([back], FT)	*H/≤ε,ɔ	*H/≤a	HEAD=H
⇒ a. (sʲi'lʲε)nʲi̯ (H on i)			*	*	
b. (sʲa'lʲε)nʲi̯ (H on a)		*!		*	*

iii. /sʲɛ'l+a/ *sela*	*H/≤e,o	ALIGN-L([back], FT)	*H/≤ɛ,ɔ	*H/≤a	HEAD=H
⇒ a. (sʲa'la) [H on la]				*	
b. (sʲi'la) [H on la]		*!		*	

The Kultuki pattern is minimally different from Orexovo in that both [e] and [ɛ] condition backness assimilation of the pretonic vowel. This difference is modelled by placing the constraint ALIGN-L([back], FT) one step higher in the constraint hierarchy, like in the Mosal'sk pattern (*cf.* Tableau (5) in section 6.2). In Kultuki, but not in Mosal'sk, [i]-reduction is blocked by ALIGN-L([low], FT) before the vowel [a] in the tonic syllable.

The types of reduction found in Novoselki and Kidusovo are derived by the constraint rankings established for Orexovo and Kultuki, respectively. The patterns attested in Orexovo and Kultuki are transparent because they restrict the occurrence of the pretonic [i] to positions before the surface [ɛ] in the tonic syllable, e.g. [vʲi'sʲɛlʲjə] 'joy', *cf.* [vʲa'sʲɔlɨj̯] 'joyful'. In contrast, Novoselki and Kidusovo use [i] both before the surface [ɛ] as well as before [ɔ] which comes from the underlying /ɛ/, for instance [vʲi'sʲɛlʲjə] 'joy', [vʲi'sʲɔlɨj̯] 'joyful'. In this respect, Novoselki and Kidusovo resemble the Sudža/Ščigry patterns, which also have an opaque process of reduction before the derived vowel [ɔ]. The analysis developed above for Sudža and Ščigry (section 6.2) assumes that the evaluation of the output candidates takes place at two levels. At Level 1, pretonic vowels assimilate in backness to the vowel in the tonic syllable. The stressed vowel in words such as [vʲi'sʲɔlɨj̯] 'joyful' is represented as /ɛ/ at this stage, triggering [i]-reduction in the preceding syllable. At Level 2, /ɛ/ retracts to [ɔ], where any further changes of the pretonic vowels are blocked by the high-ranked faithfulness constraints.

6.4. Interim conclusion

This chapter has developed an OT analysis of different types of vocalic neutralizations attested in East Slavic dialects, whose variety and complexity have been argued to be shaped by two major forces. On the one hand, the presence of the underlying High tone triggers vocalic alternations in quality and quantity in pretonic positions (dissimilative patterns, pretonic length dialects). On the other hand, harmonic processes produce assimilation in backness and/or height of the vowels in the pretonic and tonic syllables (compound dissimilative and assimilative-dissimilative patterns).

The constraint rankings generating these systems are summarized in (29). Dissimilative patterns (Žizdra, Obojan', and Don) arise due to different rankings of HEAD=H with respect to the members of the *H≤V family of constraints. These reduction patterns are attested both after non-palatalized and after palatalized consonants.

Compound dissimilative patterns are found only in the context of palatalized consonants. In the present model, they derive from dissimilative patterns by means of the constraint ALIGN-L([back], FT). Located at different points in the constraint hierarchy ALIGN-L([back], FT) generates four additional patterns of reduction (Ščigry, Sudža, Mosal'sk, and Dmitrov) by inducing harmony for the feature [back]. The present assumption that compound dissimilative reduction is based on dissimilative patterns contrasts with traditional classifications which group dissimilative and compound dissimilative systems into one type, traditionally referred to as dissimilative [ja]-reduction. However, it should be noted that there are no attested systems of dissimilative [a]-reduction after non-palatalized consonants which would parallel compound dissimilative patterns of reduction after palatalized consonants (Djačenko, 2013: 337). Deriving compound dissimilative from dissimilative systems allows us to explain this asymmetry. Specifically, compound dissimilative systems are analysed as a combination of dissimilative patterns (Žizdra and Obojan') with the harmony for the feature [back]. The alignment of the feature [back] in words with pretonic vowels occurring after a non-palatalized consonant would create an illegitimate structure of a non-palatalized [+back] consonant followed by a front [-back] vowel, which is prohibited by the constraint PAL mandating agreement in backness between consonants and following vowels (as discussed in Chapter 7 below).

Assimilative-dissimilative systems are generated by means of the constraint ALIGN-L([low], FT). Since this constraint does not conflict with PAL, it is free to combine with both [ja]-reduction and [a]-reduction. Coupled with the Don type of [ja]-reduction, ALIGN-L([low], FT) yields the Bel'sk pattern, whereas its combination with the Obojan' type of [a]-reduction produces systems traditionally called assimilative-dissimilative [a]-reduction (*cf.* Kasatkin, 2005: 40).

The present model predicts the existence of two more types of assimilative-dissimilative reduction which would combine the assimilation in height (driven by ALIGN-L([back], FT)) with Dmitrov and Obojan' dissimilation patterns. The absence of Dmitrov- and Obojan'-based assimilative-dissimilative patterns can be attributed to the fact that both Obojan' and Dmitrov require archaic eight-vowel systems distinguishing between high and low mid vowels. As the two-way contrast in mid vowels is only sporadically found in the present-day dialects, fewer reduction patterns are attested which would be based on eight-vowel systems.

Another possibility would be to combine ALIGN-L([low], FT) with the Žizdra pattern of dissimilation, in which the pretonic vowel surfaces as [a] before non-low stressed vowels and as [ə] if the stressed syllable contains [a]. In this scenario, high-ranked ALIGN-L([low], FT) would eliminate the effect of dissimilation, producing a system of non-dissimilative [a]-reduction where all vowels reduce to [a] irrespective of the quality of the vowel in the tonic position.

Finally, let me point out that Chapters 5 and 6 have considered dissimilative reduction patterns attested both after non-palatalized consonants ([a]-reduction) and palatalized consonants ([ja]-reduction). These systems exhibit parallel behaviour in terms of the contexts which trigger dissimilation, i.e. [a] is found in the pretonic position before high vowels in the stressed syllable in all reduction types analysed in Chapters 5 and 6, irrespective of the quality of the consonant in the onset of the pretonic syllable. The main difference between [a]-reduction and [ja]-reduction lies in the quality of the reduced vowel: [ə] occurs in [a]-reduction and [i] in [ja]-reduction patterns, e.g. [səˈvʲe] 'owl' (dat. sg.)/[sʲiˈlʲe] 'village' (loc. sg.), *cf.* [saˈvu] 'id.' (acc. sg.)/[sʲaˈlu] 'id.' (dat. sg.). The next chapter looks at the reduction patterns attested in the context of palatalized consonants. I will demonstrate that the secondary articulation of both the leftward and the rightward consonant may affect the outcome of reduction in various ways in different dialects. For example, the patterns of reduction in the context of palatalized consonants may combine with non-dissimilative reduction by overriding the effect of H tone (as in standard Russian), or they may interact with the constraints of the *H≤V family producing additional reduction types (e.g., the so-called moderate [ja]-reduction analysed in 7.3. below).

(29) *Pretonic reduction patterns: summary*

Dissimilative reduction
FTFORM=IAMB, ALIGN-L(H, FT) >> FT=BIN

a. Žizdra: *H/≤i,u, *H/≤e,o, *H/≤ɛ,ɔ, *H/≤a >> **HEAD=H**
b. Obojan': *H/≤i,u, *H/≤e,o >> **HEAD=H** >> *H/≤ɛ,ɔ, *H/≤a
c. Don: *H/≤i,u >> **HEAD=H** >>*H/≤e,o, *H/≤ɛ,ɔ, *H/≤a

Compound dissimilative reduction
FTFORM=IAMB, ALIGN-L(H, FT) >> FT=BIN

a. Mosal'sk/Sudža (*cf.* Žizdra)
*H/≤i,u >> **ALIGN-L([back], FT)** >> *H/≤e,o, *H/≤ɛ,ɔ, *H/≤a >> **HEAD=H**

b. Ščigry (*cf.* Žizdra)
*H/≤i,u, *H/≤e,o >> **Align-L([back], Ft)** >> *H/≤ɛ,ɔ, *H/≤a >> **Head=H**

c. Dmitrov (*cf.* Obojan')
*H/≤i,u >> **Align-L([back], Ft)** >> *H/≤e,o >> **Head=H** >> *H/≤ɛ,ɔ, *H/≤a

Assimilative-dissimilative reduction
FtForm=Iamb, Ft=Bin >> Align-L(H, Ft)

[a]-reduction
*H/≤i,u, *H/≤e,o >> **Align-L([low], Ft)**, **Head=H** >> *H/≤ɛ,ɔ, *H/≤a

[ja]-reduction
a. Bel'sk (*cf.* Don)
*H/≤i,u >> **Head=H** >> **Align-L([low], Ft)**, *H/≤e,o, *H/≤ɛ,ɔ, *H/≤a

b. Orexovo/Novoselki (*cf.* Ščigry)
*H/≤i,u, *H/≤e,o >> **Align-L([back], Ft)** >> *H/≤ɛ,ɔ, *H/≤a >> **Head=H, Align-L([low], Ft)**

c. Kultuki/Kidusovo (*cf.* Mosal'sk/Sudža)
*H/≤i,u >> **Align-L([back], Ft)** >> *H/≤e,o, *H/≤ɛ,ɔ, *H/≤a >> **Head=H, Align-L([low], Ft)**

Chapter 7

Vowel reduction in the context of palatalized consonants

7.1. Introduction

Previous chapters have analysed various patterns of [a]-reduction attested after non-palatalized consonants in different East Slavic dialects. I have argued that the vocalic reduction in immediately pretonic positions is driven by High tone, whose occurrence is restricted to the head foot of the prosodic word. On this view, the neutralization of non-high vowels into the low vowel [a] takes place to accommodate High tone, which is best realized on more sonorous vowels. The present chapter considers cases in which High tone fails to trigger the lowering of a vowel in the immediately pretonic position. In most dialects with two-degree reduction patterns, [a]-reduction is blocked in the contexts of adjacent palatalized consonants and after non-palatalized stridents, where, instead of the expected lowering, non-high vowels undergo fronting and/or raising.

There are several ways in which a palatalized consonant can affect the quality of a reduced vowel. In a simple case, the non-high vowels /e/, /a/, and /ɔ/ are reduced to [i], [e], or [a]; for example, the word *reka* 'river' can be pronounced as [rʲiˈka], [rʲeˈka], or [rʲaˈka] (*cf.* the gen. pl. form [ˈrʲek]). These types of neutralization are attested in the standard variety of Russian, in the central Russian dialects, and in some southern Russian and Belarusian dialects. In a complex case, the quality of the reduced vowel depends on both the preceding and the following consonant. For instance, [a] is found before non-palatalized consonants and [i] appears before palatalized consonants in dialects with the so-called moderate *yakan'e* ([ja]-reduction), e.g. [rʲaˈka] (nom. sg.) *vs.* [rʲiˈkʲi] (gen. sg.). Or, some dialects show [e]-reduction before non-palatalized consonants, e.g. [rʲeˈka], and [i]-reduction before palatalized consonants, e.g. [rʲiˈkʲi]. A more intricate pattern is attested in dialects such as Čuxloma, which uses [i] if the following consonant is palatalized, e.g. [rʲiˈkʲi], and either [a] or [e] if the following consonant is non-palatalized, the former occurring before a non-low vowel, and the latter before a low vowel in the following stressed syllable, e.g. [rʲaˈku] (acc. sg.) *vs.* [rʲeˈka] (nom. sg.).[100]

A further complication arises in the context of the non-palatalized stridents [ʃ], [ʒ], and [t͡s], which behave inconsistently with respect to vowel reduction in the majority of the East Slavic dialects. In standard Russian, for instance, this is illustrated by the alternations such as [ˈʃopət] 'a whisper' – [ʃɨpˈtatʲ] 'to whisper' and [ˈʃok] 'a shock' – [ʃaˈkʲirəvətʲ] 'to shock', where the non-palatalized strident [ʃ] patterns together with palatalized consonants in [ʃɨpˈtatʲ] and with non-palatalized consonants in [ʃaˈkʲirəvətʲ], triggering raising of the mid vowel in the former and lowering in the latter.

These patterns are interesting for several reasons. First, the raising of the low vowel [a] to [e] or [i] refutes our previous assertion that vowels should lower in immediately pretonic position in order to be able to carry High tone. Next, the fronting of back vowels [a] and [ɔ] before palatalized consonants as well as the retraction of [e] before non-palatalized consonants are unusual from the typological perspective because Slavic languages typically show agreement in backness between vowels and the preceding, not the following, consonants (Halle, 1959; Lightner, 1972; Rubach, 2000, 2003; among others). Finally, the operation of two contradictory processes ([a]-reduction and [i]-reduction) in the context of non-palatalized stridents constitutes a non-trivial case of opacity, which cannot be resolved without resorting to derivational levels.

The present chapter is structured as follows. Section 7.2 discusses patterns of vowel fronting and raising taking place after palatalized consonants. An OT analysis pursued in this section is based on the two generalizations about Slavic phonology, concerning the tendency of consonants and the following vowels to exhibit agreement in backness and in height. Next, section 7.3 demonstrates that these generalizations also hold in the *CʲVCʲ* sequences, where a vowel changes to accommodate in backness and/or height both to the preceding and the following consonant. Apparently exceptional patterns of neutralization attested in the context of non-palatalized stridents are discussed in section 7.4. Finally, section 7.5 summarizes the main results.

---

[100] Furthermore, some northern Russian dialects retract the front vowel /e/ if the following consonant is non-palatalized, e.g. [rʲɔˈka] *vs.* [rʲeˈkʲi]. This pattern is excluded from the present analysis because it is attested in dialects lacking High tone on the pretonic vowel (see also fn. 97 in section 6.2).

7.2. Feature assimilation in C^jV contexts

As mentioned above, [a]-reduction is blocked in the context of palatalized consonants in a number of East Slavic dialects. There are two ways in which palatalized consonants can affect the outcome of vowel reduction in unstressed *CV* sequences. First, non-high back vowels /a/ and /ɔ/ front to [e] after palatalized consonants in the central Russian dialects. Second, vowel fronting can be accompanied by the raising to [i] in many dialects, including the standard variety of Russian (Avanesov and Orlova, 1965; Avanesov, 1984; Kasatkin, 2005). These processes, traditionally referred to as *ekan'e* ([e]-reduction) and *ikan'e* ([i]-reduction) in the literature are schematically presented in (1) (repeated from Chapter 2, section 2.4.2).

(1) a. [e]-reduction: a, ɔ → e /C^j_[-stress]
    b. [i]-reduction: e, a, ɔ → i /C^j_[-stress]

The following sections demonstrate that these two processes are accounted for in a straightforward way if secondary articulation is expressed in terms of the binary features [±back] and [±high], as assumed in the Halle–Sagey model of feature geometry (Sagey, 1986; Halle, 1992, 1995, 2005). The processes in (1) aim to achieve the agreement in backness and/or height between consonants and following vowels. Specifically, the dialects with [e]-reduction show an agreement in the feature [-back], and the dialects with [i]-reduction exhibit an agreement in the features [-back] *and* [+high] (Halle, 1959; Lightner, 1972). Whereas the agreement in the feature [-back] has been generally assumed in the analysis of palatalization (Rubach (2007) and references therein), phenomena requiring an analysis in terms of the [+high] agreement are rarely documented in the literature (but see Cole, 1969; Lahiri and Evers, 1991; Halle, 2005; Rubach, 2007). Section 7.2.2 adduces evidence from several languages demonstrating that [+high], just as [-back], can actively participate in phonological processes involving palatal and palatalized consonants.

7.2.1. [e]-reduction

The pattern of [e]-reduction, described in detail in section 2.4.2 in Chapter 2, consists in a neutralization of non-high vowels into the mid front vowel [e] when preceded by palatalized consonants. Illustrative example are provided below.

(2) [e]-reduction
/ˈzʲatʲ/ [ˈzʲatʲ] 'son-in-law' (nom. sg.) – /zʲaˈtʲja/ [zʲeˈtʲja] id. (nom. pl.)
/ˈrʲad/ [ˈrʲat] 'row' (nom. sg.) – /rʲaˈda/ [rʲeˈda] id. (gen. sg.)
/ˈsʲel/ [ˈsʲol] 'village' (gen. pl.) – /sʲeˈla/ [sʲeˈla] id. (gen. sg.)
/ˈsʲestrɨ/ [ˈsʲostrɨ] 'sister' (nom. pl.) – /sʲeˈstra/ [sʲeˈstra] id. (nom. sg.)

An overarching generalization about Russian is that consonants and following vowels agree in backness (Halle, 1959; Lightner, 1972; Rubach, 2000 *et seq.*; Kochetov, 2002). That is, consonants are usually palatalized before following front vowels, both inside words and at morpheme boundaries,[101] whereas across word boundaries, the front vowel [i] is retracted to [ɨ] when preceded by non-palatalized consonants (Rubach, 2000).[102] The two processes are illustrated below with the examples from the standard Russian.

(3) a. *Consonant palatalization*
[ˈrot] 'mouth' – [ˈrotʲɪk] id. (dim.)
[pɨlʲiˈsos] 'hoover' – [pɨlʲiˈsosʲɪtʲ] 'to hoover'
[raˈbotə] 'job' – [rəbaˈtʲei̯kə] id. (perjor.)
[kaˈsa] 'scythe' (nom. sg.) – [kaˈsʲe] 'scythe' (dat. sg.)
b. *Vowel retraction*
[i] 'and' – [ˈkot ɨ saˈbakə] 'cat and dog'
[iˈvan] 'Ivan' (proper name) – [ˈgoləs ɨˈvanə] 'Ivan's voice'

Both palatalization (3a) and retraction (3b) conspire to avoid sequences of a consonant and a vowel which disagree in the feature [±back]. Rubach (2000, 2003) expresses this generalization in terms of the following OT constraint (Rubach, 2003: 217).

(4) PAL: A consonant and a following vowel agree in backness.

Besides constituting the main driving force of various palatalization processes, PAL motivates the fronting of back non-high vowels in unstressed syllables (as shown in (2) above). The change of /a/ and /ɔ/ to [e] improves on markedness because it creates a sequence of two segments with the same specification of the feature [-back].

---

101 Consonants in some borrowings, mostly recent and unassimilated ones, lack palatalisation before the mid front vowel [ɛ], e.g. *fonetika* [fəˈnɛtʲikə] 'phonetics' (Avanesov, 1984).

102 Unlike [ɨ], the back high rounded vowel [u] can be preceded by a palatalized consonant, both in stressed and unstressed syllables, for instance [vaˈlʲutə] 'currency', [t͡ʃʲuˈdʲitʲ] 'fool around', [utʲuˈga] 'iron' (gen. sg.). The back vowel [u] is preserved after palatalized consonants due to the undominated faithfulness constraint IDENT-V[+round] ('[+round] on a vowel in the input must be preserved on the corresponding vowel in the output').

In the central Russian dialects, the raising of the unstressed /a/ to [e] after palatalized consonants co-occurs with the lowering of /o/ to [a] after non-palatalized consonants. The examples illustrating this reduction pattern are provided below.

(5) *Dialects with [a]-reduction*
a. *Pretonic [a] after non-palatalized consonants*
[sta'lɨ] 'table' (nom. pl.) *cf.* ['stol] (nom. sg.)
[sa'dɨ] 'garden' (nom. pl.) ['sat] (nom. sg.)
b. *Pretonic [e] after palatalized consonants*
[rʲe'dɨ] 'row' (nom. pl.) ['rʲat] (nom. sg.)
[rʲe'kʲi] 'river' (gen. sg.) ['rʲekʲi] (nom. pl.)

It has been argued in this book that vowels in immediately pretonic positions carry High tone in dialects with [a]-reduction, and the lowering of /ɔ/ to [a] is induced by the constraint *H/≤a, ensuring that High tone docks on intrinsically longer low vowels. From the perspective of *H≤V, the raising of /a/ to [e] is an unwelcome change as High tone ends up linked to the mid vowel [e], which is a worse carrier of High tone than the low vowel [a]. The reduction to [e] in dialects with [a]-reduction after non-palatalized consonants is achieved if PAL outranks *H/≤e,o. Let us note that both PAL and *H/≤e,o would be satisfied if the consonant in the *Cʲa* sequence changed its backness specification. However, the fact that none of the East Slavic dialects depalatalizes consonants before [a] demonstrates that faithfulness to the underlying consonantal [-back] specification is more important than the preservation of the vocalic feature [+back].[103] Formally, this is expressed by ranking IDENT-C[-back] above IDENTV[+back] (Rubach, 2000). Furthermore, instead of retracting under the pressure of PAL, front vowels retain their [-back] quality and comply with PAL by palatalizing the preceding consonant.[104] Given that the identity of the consonant is protected by the high-ranked IDENT-C[-back], the sequence *Cʲa* can change either to *Cʲe* or *Cʲi* to ensure that the consonant and the following vowel agree in backness. The first option is less costly as, in addition to backness adjustment, it only involves a change of the feature [+low] to [-low], while the second option requires an additional switch from [–high] to [+high]. The constraints generating the change of /a/ to [e] are

---

[103] Depalatalisation of a consonant is attested before [ɛ] in Ukrainian (see Rubach (2007) for analysis and discussion).

[104] This generalisation holds for the word-level phonology. At a postlexical level, front vowel [i] retracts to [ɨ].

displayed in Tableau (6), which shows the evaluation of the word /pʲat+ˈa/ [pʲeˈta] 'heel' (nom. sg.) (cf. dim. form [ˈpʲatkə]).

(6) *[e]-reduction*

/pʲat+ˈa/	IDENT-C [−back]	PAL	*H/≤e,o	*H/≤a	IDENT [+low]	IDENT-V [+back]
H ⇒ a. (pʲeˈta)			*	*	*	*
H b. (pʲaˈta)		*!		*		
H c. (paˈta)	*!			*		

To recapitulate, unstressed low vowels are required to raise and front under the pressure of PAL, while non-low vowels are forced to lower due to the presence of High tone. The influence of palatalized consonants overrules the pressure exerted by High tone in dialects exhibiting [e]-reduction, which is generated by the ranking PAL >> *H/≤a. The opposite ranking produces the pattern attested in dialects with the so-called *yakan'e* ([ja]-reduction), in which non-high vowels are lowered to [a] after palatalized consonants. This reduction type is observed in Standard Belarusian and in the southern parts of the central Russian dialectal area (Vajtovič, 1968; Požarickaja, 2005). In these systems, the evaluation of the word [pʲaˈta] 'heel' proceeds as follows.

(7) *[ja]-reduction*

/pʲat+ˈa/	*H/≤e,o	*H/≤a	PAL	IDENT[+low]	IDENT-V[+back]
H ⇒ a. (pʲaˈta)		*	*		
H b. (pʲeˈta)	*	*!		*	*

It should be noted that sequences violating PAL occur in stressed syllables, in which back vowels [a] and [o] are found after palatalized consonants, for instance [ˈpʲos] 'dog', [ˈtʲotʲə] 'aunt', [ˈmʲatə] 'mint', [ˈvzʲatʲ] 'take'. As noted in section 5.3 in Chapter 5, stressed segments license greater vocalic complexity and are immune to change due to the protection of positional faithfulness (Beckman, 1997; Casali, 1997). The palatalization of consonants and the vowel quality of the stressed syllables is retained due to the following constraints.

(8) a. IDENT-C[-back]$_{\text{HDFT}}$: [-back] on a consonant in the input must be preserved on the corresponding consonant in the stressed syllable in the output.
b. IDENT-V[+low]$_{\text{HDFT}}$: In stressed syllables, [+low] on a vowel in the input must be preserved on the corresponding vowel in the stressed syllable in the output.

c. IDENT-V[+round]$_{HdFt}$: In stressed syllables, [+round] on a vowel in the input must be preserved on the corresponding vowel in the stressed syllable in the output.

To prevent the change in stressed syllables, the constraints in (8) have to be ranked above the markedness constraint PAL. The ranking choosing the optimal output for the word /'pʲatʲ/ ['pʲatʲ] 'five' is shown in Tableau (9). Here and below, tone is not shown when not relevant for the evaluation of candidates.

(9) *Lack of reduction in stressed syllables*

/'pʲatʲ/	IDENT-V[+back]$_{HdFt}$	IDENT-C[-back]$_{HdFt}$	PAL
⇒ a. ('pʲatʲ)			*
b. ('pʲitʲ)	*!		
c. ('patʲ)		*!	

Candidates (9b) and (9c) represent two different strategies: in (9b) the vowel is fronted, and in (9c) the consonant is depalatalized. Both of them lose due to the fatal violations of the undominated positional faithfulness constraints. The next section looks at [i]-reduction, another process attested in the context of palatalized consonants.

7.2.2. [i]-reduction

In the contemporary standard Russian, the vowels [a], [e] and [o] reduce to [i] in immediately pretonic positions (see section 2.4.2 in Chapter 2 for a detailed description). Some examples are given below (repeated from (16) in section 2.4.2).

(10) *[i]-reduction*

['svʲasʲ] 'connection' – [svʲi'zatʲ] 'connect'
[xa'mʲak] 'hamster' (nom. sg.) – [xəmʲi'ka] id. (gen. sg.)
['dʲel] 'business' (gen. pl.) – [dʲi'la] id. (nom. pl.)
['mʲestə] 'place' (nom. sg.) – [mʲi'sta] id. (nom. pl.)
['nʲos] 'carry' (past. masc. sg.) – [nʲi'sʲi] id. (imp.)
['mʲot] 'honey' (noun) – [mʲi'dovɨj̯] id. (adj.)

In the analysis developed so far, reduction after palatalized consonants is assumed to be driven by PAL, a constraint mandating agreement in backness between adjacent segments. As [i] is a front vowel, reduction to [i] after palatalized consonants creates a sequence conforming to the requirements of PAL. However, PAL alone is insufficient to derive the change of unstressed non-high vowels [a], [e] and [o] to a high vowel [i], as shown by the evaluation of the first syllable of the word /pʲat+'a/ [pʲi'ta] 'heel' (nom. sg.) (*cf.* the dim. form ['pʲatkə]).

(11) *[i]-reduction: failed evaluation*

/pʲat+'a/	PAL	IDENT-C[-back]	IDENT-V[+back]	IDENT-V[–high]
a. (pʲa'ta)	*!			
☹ b. (pʲi'ta)			*	*
⇐ c. (pʲe'ta)			*	
d. (pa'ta)		*!		

The faithful candidate (11a) is excluded by the high-ranked PAL. Candidates (11b) and (11c) fare equally well on PAL because in both of them, a palatalized consonant is followed by a front vowel. However, candidate (11c) wins because the intended winner (11b) turns the underlying low vowel into a high vowel and in doing so runs afoul of IDENT-V[–high].

Since [i] is less sonorous than [e], it might be argued that the choice in favour of [i] is motivated by the constraint $*\text{-}\Delta_{\omega}\geq\{e,o\}$ (defined in (6) in section 1.2.1, Chapter 3) forcing the reduction of vowel prominence in an unstressed position.[105] The point is illustrated by the evaluation shown in (12) below.

(12) *[i]-reduction*

/pʲat+'a/	PAL	$*\text{-}\Delta_{\omega}\geq\{e,o\}$	$*\text{-}\Delta_{\omega}\geq\{i,u\}$
⇒ a. (pʲi'ta)			*
b. (pʲe'ta)		*	*!
c. (pʲa'ta)	*!		

However, the use of $*\text{-}\Delta_{\omega}\geq\{e,o\}$ to derive [i]-reduction is not a viable option because dialects with [i]-reduction (such as standard Russian) also have [a]-reduction after non-palatalized consonants in the immediately pretonic positions and reduction to [ə] in other unstressed syllables. It has been assumed earlier in this book (see Chapter 4 and 5) that the two types of reduction taking place after non-palatalized consonants are generated by the *H≤V family of constraints and $*\text{-}\Delta_{\omega}\geq\{e,o\}$. In order to induce lowering of vowels associated with H tone, H≤V has to outrank $*\text{-}\Delta_{\omega}\geq\{e,o\}$. However, this ranking does not produce the correct output when the vowel in the immediately pretonic position is preceded by a palatalized consonants. Given the choice between the high vowel [i] and the mid vowel [e], *H/≤i,u opts for the latter, as illustrated in Tableau (13) below.

---

[105] An analysis along these lines has been developed by Crosswhite (2001).

(13) *[i]-reduction: failed evaluation*

/pʲat+'a/	PAL	*H/≤i,u	*H/≤e,o	*H/≤a	*-Δ_ω≥{e,o}	*-Δ_ω≥{i,u}
H a. (pʲa'ta)	*			*	*	*!
H ⇐ b. (pʲe'ta)			*	*	*	
H ☹ c. (pʲi'ta)		*	*	*!	*	*

To conclude, the process of [i]-reduction cannot be analysed, on a par with palatalization, as an assimilation in backness between a vowel and the preceding consonant. Instead, [i]-raising is more adequately analysed as an adjustment in height between two neighbouring segments (cf. Mołczanow, 2015). In the Halle–Sagey model of feature geometry, the contrast between palatalized and non-palatalized consonants is expressed utilising the feature [±back] (Kenstowicz, 1994: 41). As both series are produced by raising of tongue body which accompanies primary articulation, the feature [+high] has been assumed to be redundantly present in both palatalized and non-palatalized consonants in Russian (Rubach, 2002: 171). However, phonetic studies have demonstrated that the most salient characteristics distinguishing palatalized and non-palatalized series is a widening *vs.* a narrowing of the pharynx (Koneczna and Zawadowski, 1956; Halle, 1959; Fant, 1960; Kochetov, 2002). So while palatalized consonants are produced with a raising of the front of the tongue which is accompanied by a widened pharynx, non-palatalized consonants are articulated by retracting the tongue which results in a narrowing in the region of the uvula, and in the upper part of the pharynx (Fant, 1960: 171). In view of these facts, it is questionable whether the feature [+high] is present in both palatalized and non-palatalized consonants. Rather, it appears that palatalized consonants should be specified for both [-back] and [+high], whereas non-palatalized consonants are only defined by the feature [+back].[106]

An additional argument for the feature [+high] being present in palatalized consonants comes from the West Ukrainian dialects exhibiting vowel harmony. In Synevir, a dialect spoken in the Carpathian mountains, palatalized consonants pattern together with high vowels in triggering vowel

[106] Since non-palatalized consonants are produced with a constriction in the pharynx, they are sometimes called pharyngealized (Sawicka and Grzybowski, 1999). However, there is no evidence showing that these segments bear the redundant specification [pharyngeal].

raising (Nikolaev, 2006; Tolstaja, 2009). This is illustrated by the data in (14), taken from Tolstaja (2009).[107]

(14) *Synevir vowel raising*

ɛ → ɪ	
a. [ˈdɛ] ‘where’	b. [ˈdɪsʲ] ‘somewhere’
[ˈbɛrɛx] ‘shore’	[ˈbɪrɪzʲi] id. (loc. sg.)
[ˈčɛrɛs] ‘belt’	[ˈčɪrɪsʲi] id. (loc. sg.)
	[ˈčɪrɪsü] id. (gen. pl.)
[ˈsvɛtɛr] ‘jumper’	[ˈsvɪtɪrʲi] id. (loc. sg.)
	[svɪtɪˈrü] id. (gen. pl.)
ɔ → ʊ	
[ˈnɔsa] ‘nose’	[ˈnʊsʲi] id. (loc. sg.)
[ˈkɔlɛsɔ] ‘wheel’	[ˈkʊlɪsʲi] id. (loc. sg.)
[ɦɔlɔˈva] ‘head’	[ˈpʊ ɦʊlʊvʲi] id. (loc. sg.)
	[ɦʊlʊˈvʊw] id. (instr. sg.)
[bɔrɔˈda] ‘beard’	[ˈbʊrʊdu] id. (acc. sg.)

The examples above show that mid vowels [ɛ] and [ɔ] in the left-hand column (14a) change into the high vowels [ɪ] and [ʊ] when followed by palatalized consonants or high vowels in the next syllable (14b). This generalization is expressed in simple terms if palatalized consonants, like high vowels, are specified for the feature [+high]. Thus, the raising of non-high vowels in the vicinity of palatalized consonants can be analysed as a case of assimilation in height (Lahiri and Evers, 1991; Rubach, 2007; Mołczanow, 2015).

In contrast to Synevir leftward spreading of the feature [+high], [i]-raising in dialects with vowel reduction propagates from the consonant to the following vowel. In terms of OT, this generalization can be expressed by means of the markedness constraint Agree[+high]:

(14) Agree[+high]: A consonant and a following vowel agree in height.[108]

The constraint Agree[+high] is motivated cross-linguistically. In English, alveolar obstruents /s/, /z/, /t/ and /d/ become palatoalveolar [ʃ], [ʒ], [tʃ], and [dʒ] before the palatal glide [j], e.g. *habit* – *habitual.* As both palatoalveolar segments and the front glide [j] are specified for the feature

[107] It should be noted that mid vowel raising is not conditioned prosodically because it occurs in both stressed and unstressed syllables.

[108] Like Pal, Agree[+high] belongs to the Agree(Place) family of constraints (Gnanadesikan, 1997; Baković, 1999). Besides Agree constraints, OT offers several other approaches to modelling assimilation, such as feature alignment (Kirchner, 1993), feature spreading (Padgett, 2002), feature sharing (McCarthy, 2011), among others. From the perspective of the present data, the choice of a model is not essential.

[+high] (Chomsky and Halle, 1968), English palatalization can be analysed as spreading of the feature [+high] from a glide to the preceding consonant. Halle (2005: 38) and Rubach (2007: 107) discuss a similar phenomenon in the Bantu language Tswana, where labials undergo palatalization before the passive suffix *–wa*, e.g. *lop+a - lotʃ+wa* 'request'. Rubach (2007) argues that this process is best explained in terms of agreement in [+high] between the consonant and the glide.

Returning to the raising of non-high vowels attested in Russian, let us consider the evaluation shown in Tableau (15), which demonstrates how the constraint system established so far derives [i]-reduction in the word *pjata* [pʲi'ta] 'heel' (nom. sg.).

(15) *[i]-reduction: standard Russian*

/pʲat+'a/	AGREE [+high]	PAL	*H/≤i,u	*H/≤e,o	*H/≤a	IDENT [+low]	IDENT-V [–high]
H ⇒ a. (pʲi'ta)			*	*	*	*	*
H b. (pʲa'ta)	*!	*			*		
H c. (pʲe'ta)	*!			*	*	*	

The winning candidate (15a) raises /a/ to [i], which leads to the violation of a host of constraints. In particular, it runs afoul of the markedness constraint *H/≤i,u disallowing High tone to be realized on high vowels and two faithfulness constraints banning the underlying feature modifications. Nevertheless, it fares better than the faithful contender (15b), which fatally violates AGREE[+high]. In addition, candidate (15b) does not comply with PAL as it contains a sequence of a palatalized consonant followed by a back vowel. Candidate (15c) avoids violating PAL by turning /a/ into the front vowel [e]. Like the faithful candidate (15b), it is excluded by AGREE [+high], which penalizes the combination of the palatalized [+high] consonants with non-high vowels.

7.2.3. Interim summary

The preceding sections have considered neutralization patterns attested after palatalized consonants in different East Slavic dialects. Given that palatalized consonants are defined as [-back] and [+high], the presence of either [e]-reduction or [i]-reduction in a given dialect has been analysed to derive from the relative ranking of the markedness constraints PAL, AGREE[+high] and *H≤V. Figure 7.1 shows ranking schemata which generate different types of vowel neutralization after palatalized consonants (the constraints whose re-rankings produce different types of reduction are set in bold type). As can *[e]-reduction*

IDENT-V[feature]HDFT IDENT-C[-back]HDFT
PAL
*H≤V
IDENT-C[-back]
*-Δω≥{e,o}
IDENT-V[+back] IDENT-V[-high] IDENT[+low]
AGREE[+high]

[i]-reduction

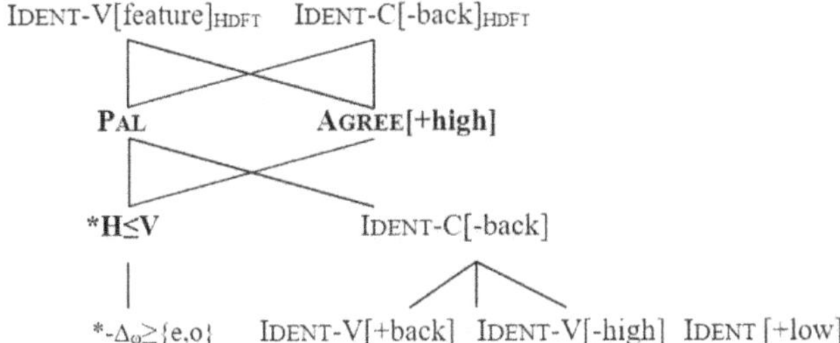

[ja]-reduction

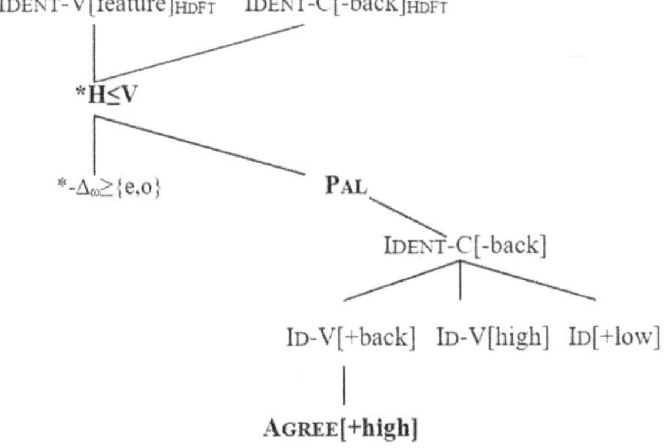

Figure 7.1: Reduction patterns after palatalized consonants.

be seen in Figure 7.1, [e]-reduction is triggered by PAL ranked above *H≤V, while [i]-reduction is derived when both PAL and AGREE[+high] outrank *H≤V. The opposite scenario, with *H≤V dominating PAL and AGREE[+high], yields [ja]-reduction. This system neutralizes non-high vowels into [a], after palatalized and non-palatalized consonants alike. In the next section I turn to more complex patterns of reduction, in which not only preceding, but also the following consonants affect the quality of unstressed vowels.

7.3. Feature assimilation in C^jVC^j contexts

Some dialects with non-dissimilative [a]-reduction after non-palatalized consonants exhibit a mixed neutralization pattern after palatalized consonants. In this system, called moderate [ja]-reduction in traditional sources, non-high vowels neutralize to [a] before non-palatalized consonants and to [i] or [e] before palatalized consonants (see section 2.8 in Chapter 2 for references and further description). The illustrative examples are repeated from (28) in section 2.8.

(16) *Moderate [ja]-reduction*

a. Stressed syllable	b. CVCʲ	c. CʲVCʲ *[i]-reduction*	*[e]-reduction*
[ˈnʲos] ‘carry’ (masc. past)	[nʲaˈsla] (fem. past)	[nʲiˈsʲi]	[nʲeˈsʲi] ‘carry’ (imp.)
[ˈlʲes] ‘forest’ (nom. sg.)	[lʲaˈsu] (loc. sg.)	[lʲiˈsʲina]	[lʲeˈsʲina] ‘piece of wood’

These data show that non-high vowels lower to [a] in the immediately pretonic position before a non-palatalized consonant in the stressed syllable (16b). When the following consonant is palatalized (16c), the non-high vowels neutralize either into [e] or [i]. Crosswhite (2001) analyses the reduction to [e] and [i] by means of a phonotactic constraint requiring a vowel flanked by two palatalized consonants to be front:

(17) Cʲ_Cʲ/[+front]: A vowel may not occur between two palatalized consonants unless it is [+front] (Crosswhite, 2001: 93).

The choice between [e] or [i] in a given dialect is made by the mutual ranking of the two constraints, LIC-NONPERIPH/STRESS and MAX[–high], defined below:

(18) a. LIC-NONPERIPH/STRESS: A nonperipheral vowel may not occur in the output unless under stress (Crosswhite, 2001: 83).
b. MAX[–high]: no deletion of [–high] (Crosswhite, 2001: 16).

High-ranked LIC-NONPERIPH/STRESS eliminates unstressed mid vowels, whereas Cʲ_Cʲ/[+front] induces the fronting of a back vowel. Both constraints outrank MAX[–high] in dialects exhibiting [i]–raising before palatalized consonants. The operation of LICNONPERIPH/STRESS and Cʲ_Cʲ/[+front] is illustrated in Tableau (19), which shows the evaluation of the word /pʲa'tʲi/ [pʲi'tʲi] 'five' (gen.). The nominative form ['pʲatʲ] demonstrates that the vowel in question comes from the underlying /a/.

(19) *Moderate [ja]-reduction: dialects with [i]-reduction (Crosswhite, 2001)*

/pʲatʲ+'i/	Cʲ_Cʲ/[+front]	Lic-Nonperiph/Stress	Max[–high]
⇒ a. (pʲi'tʲi)			*
b. (pʲa'tʲi)	*!		
c. (pʲe'tʲi)		*!	

The reduction to [e] is generated by the reverse ranking of the constraints LicNonperiph/Stress and Max[–high]. In this scenario, [e]-reduction (candidate (20a) in Tableau (20) below) is the optimal output because [e], unlike [i], preserves the underlying [high] specification.

(20) *Moderate [ja]-reduction: dialects with [e]-reduction (Crosswhite, 2001)*

/pʲatʲ+'i/	Cʲ_Cʲ/[+front]	Max[–high]	Lic-Nonperiph/Stress
⇒ a. (pʲe'tʲi)			*
b. (pʲa'tʲi)	*!		
c. (pʲi'tʲi)		*!	

Given that the basic architecture of OT aims at minimizing the number of constraints, employing one constraint Cʲ_Cʲ/[+front] to drive fronting in systems with [e]-reduction and [i]-reduction is a desirable move. However, while Crosswhite's model is successful in analysing systems with moderate [ja]-reduction, it cannot adequately account for the data attested in dialects with moderate [e]-reduction. In these dialects, non-high vowels preceded by palatalized consonants are reduced to [e] before non-palatalized consonants and to [i] before palatalized consonants (Kasatkin, 2005: 43). Such a pattern is attested in Čuxloma, spoken in the northern Russian dialect area in the region of Kostroma (Kasatkin, 1999b). Čuxloma has the Žizdra pattern of reduction after non-palatalized consonants, with non-high vowels neutralizing into [a] before stressed non-low vowels and into [ə] before the stressed vowel [a]. After a palatalized consonant, the choice among [a], [e], or [i] is conditioned by the quality of the following consonant and the vowel in the stressed syllable. If the consonant is non-palatalized, [a] is found before the non-low vowels, and [e] before the low vowel [a]. The high vowel [i] is attested before palatalized consonants, irrespective of the quality of the stressed vowel. This is illustrated by the examples in (21) below, taken from Kasatkin (1999: 417 420).

(21) Čuxloma reduction

a. *CʲVC*

i. [a] before non-low vowels

[prʲɪvʲa'zut]	'bring' (3rd pers. pl. future)
[pət͡ʃʲa'mu]	'why'
[dʲa'rut͡sːə]	'fight' (3rd pers. pl.)
[fʲsʲa'vo]	'whole' (gen. sg. masc.)
[sʲa'vodʲnʲə]	'today'

ii. [e] before low vowels

[xlʲe'bai̯]	'drink' (imp. sg.)
[ft͡ʃʲe'raʃnʲɪvə]	'yesterday' (adj., gen. sg.)
[pəbrʲe'la]	'ramble' (past. fem.)
[vəsʲe'mnat͡sːətʲ]	'eighteen'

b. *CʲVCʲ*

[i] in all positions

[tʲi'lʲatɨ]	'calves'
[vʲinʲ't͡ʃʲalʲɪsʲ]	'marry' (3rd pers. pl. past)
[zʲvʲi'rʲei̯]	'animal' (gen. pl.)
[vʲirʲ'xom]	'astride'
[rʲɪbʲi'tʲiʃkʲɪ]	'children'

The pattern of moderate [e]-reduction, instantiated by Čuxloma, is interesting because it shows that both [e] (21aii) and [i] (21b) can constitute the outcome of reduction in the *CʲV* context, which proves that the occurrence of either [e] or [i] is not always a matter of dialectal variation, as in the moderate [ja]-reduction systems discussed above. Crosswhite (2001) suggests the following constraint to analyse [e]-reduction taking place after palatalized consonants:

(22) Cʲ/[+front]: In unstressed syllables, a palatalized consonant must be followed by a [+front] vowel (Crosswhite, 2001: 77).

In Čuxloma, a palatalized consonant is followed by a front vowel in *Cʲi* as well as in *Cʲe*, so both sequences satisfy Cʲ/[+front]. However, *Cʲe* contains a mid vowel, which is banned from unstressed syllables by Lic-Nonperiph/Stress. In turn, the raising to [i] in *Cʲi* sequences is assumed to be blocked by a high-ranked Max[–high] (Crosswhite, 2001: 89). The two processes are incompatible in this model: [e]-reduction compels Max[–high] to outrank Lic-Nonperiph/Stress, whereas [i]-reduction requires the opposite ranking, Lic-Nonperiph/Stress >> Max[–high].

To conclude, the analysis assuming that both [i]-reduction and [e]-reduction are driven by a constraint against back vowels in the contexts of palatalized consonants (C^j_C^j/[+front]), coupled with a constraint prohibiting unstressed mid vowels (Lic-Nonperiph/Stress), fails to account for systems with moderate [e]-reduction. The main problem of this approach stems from its inability to distinguish two separate triggers for [i]-reduction and [e]-reduction. However, the ranking paradox discussed above indicates that these processes do not constitute two different strategies which are used by different dialects to avoid disagreement in backness between vowels and adjacent consonants. Rather, the fact that [i]-reduction and [e]-reduction co-occur within one system suggests that they respond to different types of markedness requirements.

Let us recall from the preceding sections that [e]-reduction and [i]-reduction are widely attested in different East Slavic dialects in the contest of the preceding palatalized consonant in the unstressed C^jV sequences. It has been argued in section 7.2.1 of this chapter that [e]-reduction is driven by the constraint Pal requiring agreement in backness, while [i]-reduction is triggered by the constraint Agree[+high] mandating agreement in height. The data furnished by the dialects with moderate [ja]-reduction and [e]-reduction suggest that similar mechanisms are at work in the VC^j and VC sequences. In particular, [i]-reduction taking place before palatalized consonants can be viewed as a regressive assimilation in height between a vowel and a following consonant. However, none of the East Slavic dialects exhibits raising before palatalized consonants when the unstressed vowel is preceded by a non-palatalized consonant, e.g. [pa'r^jit^j] 'float', [va'd^je] 'water' (dat. sg.), or when it occurs in an onsetless syllable, e.g. [a'n^ji] 'they'; the pronunciations such as *[pɨ'r^jit^j], *[vɨ'd^je], and *[ɨ'n^ji]/*[i'n^ji] are never attested. Therefore, the constraint compelling the raising of non-high vowel has to refer not only to the following, but also to the preceding segment, as in (23) below:

(23) Agree-C^jVC^j[+high]: Assign a violation mark for every non-high vowel occurring between two palatalized consonants.

Tableau (24) demonstrates how the analysis including the constraint Agree-C^jVC^j[+high] generates correct outputs for the words /p^jat+'ak/ [p^je'tak] 'five-rouble note' and /p^jat^j+'i/ [p^ji't^ji] 'five' (gen.) in dialects with moderate [e]-reduction. As noted previously, the underlying vowel /a/ in the first syllable of both words is motivated by the morphologically related form /p^jat^j/ [p^ja't^j] 'five' (nom.).

(24) *Moderate [e]-reduction*

i. /pʲat+ˈak/	PAL	AGREE-CʲVCʲ [+high]	IDENT-V [–high]	IDENT-V [+low]
⇒ a. (pʲeˈtak)				*
b. (pʲiˈtak)			*	*!
c. (pʲaˈtak)	*!			

ii. /pʲatʲ+ˈi/	PAL	AGREE-CʲVCʲ [+high]	IDENT-V [–high]	IDENT-V [+low]
⇒ a. (pʲiˈtʲi)			*	*
b. (pʲeˈtʲi)		*!		*
c. (pʲaˈtʲi)	*!	*		

A crucial difference between Crosswhite's (2001) approach employing the constraints Cʲ/[+front] and Cʲ_Cʲ/[+front] and the present model is that the analysis in (24) provides a means of distinguishing between the outputs containing the high and the non-high vowels. Tableau (24ii) shows that, while both [pʲiˈtʲi] (24iia) and [pʲeˈtʲi] (24iib) satisfy PAL, the latter does not conform to the requirements of AGREE-CʲVCʲ[+high] because it contains a [–high] vowel followed by a [+high] consonant. AGREE-CʲVCʲ[+high] is mute in (24i) since the pretonic vowel in /pʲat+ˈak/ occurs before a non-palatalized consonant, which is not specified for [+high]. In this case, the winner is determined by the lower-ranked faithfulness constraints: candidate (24ia) wins because it preserves the underlying [–high] specification.

The constraint AGREE-CʲVCʲ[+high] is also operative in dialects with moderate [ja]-reduction. As illustrated by the data in (16) at the beginning of this section, moderate [ja]-reduction consists in the raising and fronting of the immediately pretonic nonhigh vowels in the *CʲVCʲ* context and in the lowering to [a] elsewhere. The tone-based approach to vowel reduction advocated in this book assumes that pretonic reduction to [a] is motivated by High tone, which prefers to dock on low (most sonorous) vowels. Let us recall that the association of High tone with vowels of different sonority profiles is regulated by the constraints of the *H≤V family. These constraints are undominated in dialects with the so-called strong [ja]-reduction (as in standard Belarusian), where all pretonic mid vowels are lowered to [a], irrespective of the consonantal context. In dialects with moderate [ja]-reduction, lowering to [a] is blocked if the pretonic vowel is flanked by palatalized consonants: instead of the expected [a], the vowel in question surfaces as [i] or [e], *cf.* [nʲaˈsu] 'carry' (1st pers. sg.) *vs.* [nʲiˈsʲi] id. (imp.). The change to [i] is driven by AGREE-CʲVCʲ[+high] forcing the assimilation in height between the vowel and the adjacent palatalized consonants, as in the dialects with moderate [e]-reduction discussed above.

The operation of the constraint system generating moderate [ja]-reduction is illustrated in (25). The Tableau in (25i) shows the evaluation of the word /rʲek+'a/ [rʲa'ka] id. (nom. sg.), in which the underlying mid vowel /e/ (*cf.* ['rʲek] 'river' (gen. pl.)) surfaces as [a] in the pretonic syllable. The change to [a] takes place under duress of *H/≤e,o, which gives preference to candidate (25ia) with a low vowel in the pretonic syllable. The ranking *H/≤e,o >> PAL ensures that candidate (25ia) wins despite containing a marked configuration of a [-back] consonant followed by a [+back] vowel. In [rʲi'kʲe] 'id.' (dat. sg.) in (25ii), the pretonic vowel is followed by a palatalized consonant, so the change to [a] in candidate (25iib) is blocked due to the markedness constraint AGREE-CʲVCʲ[+high]. This constraint also rules out the faithful contender (25iib) and chooses candidate (25iia), in which a palatalized consonant is preceded by a high vowel.

(25) *Moderate [ja]-reduction, [i]-reduction*

i. /rʲek+'a/	AGREECʲVCʲ [+high]	*H/≤i,u	*H/≤e,o	*H/≤a	PAL	IDENT-V [-high]	IDENT [-low]
H ⇒ a. (rʲa'ka)				*	*		*
H b. (rʲe'ka)			*	*!			
H c. (rʲi'ka)		*	*	*!		*	

ii. /rʲek+'e/	AGREE-CʲVCʲ [+high]	*H/≤i,u	*H/≤e,o	*H/≤a	PAL	IDENT-V [-high]	IDENT [-low]
H ⇒ a. (rʲi'kʲe)		*	*	*		*	
H b. (rʲa'kʲe)	*!			*	*		*
H c. (rʲe'kʲe)	*!		*	*			

As mentioned previously, non-low vowels neutralize to [e] when followed by a palatalized consonant in a number of dialects with moderate [ja]-reduction, e.g. [pʲa'tak] 'five-rouble note' – [pʲe'tʲi] 'five' (gen.) (for further illustration, see data in (28c) in section 2.8 in Chapter 2). This process mirrors [e]-reduction occurring in the unstressed *CʲV* sequences described earlier in this chapter (in section 7.2.1), e.g. ['t͡ʃʲas] 'hour' (nom. sg.) – [t͡ʃʲe'sa] id. (gen. sg.). In both cases, a pretonic vowel assimilates in backness to an adjacent consonant, the difference between the two patterns consisting in the direction of assimilation: the trigger is located in the preceding consonant in [t͡ʃʲe'sa] and in the following consonant in [pʲe'tʲi]. At first blush, then, it would seem that the latter change instantiates a case of backness assimilation between a vowel and the immediately following consonant. However, dialects showing moderate [ja]-reduction after palatalized consonants also exhibit [a]-reduction after non-palatalized consonants and in word-initial positions, e.g. [ˈkonʲ] ‘horse’ (nom. sg.) – [kaˈnʲa] id. (gen. sg.), [ˈon] ‘he’ – [aˈnʲi] ‘they’, where lowering to [a] takes place irrespective of the quality (or the presence) of the following consonant. If the consonant following the pretonic vowel were to trigger fronting in these words, one would expect to attest forms such /konʲ+ˈa/ *[kʲeˈnʲa] and /on+ˈi/ *[eˈni], similar to /pʲatʲ+ˈi/ [pʲeˈtʲi]. Therefore, the constraint driving fronting needs to make reference to the consonants at both sides of the vowel. The relevant constraint is stated in (26) below.

(26) Agree-CʲVCʲ[-back]: Assign a violation mark for every back vowel occurring between two palatalized consonants.

Besides the switch in backness, the change of /a/ to [e] in words such as [pʲeˈtʲi] involves raising to a less sonorous vowel. Let us recall that dialects with moderate [ja]-reduction lower non-high vowels in all pretonic positions except before palatalized consonant, *cf.* the data in (16). It has been argued in this book that reduction to [a] is triggered by High tone, favouring low vowels in immediately pretonic positions. On this view, moderate [ja]-reduction is modelled by ranking Agree-CʲVCʲ[-back] above the *H≤V constraints, thus ensuring that Agree-CʲVCʲ[-back] overrides the pressure exerted by High tone. This is illustrated by Tableau (27), which shows the evaluation of the words /pʲatʲ+ˈi/ [pʲeˈtʲi] ‘five’ (gen.) and /pʲat+ˈak/ [pʲaˈtak] ‘five-rouble note’ in dialects exhibiting [e]-reduction in the context of palatalized consonants and [a]-reduction elsewhere.

(27) *Moderate [ja]-reduction, [e]-reduction*

i. /pʲatʲ+ˈi/	Agree-CʲVCʲ [-back]	*H/≤i,u	*H/≤e,o	*H/≤a	Pal	Ident-V [+back]
H ⇒ a. (pʲeˈtʲi)			*	*		*
H b. (pʲiˈtʲi)		*	*	*!		*
H c. (pʲaˈtʲi)	*!			*	*	
ii. /pʲat+ˈak/	Agree-CʲVCʲ [-back]	*H/≤i,u	*H/≤e,o	*H/≤a	Pal	Ident-V [+back]
H ⇒ a. (pʲaˈtak)				*	*	
H b.(pʲiˈtak)	*!	*	*	*		*
H c.(pʲeˈtak)	*!		*	*		*

In (27i), Agree-CʲVCʲ[-back] excludes candidate (27ic) because it retains the back vowel [a] before a palatalized consonant. The remaining candidates (27ia) and (27ib) fare equally well on Agree-CʲVCʲ[-back], so the choice in favour of (27ia) is made by the lower-ranked *H/≤a. In (27ii), the pretonic vowel is followed by a non-palatalized consonant, so in this case, the back vowel [a] in (27iia) is the most optimal output, both from the perspective of AGREE-CʲVCʲ[-back] as well as *H/≤i,u.

To conclude, the data discussed in this section has demonstrated that East Slavic dialects show backness agreement not only between consonants and the following vowels, but also in the environments in which a vowel in the immediately pretonic position is flanked on both sides by palatalized consonants. I have suggested that both [e]-reduction and [i]-reduction instantiate two distinct assimilation processes: reduction to [e] is the result of backness assimilation, while the reduction to [i] is the effect of the assimilation in height. The mechanisms deriving [e]-reduction and [i]-reduction in the *CʲVCʲ* contexts parallel the ones responsible for the palatalization and raising in consonant-vowel sequences. The presence of palatalized consonants in both *CʲV* and *CʲVCʲ* contexts inhibits tone-induced vowel lowering attested after non-palatalized consonants in many East Slavic dialects. In the next section I turn to one more context in which the consonantal neighbourhood obscures the effect of H tone.

7.4. Reduction after non-palatalized stridents

7.4.1. Introduction

In most Russian dialects, as well as in the standard variety, stridents [ʃ], [ʒ], and [t͡s] are phonetically non-palatalized and, unlike other non-palatalized consonants, do not have palatalized counterparts (Avanesov, 1984; Kasatkin, 2005).[109] Given this fact, non-palatalized stridents are expected to pattern together with other non-palatalized consonants with respect to vowel reduction. However, [a]-reduction is blocked after non-palatalized stridents in the majority of Russian dialects, where, instead of lowering, non-high vowels exhibit raising to [i] when preceded by the consonants [ʃ], [ʒ], or [t͡s]. For instance, dialects with moderate [ja]-reduction use a high vowel after a non-palatalized strident and a low vowel after other non-palatalized consonants. The examples in (28) demonstrate that non-palatalized stridents in (28a) pattern together with palatalized consonant (28b) and not with non-palatalized consonants (28c).

[109] The discussion in this section draws on Molczanow (2015).

(28) *Non-palatalized stridents in dialects with moderate [ja]-reduction* (data from Kasatkin, 2005: 50)

a. [pʃaˈno] 'millet' – [pʃɨˈnʲi͡tsə] 'wheat'
   [ʒaˈna] 'wife' – [ʒɨˈnʲix] 'bridegroom'
   [͡tsaˈna] 'price' – [͡tsɨˈnʲe] id. (dat. sg.)
   [ʒaˈra] 'heat' – [ʒɨˈrʲe] id. (dat. sg.)
b. [nʲaˈsu] 'I carry' – [nʲiˈsʲi] id. (imp.)
   [lʲaˈsok] 'forest' (dim.) – [lʲiˈsʲnʲk] 'forester'
c. [vaˈda] 'water' – [vaˈdʲe] id. (dat. sg.)
   [traˈva] 'grass' – [traˈvʲe] id. (dat. sg.)

The data in (28) is not problematic if one assumes that non-palatalized stridents are underlyingly palatalized and become non-palatalized at a later derivational level, after the neutralization of vowels has taken effect. An analyses along these lines has been proposed for standard Russian by Halle (1959), Lightner (1972), and Rubach (2000). The basic idea is that non-palatalized stridents group together with palatalized consonants because both are [-back] when non-high vowels undergo pretonic reduction. However, while this analysis explains the presence of a high vowel in (28a) above, it actually fails to account for neutralization patterns attested after non-palatalized consonants in standard Russian. Unlike in the pattern presented in (28), consonants [ʃ], [ʒ], and [͡ts] do not behave consistently with respect to vowel reduction in standard Russian. As illustrated in (29) below, the pretonic vowel can surfaces either as [a] (29a) or as [ɨ] in a similar consonantal environment (29b).

(29) *Non-palatalized stridents in standard Russian* (data from Avanesov, 1984)

a. [ˈʃar] 'ball' – [ʃaˈrɨ] id. (nom. pl.)
   [ˈʃok] 'shock' – [ʃaˈkʲirəvətʲ] 'to shock'
b. [ˈʒaləstʲ] 'pity' – [ʒɨˈlʲetʲ] 'to pity'
   [ˈʃopət] 'a whisper' – [ʃɨpˈtatʲ] 'to whisper'

The fact that non-high vowels are raised in (29b) but not in (29a) is problematic on the assumption that stridents are phonologically palatalized consonants. The following section develops an alternative analysis, in which non-palatalized sibilants are argued to be underlyingly non-palatalized and neutralization to [a] in (29a) is assumed to constitute the default pattern.

7.4.2. Basic facts

As mentioned previously, consonants [ʃ], [ʒ], and [͡ts] exhibit inconsistent behaviour with respect to vowel reduction in standard Russian. This pattern is interesting because the outcome of reduction depends not only on the quality of the adjacent consonant, but also on the input quality of the vowel undergoing reduction. The underlying vowel /a/ surfaces as [a] after non-palatalized stridents in the immediately pretonic position, which is illustrated in (30).[110]

(30) *šar* /ˈʃar/ [ˈʃar] 'ball' (nom. sg.) – *šary* /ʃaˈrɨ/ [ʃaˈrɨ] id. (nom. pl.)
žar /ˈʒar/ [ˈʒar] 'feaver' – *žara* /ʒaˈra/ [ʒaˈra] 'heat'
car' /ˈt͡sarʲ/ [ˈt͡sarʲ] 'tsar' (nom. sg.) – *car'a* /t͡saˈrʲa/ [t͡saˈrʲa] id. (gen. sg.)

Non-palatalized stridents were historically palatalized and, similar to other palatalized consonants, caused vowel raising. The vowel /a/ was still raised to [ɨ] after [ʃ] and [ʒ] in the Old Moscow pronunciation, e.g. /ʒaˈra/ [ʒɨˈra] 'heat', /ʃaˈrɨ/ [ʃɨˈrɨ] 'balls'. However, standard Russian has [a] in these positions and Avanesov (1984: 93) explicitly warns against the pronunciation with [ɨ]. However, a handful of words have retained [ɨ] in immediately pretonic positions after non-palatalized stridents; the complete list is provided below.

(31) *žalet'* /ʒaˈlʲetʲ/ [ʒɨˈlʲetʲ] 'to pity' and derivatives; oblique plural forms of the word *lošad'* /ˈloʃadʲ/ [ˈloʃətʲ] 'horse': *lošadej* [ləʃɨˈdʲej̯] (gen. pl.), *lošad'am* [ləʃɨˈdʲam] (dat. pl.), etc.; *ržanoj* /rʒaˈnoj̯/[111] [rʒɨˈnoj̯] 'rye' (adj.); oblique forms of the numerals *dvadcat'* /ˈdvat͡satʲ/ [ˈdvat͡sətʲ] 'twenty' and *tridcat'* /ˈtrʲit͡satʲ/ [ˈtrʲit͡sətʲ] 'thirty': *dvadcati* [dvət͡sɨˈtʲi] (gen.), *tridcati* [trʲɪt͡sɨˈtʲi] (gen.).

The pronunciation of pretonic [ɨ] in the words in (31) above constitutes a prescriptive norm, which is not always followed. According to Shapiro (1968), most speakers fail to observe this norm and pronounce [a] after non-palatalized stridents. Shapiro's observation is confirmed by Avanesov and Ožegov (1959: 671), who note that 'the frequently occurring pronunciation [ʃa], [ʒa], [t͡sa] is incorrect in these words' (translation is mine).

The low vowel [a] is reported to occur after non-palatalized stridents in the immediately pretonic position in loan words (32a), among which only four words, shown in (32b), have [ɨ] in the pretonic position (Avanesov, 1984:

[110] Data in (30)–(34) below are reprinted from Lingua, 163, J. Mołczanow, *The Interaction of Tone and Vowel Quality in Optimality Theory: A Study of Moscow Russian Vowel Reduction*, Pages No. 114–115, Copyright 2015, with permission from Elsevier.

[111] This word also contains a yer vowel, cf. the nom. sg. nominal form /ˈroʒ/. As the issue of yer vocalisation is not relevant to the discussion of vowel reduction, yers which fail to vocalize are not shown in the inputs.

93).[112] As these words have fixed stress and do not exhibit alternations, the quality of the unstressed input vowels cannot be determined; input forms are not shown.

(32) a. *šofer* [ʃaˈfʲor] 'driver', *šotlandec* [ʃaˈtlandʲɪt͡s] 'Scot', *žokej* [ʒaˈkʲej̯] 'jockey', *žongl'or* [ʒanˈglʲor] 'juggler'
b. *žaket* [ʒɨˈkʲet] 'jacket', *žasmin* [ʒɨˈsmʲin] 'jasmine', *žavel'* [ʒɨˈvʲelʲ] 'bleach', *bešamel'* [bʲɪʃɨˈmʲelʲ] 'bechamel'

Unlike /a/, the front mid vowel /ɛ/ is raised to [ɨ] after [ʃ], [ʒ], and [t͡s]. Some examples are given in (33).

(33) *šest'* /ˈʃɛsʲtʲ/ [ˈʃɛsʲtʲ] 'six' – *šestoj* /ʃɛˈstoj̯/ [ʃɨˈstoj̯] 'sixth', *žemčug* /ˈʒɛmt͡ʃʲug/ [ˈʒɛmt͡ʃʲuk] 'pearl' (masc.) – *žemčužyna* /ʒɛmˈt͡ʃʲuʒɨna/ [ʒɨmˈt͡ʃʲuʒɨnə] (fem.), *ceny* /ˈt͡sɛnɨ/ [ˈt͡sɛnɨ] 'price' (nom. pl.) – *cena* /t͡sɛˈna/ [t͡sɨˈna] (nom. sg.)

In words not showing alternations, the sound spelled with the letter 'e' is pronounced [ɨ], for instance šeršavyj [ʃɨrˈʃavɨj̯] 'rough', žeton [ʒɨˈton] 'jetton', žemannyj [ʒɨˈmannɨj̯] 'affected'.

The mid vowel [o] alternates with both [a] and [ɨ] after non-palatalized stridents, as exemplified in (34a) and (34b)[113], respectively.

(34) a. *šok* /ˈʃok/ [ˈʃok] 'shock' – *šokirovat'* /ʃoˈkʲirovatʲ/ [ʃaˈkʲirəvətʲ] 'to shock'
b. *šepot* /ˈʃɛpət/ [ˈʃopət] 'a whisper' – *šeptat'* /ʃɛpˈtatʲ/ [ʃɨpˈtatʲ] 'to whisper'
ženy /ˈʒɛnɨ/ [ˈʒonɨ] 'wife' (nom. pl.) – *žena* /ʒɛˈna/ [ʒɨˈna] (nom. sg.)

To sum up, the outcome of reduction after non-palatalized consonant is determined to a large extent by the quality of the input vowel. The underlying vowel /a/, except for a handful of exceptions in (32b), predominantly surfaces as [a] after non-palatalized stridents. The mid vowel /ɛ/ is consistently realized as [ɨ], and /o/ appears to reduce to both [a] and [ɨ].

[112] Borrowings which are not fully assimilated into the Russian phonological system may be exempt from vowel neutralisation, e.g., the word *šosse* 'highway' can be pronounced either [ʃoˈsɛ] or [ʃaˈsɛ].

[113] The underlying /ɛ/ in the forms in (34b) is motivated by forms such as [ˈʃɛpt͡ʃʲɪt] 'whisper' (3rd pers. sg.), and [ˈʒɛnskʲɪj̯] 'female', see also fn. 21 in section 2.4.2.

7.4.3. Analysis

Given the fact that non-palatalized stridents, similarly to other non-palatalized consonants, are not [+high] and [back], they are not expected to trigger vowel raising and to block tone-induced lowering in the immediately pretonic syllable. However, only the behaviour of the underlying vowel /a/ is in line with these predictions. In contrast, the mid vowel /ɛ/ is raised to [ɨ] after non-palatalized stridents, as in [ˈʃɛsʲtʲ] 'six' (nom.) – [ʃɨˈstʲi] 'six' (gen.), whereas /o/, exhibits either raising or lowering after non-palatalized stridents, e.g. [ˈʃopət] 'a whisper' – [ʃɨpˈtatʲ] 'to whisper', [ˈʃok] 'a shock' – [ʃaˈkʲirəvatʲ] 'to shock'.

First, let us consider the alternation [o] – [ɨ], as in [ˈʃopət] – [ʃɨpˈtatʲ]. It should be noted that the vowel [o] found after non-palatalized sibilants is the result of a historical process which changed stressed *e* into *o* before non-palatalized consonants.[114] As a result, morphologically related forms may exhibit the alternation [o] – [ɛ] – [ɨ], illustrated in (35).

(35) *Vowel alternations after non-palatalized stridents*

[o]	[ɛ]	[ɨ]
[ˈʃopət]	[ˈʃɛpt͡ʃʲɪʃ]	[ʃɨpˈtatʲ]
'whisper'	'whisper' (2nd pers. sg.)[115]	'whisper' (inf.)
[ˈʒonɨ]	[ˈʒɛnskʲɪj̯]	[ʒɨˈna]
'wife' (nom. pl.)	'female	'wife' (nom. sg.)

In some cases, only the alternation [o] – [ɨ] is present, without the form in which the vowel [ɛ] occurs under stress before a palatalized consonant, e.g. [ʃolk] 'silk' (nom. sg.) – [ʃɨlˈka] 'silk' (nom. pl.). I assume, after Crosswhite (2001), that the alternation [o] – [ɛ] is conditioned morphologically and the forms such as [ʃolk] 'silk' (nom. sg.) and [ʃɨlˈka] 'silk' (nom. pl.) are derived from two different allomorphs, /ʃolk/ and /ʃɛlk/, respectively.[116] In this view, the unstressed vowel [ɨ] in words such as [ʃɨlˈka] 'silk' (nom. pl.) and [ʃɨpˈtatʲ] 'to whisper' comes from /ɛ/. In effect, there are no cases of the raising of /o/ to [ɨ] or [i] as only /ɛ/ is raised to [ɨ], whereas /o/ can only be lowered to [a].

---

[114] Note that the difference between the original vowel [o] and the one which is historically derived from /e/ is reflected in orthography: the former is spelled with the letter *o* and the latter with *e* or ë.

[115] The consonants [p] in [ˈʃɛpt͡ʃʲɪʃ] and [n] in [ˈʒɛnskʲɪj̯] used to be palatalized because they were followed by a front vowel, which was subsequently deleted.

[116] For an alternative view, see Melvold (1990) and Plapp (1996), who assume that the stressed vowel [o] preceded by a palatalized consonant is synchronically derived from the underlying front mid vowel /ɛ/.

The next problematic issue to be addressed concerns the raising of /ɛ/ to [ɨ] in the context of non-palatalized sibilants. In the current model, [i]-reduction is driven by the markedness constraint AGREE[+high] requiring [+high] palatalized consonants to be followed by high vowels. As non-palatalized stridents, similarly to other non-palatalized consonants, are not specified for the feature [+high], the constraint AGREE[+high] is not violated when [ʃ], [ʒ], and [t͡s] are followed by non-high vowels. This problem does not arise if one assumes, together with Halle (1959), Lightner (1972), and Rubach (2000), that stridents are underlyingly palatalized in Russian. In this conception, /ɛ/ is raised to [ɨ] because [ʃ], [ʒ], and [t͡s] are [+high] and [-back] in the underlying representation. However, this solution is unacceptable for a number of reasons. First, the vowel /a/ would raise to [i] after [ʃ], [ʒ], and [t͡s] if non-palatalized stridents were underlyingly palatalized. It has been demonstrated above that while the low vowel /a/ changes to [i] after palatalized consonants, e.g. [ˈt͡ʃʲas] 'hour' (nom. sg.) – [t͡ʃʲiˈsa] (gen. sg.), /a/ does not raise after [ʃ], [ʒ], and [t͡s], e.g. [ʃaˈrɨ] 'ball' (nom. pl.), [ʒaˈra] 'heat', [t͡saˈrʲa] 'tsar' (gen. sg.).

Moreover, the vowel /o/ which is not historically derived from /e/ lowers both after non-palatalized consonants and after non-palatalized stridents, for instance, [ˈdom] 'house' (nom. sg.) – [daˈma] (nom. pl.), [ˈʃok] 'a shock' – [ʃaˈkʲirəvatʲ] 'to shock'. The parallel patterning of non-palatalized stridents and non-palatalized consonants would be unaccounted for if non-palatalized stridents were underlyingly palatalized.

To summarize, non-palatalized stridents act as palatalized consonants before the front vowel /ɛ/ and as non-palatalized consonants when followed by the back vowels /o/ and /a/. This contradictory behaviour can be explained assuming that evaluation of candidates is carried out in two steps, as assumed in Stratal OT (Kiparsky, 1997, 2000; Rubach, 1997, *et seq.*; Bermúdez-Otero, 1999, 2003). At the fist level, the underlyingly non-palatalized sibilants [ʃ], [ʒ], and [t͡s] get palatalized when followed by a front vowel. The palatalized stridents lose palatalization at a subsequent derivational level due to the constraint HARD-C, which requires that the output [ʃ], [ʒ], and [t͡s] are non (Rubach, 2000: 59).[117]

(36) HARD-C: a. *t͡sʲ: Anterior affricates cannot be [-back].
b. *ʃʲ ʒʲ: Non-anterior coronal continuants cannot be [-back].

[117] The current model is different from Rubach's (2000a) analysis, who assumes that non-palatalized stridents are palatalized in the underlying representation.

HARD-C is low-ranked at the first level, which allows stridents to get palatalized before front vowels. Tableau (37) shows the level 1 evaluation of the word /ʃɛstʲ+ˈi/ [ʃɨˈstʲi] 'six' (gen.), *cf.* /ˈʃɛstʲ/ [ˈʃɛstʲ] 'id.' (nom.).

(37) *Reduction of /ɛ/ after non-palatalized stridents: Level 1*

/ʃɛstʲ+ˈi/	AGREE [+high]	PAL	ID-V [-back]	HARD-C	ID-C [+back]	*H/≤i,u	*H/≤ɛ,ɔ
H ⇒ a. (ʃʲiˈstʲi)				*	*	*	*
H b. (ʃʲɛˈstʲi)	*!			*	*		*
H c. (ʃɛˈstʲi)		*!					*
H d. (ʃaˈstʲi)			*!				

High-ranked PAL eliminates the faithful candidate (37c) because it contains a sequence of a non-palatalized consonant followed by a front vowel. The palatalization of the strident in (37b) satisfies PAL but violates AGREE[+high], since /ʃʲ/, which is [+high], is followed by a non-high vowel. Non-palatalized consonants are not specified for height, so AGREE[+high] is mute in (37c) and (37d). Candidate (37d) satisfies both markedness constraints but fatally violates ID-V[−back]. The optimal candidate (37a) runs afoul of a host of lower-ranked constraints, it still wins because the raising to [i] leads to a considerable improvement in markedness.

At level 2, HARD-C is re-ranked above the markedness constraints AGREE[+high] and PAL, which jointly drive raising at level 1. The input to level 2 is the optimal output from level 1. The evaluation is shown in (38).

(38) *Reduction of /ɛ/ after non-palatalized stridents: Level 2*

H (ʃʲiˈstʲi)	HARD-C	PAL	ID-V [−back]	ID-V [+high]	ID-C [−back]	*H/≤ɛ,ɔ
H ⇒ a. (ʃɨˈstʲi)			*		*	*
H b. (ʃʲiˈstʲi)	*!					*
H c. (ʃiˈstʲi)		*!			*	*
H d. (ʃɛˈstʲi)		*!			*	*
H e. (ʃaˈstʲi)			*	*!	*	

Only a minimal re-ranking of HARD-C between the two levels is sufficient to ensure the correct output. The promoted HARD-C eliminates the palatalized strident in candidate (38b). The optimal candidate (38a) retains the high vowel, which is retracted to [ɨ] after the non-palatalized strident in order to comply with PAL. Candidate (38e) and the winner (38a) tie on the high-ranked IDENT-V[-back], and candidate (38a) is chosen by the faithfulness constraint IDENT-V[+high].

The lowering of the vowel /o/ after non-palatalized stridents is generated at level 1. This is as illustrated in Tableau (39) displaying the evaluation of the word /ʃok+'ir+ova+tʲ/ [ʃa'kʲirəvətʲ] 'to shock'.

(39) *Reduction of /o/ after non-palatalized stridents: Level 1*

/ʃok+'ir+ova+tʲ/	AGREE [+high]	PAL	HARD-C	*H/≤i,u	*H/≤e,o	*H/≤ε,ɔ	*H/≤a	ID-V [–low]
H ⇒a. (ʃa'kʲi)rəvətʲ							*	*
H b. (ʃo'kʲi)rəvətʲ					*	*!	*	
H c. (ʃε'kʲi)rəvətʲ		*!				*	*	
H d. (ʃɨ'kʲi)rəvətʲ				*	*!	*	*	
H e. (ʃʲε'kʲi)rəvətʲ	*!		*			*	*	
H f. (ʃʲi'kʲi)rəvətʲ			*	*!	*	*	*	

Vowel lowering in the optimal candidate (39a) maximizes the sonority of a vowel linked to a High tone. Other candidates (39c-f) are excluded because their violations of faithfulness do not lead to the improvement in markedness. As the strident /ʃ/ is non-palatalized in the optimal output at level 1, the re-ranking of HARD-C does not affect the evaluation at level 2 and the optimal candidate from level 1 also wins at level 2.

To conclude, this section has argued that the reduction pattern found after non-palatalized stridents is not exceptional and that non-palatalized stridents behave like other non-palatalized consonants with respect to vowel reduction. In particular, the change of /o/ to [a] in words such as /ʃok+'ir+ova+tʲ/ [ʃa'kʲirəvətʲ] 'to shock' is brought about by the need to increase the sonority of immediately pretonic vowels, and /a/ surfaces as [a] after non-palatalized stridents. In a handful of words, /a/ is raised to [i] after non-palatalized sibilants, for example [ləʃɨ'dʲej] 'horse' (gen. pl.), cf. [lə'ʃatkə] (dim.). However, these forms are exceptional and do not constitute counterevidence to the present model. The low vowel /a/ was regularly raised after non-palatalized stridents in Old Moscow pronunciation and the words which have retained the high vowel in the standard language are the lexicalized remnants of the old norm. Their exceptional status is confirmed by the increasing tendency to pronounce these words with [a] (Shapiro, 1968). Similarly, the existence of the alternation of [o] with [ɨ], as in ['ʒonɨ] 'wife' (nom. pl.) – [ʒɨ'na] (nom. sg.), does not argue against the proposed analysis because the forms with the reduced vowel [i] come from the allomorphs containing the front vowel /e/ in the immediately pretonic position. Yet, the raising of /e/ to [ɨ] after the non-palatalized stridents is not expected given that [ʃ], [ʒ], and [t͡s] are [+back] consonants not specified for the feature [+high]. Let us note that the front mid vowel /ɛ/ has a palatalizing effect on all consonants except [ʃ], [ʒ], and [t͡s]. The idea behind the present analysis is that non-palatalized stridents are also palatalized when followed by /ɛ/, but lose their palatalization on the surface. Contrary to previous analyses which postulated that [ʃ], [ʒ], and [t͡s] are palatalized underlyingly (Halle, 1959; Lightner, 1972; Rubach, 2000), I assume that sibilants are underlyingly non-palatalized and acquire palatalization only before front vowels. This assumption accounts for a fact that /a/ is exempt from raising after [ʃ], [ž], and [t͡s].

7.5. Conclusion

This chapter has considered contexts in which tone-induced lowering is blocked due to the presence of a palatalized consonant. In most cases, palatalized consonants induce fronting and raising of the following unstressed vowels. However, a number of East Slavic dialects exhibit a pattern in which not only the preceding, but also the following consonants affect the quality of unstressed vowels. It has been argued that the processes operating in the vicinity of palatalized consonants are triggered by the features [+high] and [-back] which are present both in vowels and in consonants. While [+high] and [-back] constitute definitional properties of high and front vowels, these features also serve to define secondary place of articulation in palatalized consonants, and so vowel fronting and raising are triggered by the constraints requiring agreement in backness and/or height between a consonant and a following vowel, or between a vowel and both the preceding and the following consonant.

Furthermore, I have argued that non-palatalized stridents pattern together with other non-palatalized consonants with respect to vowel reduction. An apparently exceptional raising of /ɛ/ after non-palatalized consonants has been analysed in terms of Stratal OT, the basic assumption being that underlyingly non-palatalized stridents are palatalized when followed by /ɛ/, and subsequently lose their palatalization on the surface. This account allows us to explain why /a/ does not undergo raising after non-palatalized stridents.

Chapter 8

Concluding remarks

This study has set out to design a theoretical model which would account for the crosslinguistically attested patterns of the interaction between vocalic sonority and tone. The model of the tone-sonority interaction has been developed within the framework of Optimality Theory (Prince and Smolensky, 1993/2004; McCarthy and Prince, 1995). The present book argues that tone can interact directly with vowel quality without mediating factors such as syllable structure or duration. The basic assumption is that tonally prominent units co-occur with prominent segments. In terms of Optimality Theory, this generalization is expressed by a family of markedness constraints *H≤V and *M/≥V, which are derived by harmonic alignment of two natural linguistic scales, the tonal scale and the sonority scale.

The proposed constraints are used in the analysis of vowel neutralizations found in immediately pretonic positions in standard Russian and in different East Slavic dialects. A characteristic trait of these systems is that they exhibit two degrees of vowel reduction: moderate reduction is found in immediately pretonic positions, while extreme reduction is found in atonic positions. Previous accounts have unanimously agreed that different degrees of reduction are due to iambic foot structure, with moderate reduction taking place in the syllable parsed into the iambic foot, and extreme reduction occurring in unparsed syllables.

Drawing on the insight originally expressed by Bethin (2006), this book has developed an alternative model in which pretonic reduction to [a] is a direct consequence of the shift of the tonal prominence (High tone) from the stressed syllable to the immediately preceding syllable. Neutralization of non-high vowels to [a] is driven by a family of functionally grounded markedness constraints *H≤V requiring High tone to be realized on the most sonorous vowel [a]. The location of High tone determines whether a given system exhibits non-dissimilative or dissimilative reduction type. In the former, High tone is linked to both the tonic and the immediately pretonic syllables. In the latter, High tone docks on the tonic syllable if it contains a low sonorous vowel, otherwise, tone shifts to the pretonic position. Additionally, it has been demonstrated that the pressure to maximize sonority of high-toned vowels can be overruled by the harmonic processes affecting vowels in the immediately pretonic and tonic syllables. The influence of High tone is also supressed in the presence of palatalized consonants. It has been argued in Chapters 5, 6, and 7 that all these cases can be accounted for in an elegant way in terms of the agreement in the features [high], [back] and [low]. The present model is conceptually parsimonious in that it provides a common denominator (tone) for such diverse processes as lengthening, non-dissimilative reduction, and different types of dissimilative reduction attested in the pretonic position across East Slavic. It is demonstrated that the subtle differences between vowel patterns attested in various East Slavic dialects can be modelled based on minimal variations in the rankings of the same constraints.

The central claim of this book is that, synchronically, H tone interacts with segmental quality and quantity without the mediation of phonetic pitch. Historically, however, it is likely that phonological tone was expressed through phonetic pitch, and segmental and suprasegmental adaptations occurred in response to the requirements of the rising pitch contour. As argued in Chapter 5, these adaptations could have been grounded in both articulation and perception. As the results of acoustic studies do not provide conclusive evidence for the presence of contrastive pitch contours in the East Slavic dialects in question, it is plausible that the transparent link in the form of the F_0 excursion has been lost in the present-day dialects, and the underlying tonal contrast has developed into productive alternations in quality and length.

The proposed theory of tone–vowel interactions carries a series of implications for the typology. While the Low tone is predicted not to interact with segmental sonority, it is expected that High tone should co-occur with lower vowels and Mid tone should be associated with higher vowels. As discussed in section 1.3, Chapter 1, these predictions are borne out by the attested cases of tone-sonority interactions. The present model also predicts that there should be no languages with High tone favouring high vowels and/or Mid tone favouring low vowels. However, there are systems in which High tone is correlated with higher vowels. For instance, Becker and Jurgec (2017) report a synchronic interaction of tone with vowel quality in Slovenian, where High tone co-occurs with tense vowels and Low tone with lax vowels. This pattern is not predicted by the present analysis. However, experimental studies reveal a phonetic affinity between High tones and high vowels: higher vowels have higher fundamental frequency than lower vowels (Ladefoged, 1968; Ohala, 1973). It might then be the case that there is a constraint which forces high tones to be associated to high vowels. This type of constraint, *H[-ATR -low], has been postulated by Becker and Jurgec (2017) to account for the Slovenian data.

Finally, it should be noted that the constraints *H≤V and *M/≥V also predict the existence of tonal systems in which High tone would seek out low vowels and Mid tone would dock on high vowels· Such languages have not been documented in the literature. Needless to say, more empirical research on tonal and pitch-accent languages is needed to validate the theory presented in this book.

To conclude, I hope that the present study has shed new light on a number of theoretical and descriptive issues and produced a more explanatory and coherent description of the complex vowel patterns attested in East Slavic. The future research shall demonstrate whether (and how) the theory of tone-sonority interaction developed here can be implemented in the analyses of tone-related phenomena in other languages.

References

Abercrombie, David. 1976. 'Stress and Some Other Terms.' in *Work in progress 9: 51-3. Rpt. in D. Abercrombie, 1991. Fifty years in phonetics.* Edinburgh: Edinburgh University Press.

Alber, Birgit. 2005. Clash, lapse and directionality. *Natural Language and Linguistic Theory 23*:485–542.

Al'muxamedova, Z. M., and R. E. Kul'šaripova. 1980. *Redukcija Glasnyx i Prosodija Slova v Okajuščix Russkix Govorax.* Kazan': Izdatel'stvo Kazanskogo Universiteta.

Alderete, John D. 1995. 'Faithfulness to Prosodic Heads.' *Rutgers Optimality Archives* 751:1–46.

Alderete, John D. 1999. 'Morphologically Governed Accent in Optimality Theory.' UMass dissertation.

Anderson, Gregory D. S., and K. David. Harrison. 1999. *Tyvan.* LINCOM Europa.

Anderson, Stephen R. 1982. 'The Analysis of French Shwa: Or, How to Get Something for Nothing.' *Language* 58(3):534–73.

Anttila, Arto. 1997. 'Deriving Variation from Grammar: A Study of Finnish Genitives.' Pp. 35–68 in *Variation, Change, and Phonological Theory*, edited by F. Hinskens, R. van Hout, and L. Wetzels. Amsterdam: Benjamins.

Archangeli, Diana, and Douglas Pulleyblank. 1994. *Grounded Phonology.* Cambridge MA: MIT Press.

Archangeli, Diana, and Douglas Pulleyblank. 2007. 'Harmony.' Pp. 353–78 in *The Cambridge Handbook of Phonology*, edited by P. de Lacy. Cambridge: Cambridge University Press.

Avanesov, R. I. 1952. 'Lingvističeskaja Geografija i Istorija Russkogo Jazyka.' *Voprosy Jazykoznanija* 6:25–47.

Avanesov, R. I. 1974. *Russkaja Literaturnaja i Dialektnaja Fonetika.* Moskva: Prosveščenie.

Avanesov, R. I. 1984. *Russkoe Literaturnoe Proiznošenie.* 6th ed. Moskva: Prosveščenie.

Avanesov, R. I., and S. V. Bromlej, eds. 1986. *Dialektologičeskij Atlas Russkogo Jazyka. Vol. 1: Fonetika.* Moskva: Nauka.

Avanesov, R. I., and V. G. Orlova. 1965. *Russkaja Dialektologija.* 2nd ed. Moskva: Prosveščenie.

Avanesov, R. I., and S. Ožegov. 1959. *Russkoe Literaturnoe Proiznošenie i Udarenie.* Moskva: Gosudarstvennoe izdatel'stvo inostrannyx i nacional'nyx slovarej.

Bagemihl, Bruce. 1995. 'Language Games and Related Areas.' Pp. 697–712 in *The Handbook of Phonological Theory*, edited by J. A. Goldsmith. Oxford and Cambridge, MA: Blackwell Publishers.

Baković, Eric. 2000. 'Harmony, Dominance and Control.' Rutgers University dissertation.

Baković, Eric J. 1999. 'Assimilation to the Unmarked.' Proceedings of the 23rd Annual Penn Linguistics Colloquium (Penn Working Papers in Linguistics 6.1), University of Pennsylvania, Philadelphia. 1–16.

Barnes, Jonathan. 2006. *Strength and Weakness at the Interface: Positional Neutralization in Phonetics and Phonology.* Berlin: Mouton de Gruyter.

Barnes, Jonathan. 2007. *Phonetics and Phonology in Russian Unstressed Vowel Reduction: A Study in Hyperarticulation.* Boston University.

Becker, M., and P. Jurgec. 2017. 'Interactions of Tone and ATR in Slovenian.' Pp. 11–26 in *Segmental Structure and Tone*, edited by W. Kehrein, B. Köhnlein, P. Boersma, and M. van Oostendorp. Bernin, Boston: Niemeyer.

Beckman, Jill N. 1997. 'Positional Faithfulness, Positional Neutralisation and Shona Vowel Harmony.' *Phonology* 14(1):1–46.

Beckman, Mary E. 1986. *Stress and Non-Stress Accent.* Dordrecht, Holland; Riverton, U.S.A.: Foris Publications.

Belaja, A. S. 1974. 'K Xarakteristike Kvantitativno-Prosodičeskix Različij v Nadsnovskix Govorax na Černigovščine.' Pp. 22–31 in *Obščeslavjanskij lingvističeskij atlas: materialy i issledovanija, 1971*, edited by R. I. Avanesov, S. B. Bernštejn, S. K. Požarickaja, and F. P. Filin. Moskva: Nauka.

Benua, Laura. 1997. 'Transderivational Identity: Phonological Relations between Words.' UMass dissertation.

Bermúdez-Otero, Ricardo. 1999. 'Constraint Interaction in Language Change: Quantity in English and Germanic.' University of Manchester dissertation.

Bermúdez-Otero, Ricardo. 2003. 'The Acquisition of Phonological Opacity.' Pp. 25–36 in *Variation within Optimality Theory: Proceedings of the Stockholm Workshop on `Variation within Optimality Theory´*, edited by J. Spenader, A. Eriksson, and Ö. Dahl. Stockholm: Department of Linguistics, Stockholm University.

Bermúdez-Otero, Ricardo. 2007. 'Diachronic Phonology.' Pp. 497–517 in *The Cambridge Handbook of Phonology*, edited by P. de Lacy. Cambridge: Cambridge University Press.

Bethin, Christina Y. 1998. *Slavic Prosody: Language Change and Phonological Theory.* Cambridge: Cambridge University Press.

Bethin, Christina Y. 2005. 'On Pretonic Length in Belarusian and Ukrainian Nadsnovs'ki Dialects.' Pp. 52–67 in *Formal Approaches to Slavic Linguistics 13: the South Carolina Meeting*, edited by S. Franks, F. Y.

Gladney, and M. Tasseva-Kurktchieva. Ann Arbor: Michigan Slavic Publications.

Bethin, Christina Y. 2006. 'Stress and Tone in East Slavic Dialects.' *Phonology* 23(2):125–56.

Bethin, Christina Y. 2012. 'A Question of Timing: Raising /a/ to /o/ in East Slavic.' Pp. 1–14 in *Sound, Structure and Sense: Studies in Memory of Edmund Gussmann*, edited by E. Cyran, H. Kardela, and B. Szymanek. Lublin: KUL.

Bidwell, Charles E. 1969. *Outline of Slovenian Morphology.* Pittsburgh: University Center for International Studies, University of Pittsburgh.

Blevins, Juliette, and Andrew Garrett. 2004. 'The Evolution of Metathesis.' Pp. 117–56 in *Phonetically Based Phonology*, edited by B. Hayes, D. Steriade, and R. Kirchner. Cambridge: Cambridge University Press.

Bondarko, L. V. 1977. *Zvukovoj Stroj Sovremennogo Russkogo Jazyka.* Moskva: Prosveščenie.

Booij, Geert E. 1995. *The Phonology of Dutch.* Oxford: Clarendon Press.

Borise, Lena. 2015. 'Prominence Redistribution in the Aŭciuki Dialect of Belarusian.' in *Proceedings of the 24th Meeting of Formal Approaches to Slavic Linguistics*, edited by Y. Oseki, M. Esipova, and S. Harves. Ann Arbor, Michigan: Michigan Slavic Publications.

Bradshaw, Mary M. 1999. 'A Crosslinguistic Study of Consonant-Tone Interaction.' Ohio State University dissertation.

Broch, Olaf. 1916. *Govory k Zapadu ot Mosal'ska.* Petrograd: Imperatorskaja Akademija Nauk.

Burova, E. G., and L. L. Kasatkin. 1977. 'Čuxlomskoe Akan'e.' Pp. 64–85 in *Dialektologičeskije issledovanija po russkomu jazyku*, edited by R. I. Avanesov, J. S. Azarx, L. N. Bulatova, and V. V. Ivanov. Moskva: Nauka.

Casali, Roderic F. 1997. 'Vowel Elision in Hiatus Contexts: Which Vowel Goes?' *Language* 73(3):493–533.

Čekmonas, V. H. 1987. 'Territorija Zaroždenija i Etapy Razvitija Vostočnoslavjanskogo Akan'ja v Svete Dannyx Lingvogeografii.' *Russian Linguistics* 11:335–49.

Čekmonas, V. H. 1999. 'Akan'e i Jakan'e v Govorax Pskovskogo Rajona (Sovremennoje Sostojanie i Problemy Istorii).' *Slavistica Vilnensis (Kalbotyra)* 48(2):89–146.

Chen, Leo, and Jerry Norman. 1965. 'An Introduction to the Foochow Dialect.' San Francisco State College in cooperation with the U.S. Office of Education.

Chomsky, Noam, and Morris Halle. 1968. *The Sound Pattern of English.* New York: Harper & Row.

Clements, George N. 1985. 'The Geometry of Phonological Features.' *Phonology Yearbook* 2:225–52.

Clements, George N. 1991. 'Vowel Height Assimilation in Bantu Languages.' Pp. 25–64 in *Proceedings of the 17th Annual Meeting of the Berkeley Linguistics Society, Feb. 15–18, 1991: Special Session on African Language Structures*, edited by K. Hubbard. Berkeley: University of California Press.

Clements, George N., and Elizabeth V. Hume. 1995. 'The Internal Organisation of Speech Sounds.' Pp. 245–306 in *The Handbook of Phonological Theory*, edited by J. A. Goldsmith. Oxford: Blackwell.

Clements, George N., and Engin Sezer. 1982. 'Vowel and Consonant Disharmony in Turkish.' Pp. 213–55 in *The Structure of Phonological Representations*, edited by H. van der Hulst and N. Smith. Dordrecht: Foris.

Coetzee, Andries W., and Joe Pater. 2011. 'The Place of Variation in Phonological Theory.' Pp. 401–34 in *The Handbook of Phonological Theory*, edited by J. A. Goldsmith, J. Riggle, and A. C. L. Yu. Wiley-Blackwell.

Cole, Desmond. 1969. *An Introduction to Tswana Grammar*. London: Longmans, Green.

Crosswhite, Katherine. 1998. 'Segmental vs. Prosodic Correspondence in Chamorro.' *Phonology* 15(3):281–316.

Crosswhite, Katherine. 2000. 'Vowel Reduction in Russian: A Unified Account of Standard, Dialectal, and 'Dissimilative" Patterns.' Pp. 107–71 in *University of Rochester Working Papers in the Language Sciences, Vol. Spring 2000*, edited by K. M. Crosswhite and J. McDonough.

Crosswhite, Katherine. 2001. *Vowel Reduction in Optimality Theory*. New York and London: Routledge.

Crosswhite, Katherine, John Alderete, Tim Beasley, and Vita Markman. 2003. 'Morphological Effects on Default Stress in Novel Russian Words.' *WCCFL 22 Proceedings* 151–64.

Cumming, Ruth. 2011. 'The Effect of Dynamic Fundamental Frequency on the Perception of Duration.' *Journal of Phonetics* 39:375–87.

Cutler, Anne. 1984. 'Stress and Accent in Language Production and Understanding.' Pp. 77–90 in *Intonation, Accent and Rhythm. Studies in Discourse Phonology.*, edited by D. Gibbon and H. Richter. Berlin: de Gruyter.

Czekman, Walery, and Elżbieta Smułkowa. 1988. *Fonetyka i Fonologia Języka Białoruskiego z Elementami Fonetyki i Fonologii Ogólnej*. Warszawa: Państwowe Wydawnictwo Naukowe.

Cyran, Eugeniusz. 2010. *Complexity Scales and Licensing Strength in Phonology*. New York/Berlin: Mouton de Gruyter.

D'jačok, M. T. 2002. 'Akcentnaja Baza (k Postanovke Problemy).' Pp. 16–19 in *Opuscula glottologica professori Cyrillo Timofeiev ab discipulis dedicata*, edited by M. T. D'jačok and V. V. Šapoval. Moskva: Sputnik+.

Davis, Philip W. 1970. 'A Classification of Dissimilative Jakan'e Dialects of Russian.' *Orbis* 19:360–76.

Djačenko, S. V. 2013. 'Razvitie Sistemy Glasnyx Posle Tvjordyx i Mjagkix Soglasnyx v Govorax s Arxaičeskim Tipom Vokalizma.' Pp. 335–57 in *Russkaja fonetika v razvitii. Fonetičeskije 'otcy' i 'deti' načala XXI veka*, edited by M. L. Kalenčuk and R. F. Kasatkina. Moskva: Jazyki slavjanskoj kul'tury.

Dubina, Andrei. 2012. 'Towards a Tonal Analysis of Free Stress.' Doctoral dissertation, Radboud University.

Durnovo, N. N. 1917. *Dialektologičeskie Razyskanija v Oblasti Velikorusskix Govorov. I. Južnovelikorusskoje Narečie.* Moskva: Sinod. tipog. (Trudy Postojannoj Komissij po Dialektologii Russkogo Jazyka Akademii Nauk, vyp.6–7.).

Edmondson, Jerold A., and Kenneth J. Gregerson. 1993. 'Western Cham as a Register Language.' Pp. 61–74 in *Tonality in Austronesian Languages*, edited by J. A. Edmondson and K. J. Gregerson. Honolulu: University of Hawaii Press.

Fant, Gunnar. 1960. *Acoustic Theory of Speech Production.* The Hague: Mouton.

Fomina, T. G. 1985. 'Prosodija Slova v Južnorusskom Govore s Dissimiljativnym Vokalizmom.' Pp. 101–30 in *Gradacionnaja fonologija jazyka i prosodija slova russkoj dialektnoj reči*, edited by Z. M. Al'muxamedova. Kazan': Izdatel'stvo Kazanskogo Universiteta.

Fox, Anthony. 2000. *Prosodic Features and Prosodic Structure: The Phonology of Suprasegmentals.* Oxford: Oxford University Press.

Gandour, J. 1977. 'On the Interaction between Tone and Vowel Length: Evidence from Thai Dialects.' *Phonetica* 34:54–65.

Gimson, Alfred C. 1970. *Introduction to the Pronunciation of English.* London: Arnold.

Gnanadesikan, Amalia. 1997. 'Ternary Scales in Phonology.' UMass dissertation.

Goldsmith, John A. 1976. 'Autosegmental Phonology.' MIT dissertation.

Goldsmith, John A. 1990. *Autosegmental and Metrical Phonology.* Oxford: Blackwell.

Golston, Chris. 1990. 'Floating L* (and H) Tones in Ancient Greek.' Pp. 66–82 in *Arizona Phonology Conference: Volume 3*, edited by J. Myers and P. Pérez.

Gordon, Matthew Kelly. 2006. *Syllable Weight: Phonetics, Phonology, Typology.* New York and London: Routledge.

Gorškova, K. V., and G. A. Xaburgaev. 1981. *Istoričeskaja Grammatika Russkogo Jazyka.* Moskva: Vysšaja škola.

Gouskova, Maria. 2003. 'Deriving Economy: Syncopy in Optimality Theory.' UMass dissertation.

Gouskova, Maria. 2010. 'The Phonology of Boundaries and Secondary Stress in Russian Compounds.' *Linguistic Review* 27(4):387–448. doi: 10.1515/tlir.2010.015.

Gouskova, Maria, and Kevin Roon. 2013. 'Gradient Clash, Faithfulness, and Sonority Sequencing Effects in Russian Compound Stress.' *Laboratory Phonology* 4(2):383–434.

Gregerson, Kenneth J. 1976. 'Tongue-Root and Register in Mon-Khmer.' Pp. 323–69 in *Austroasiatic Studies, vol.1*, edited by P. N. Jenner, L. C. Thompson, and S. Starosta. Honolulu: University of Hawaii Press.

Gussenhoven, Carlos, and Wilske Driessen. 2004. 'Explaining Two Correlations between Vowel Quality and Tone: The Duration Connection. Paper Presented at the ISCA Workshop on Prosody 2004.'

Gussmann, Edmund. 2002. *Phonology: Analysis and Theory.* Cambridge: Cambridge University Press.

Halle, Morris. 1959. *The Sound Pattern of Russian.* The Hague: Mouton.

Halle, Morris. 1965. 'Akan'e: The Treatment of Unstressed, Nondiffuse Vowels in Southern Great Russian Dialects.' Pp. 103–9 in *Symbolae Linguisticae in Honorem Georgii Kuryłowicz*, edited by W. Taszycki. Wrocław: Polska Akademia Nauk.

Halle, Morris. 1973. 'The Accentuation of Russian Words.' *Language* 49(2):312–48.

Halle, Morris. 1992. 'Phonological Features.' Pp. 207–12 in *International encyclopedia of linguistics*, edited by W. Bright. Oxford: Oxford University Press.

Halle, Morris. 1995. 'Feature Geometry and Feature Spreading.' *Linguistic Inquiry* 26:1–46.

Halle, Morris. 1997. 'On Stress and Accent in Indo-European.' *Language* 73(2):275–313.

Halle, Morris. 2005. 'Palatalization/Velar Softening: What It Is and What It Tells Us about the Nature of Language.' *Linguistic Inquiry* 36:23–41.

Halle, Morris, and William Idsardi. 1995. 'General Properties of Stress and Metrical Structure.' Pp. 403–43 in *The handbook of phonological theory*, edited by J. A. Goldsmith. Oxford and Cambridge, MA: Blackwell.

Halle, Morris, and Jean-Roger Vergnaud. 1987. *An Essay on Stress.* Cambridge MA: MIT Press.

Hansson, Gunnar Ólafur. 2008. 'Diachronic Explanations of Sound Patterns.' *Language and Linguistics Compass* 2(5):859–93.

Hamilton, William S. 1980. *Introduction to Russian Phonology and Word Structure.* Columbus: Slavica Publishers, Inc.

Haraguchi, Shosuke. 1984. 'Some Tonal and Segmental Effects of Vowel Height in Japanese.' Pp. 145–56 in *Language and sound structure*, edited by M. Aronoff and R. Oehrle. Cambridge (Mass.)/London: MIT Press.

Harris, John. 1994. *English Sound Structure.* Oxford: Basil Blackwell.

Harris, John. 2005. 'Vowel Reduction as Information Loss.' Pp. 119–32 in *Headhood, elements, specification and contrastivity*, edited by P. Carr, J. Durand, and C. J. Ewen. Amsterdam: Benjamins.

Hayes, Bruce P. 1995. *Metrical Stress Theory: Principles and Case Studies.* Chicago: University of Chicago Press.

Heijmans, Linda. 2003. 'The Relationship between Tone and Vowel Length in Two Neighboring Dutch Limburgian Dialects.' Pp. 7–45 in *Development in prosodic systems*, edited by P. Fikkert and J. Haike. Berlin: Mouton de Gruyter.

Hombert, Jean-Marie. 1977. 'Development of Tones from Vowel Height.' *Journal of Phonetics* 5:9–16.

Hombert, Jean-Marie. 1978. 'Consonant Types, Vowel Quality, and Tone.' Pp. 77–112 in *Tone: A linguistic survey*, edited by V. A. Fromkin. New York: Academic Press.

Hombert, Jean-Marie, John J. Ohala, and William G. Ewan. 1979. 'Phonetic Explanations for the Development of Tones.' *Language* 55:37–58.

Hualde, José. 1991. *Basque Phonology*. London: Routledge.

Hualde, José Ignacio. 1989. 'Autosegmental and Metrical Spreading in the Vowel-Harmony Systems of Northwestern Spain.' *Linguistics* 27:773–805.

Hulst, Harry van der. 1999. 'Word Accent.' Pp. 3–116 in *Word prosodic systems in the languages of Europe.*, edited by H. van der Hulst. Berlin and New York: Mouton de Gruyter.

Hulst, Harry van der. 2011. 'Pitch Accent Systems.' Pp. 1003–26 in *Phonological compendium*, edited by C. Ewen, M. van Oostendorp, and K. Rice. Oxford: Blackwell.

Hulst, Harry van der, and Jeroen van de Weijer. 1995. 'Vowel Harmony.' Pp. 495–534 in *The Handbook of Phonological Theory*, edited by J. A. Goldsmith. Oxford: Blackwell.

Hyde, Brett. 2002. 'A Restrictive Theory of Metrical Stress.' *Phonology* 19:313–59.

Hyde, Brett. 2016. *Layering and Directionality: Metrical Stress in Optimality Theory*. London: Equinox.

Hyman, Larry M. 2006. 'Word-Prosodic Typology.' *Phonology* 23(2):225–57.

Idsardi, William. 1992. 'The Computation of Prosody.' MIT dissertation.

Inkelas, Sharon, and Cemil Orhan Orgun. 1995. 'Level Ordering and Economy in the Lexical Phonology of Turkish.' *Language* 71:763–93.

Inkelas, Sharon, and Draga Zec. 1988. 'Serbo-Croatian Pitch Accent: The Interaction of Tone, Stress, and Intonation.' *Language* 64(2):227–48.

Iosad, Pavel. 2012. 'Vowel Reduction in Russian: No Phonetics in Phonology.' *Journal of Linguistics* 48:521–571.

Ito, Junko, and Armin Mester. 2001. 'Structure Preservation and Stratal Opacity in German.' Pp. 261–95 in *Segmental Phonology in Optimality Theory*, edited by L. Lombardi. Cambridge: Cambridge University Press.

Ito, Junko, and Armin Mester. 2003. 'Lexical and Postlexical Phonology in Optimality Theory: Evidence from Japanese.' *Linguistische Berichte. Sonderheft 11: Resolving Conflicts in Grammars* 183–207.

Jakobson, Roman. 1929. 'Remarques Sur l'evolution Phonologique de Russe Comparée à Celle Des Autres Langues Slaves.' Travaux Du Cercle Linguistique de Prague 2. Rpt. in *Selected Writings*, Vol. 1: Phonological Studies (1971), 2nd Exp. Edn. Pp. 7–116. The Hague: Mouton.

Jakobson, Roman. 1931. 'Die Betonung Und Ihre Rolle in Der Wort- Und Syntagmaphonologie.' Travaux Du Cercle Linguistique de Prague 4 (Pp. 164–182). Rpt. in *Selected Writings*, Vol. 1: Phonological Studies (1971), 2nd Exp. Edn.' Pp. 117–36. The Hague: Mouton.

Jakobson, Roman. 1963. 'Opyt Fonologičeskogo Podxoda k Istoričeskim Voprosam Slavjanskoj Akcentologii. Pozdnij Period Slavjanskoj Jazykovoj

Praistorii.' American Contributions to the Fifth International Congress of Slavists, Vol.I: Linguistic Contributions, Pp. 153–178. The Hague: Mouton.

Jakobson, Roman. 1971. 'Fonetika Odnogo Severnorusskigo Govora s Namečajuščejsja Perexodnostju.' Pp. 571–613 in *Selected writings, Vol. 1, 2nd exp. ed.* The Hague: Mouton.

Jassem, Wiktor, and Dafydd Gibbon. 1980. 'Re-Defining English Accent and Stress.' *Journal of the International Phonetic Association* 10:2–16.

Jespersen, Otto. 1904. *Lehrbuch Der Phonetik.* Leipzig and Berlin: Teubner.

Jiang-King, Ping. 1999. *Tone–Vowel Interaction in Optimality Theory.* München: LINCOM Europa.

Jiménez, Jesús, and Maria-Rosa Lloret. 2007. 'Andalusian Vowel Harmony: Weak Triggers and Perceptibility.' OCP 4, Rhodes. Available at ROA 901-0207.

Jones, Daniel. 1923. *The Phonetics of Russian. Revized by Ward, D., 1969.* Cambridge: Cambridge University Press.

Jouravlev, Olessia, and Stephen J. Lupker. 2015. 'Predicting Stress Patterns in an Unpredictable Stress Language: The Use of Non-Lexical Sources of Evidence for Stress Assignment in Russian.' *Journal of Cognitive Psychology* 27(8):944–66.

Kager, René. 1999. *Optimality Theory.* Cambridge: Cambridge University Press.

Kalenčuk, M. L., and R. F. Kasatkina. 2013. *Russkaja Fonetika v Razvitii. Fonetičeskije 'Otcy' i 'Deti' Načala XXI Veka.* Moskva: Jazyki slavjanskoj kul'tury.

Kasatkin, L. L. 1989. 'Fonetika.' Pp. 32–79 in *Russkaja dialektologija*, edited by L. L. Kasatkin. Moskva: Prosveščenie.

Kasatkin, L. L. 1999a. 'Affrikaty na Meste Vzryvnyx Soglasnyx Pered Ščelevymi v Russkom Jazyke.' Pp. 78–84 in *Problemy fonetiki III*, edited by R. F. Kasatkina. Moskva: RAN.

Kasatkin, L. L. 1999b. *Sovremennaja Russkaja Dialektnaja i Literaturnaja Fonetika Kak Istočnik Dlja Istorii Russkogo Jazyka.* Moskva: Nauka – Škola 'Jark.'

Kasatkin, L. L. 2005. 'Fonetika.' Pp. 22–85 in *Russkaja dialektologija*, edited by L. L. Kasatkin. Moskva: Akademia.

Kasatkin, L. L. 2013. 'Akan'je i Jakan'je – Istorija i Sovremennost'.' Pp. 295–317 in *Russkaja fonetika v razvitii. Fonetičeskije 'otcy' i 'deti' načala XXI veka*, edited by M. L. Kalenčuk and R. F. Kasatkina. Moskva: Jazyki slavjanskoj kul'tury.

Kasatkina, R. F. 1995. 'O Južnorusskom Dissimiljativnom Akan'e.' Pp. 220–28 in *Filologičeskij sbornik (k 100-letiju so dnja roždenija akademika V. V. Vinogradova)*, edited by M. V. Ljapon. Moskva: RAN.

Kasatkina, R. F. 1996a. 'Mežslogovaja Assimilacija Glasnych v Russkix Govorax.' Pp. 207–21 in *Prosodičeskij stroj russkoj reči*, edited by T. M. Nikolaeva. Moskva: RAN.

Kasatkina, R. F. 1996b. 'Srednerusskie Govory i Ritmika Slova.' Pp. 222–35 in *Prosodičeskij stroj russkoj reči*, edited by T. M. Nikolaeva. Moskva: RAN.

Kasatkina, R. F. 2000. 'Južnorusskoje Narečije. Novyje Dannyje.' *Voprosy Jazykoznanija* 6:98–109.

Kasatkina, R. F. 2005. 'Moskovskoe Akan'e v Svete Nekotoryx Dialektnyx Dannyx.' *Voprosy Jazykoznanija* 53:29–45.

Kasatkina, R. F., and E. V. Ščigel'. 1995. 'Assimiljativno-Dissimiljativnoe Akan'e.' Pp. 295–309 in *Problemy fonetiki II*, edited by L. L. Kasatkin. Moskva: RAN.

Kasatkina, R. F., and E. V. Ščigel'. 1996. 'Osobennosti Prosodii Slova v Južnorusskix Govorax.' Pp. 236–55 in *Prosodičeskij stroj russkoj reči*, edited by T. M. Nikolaeva. Moskva: RAN.

Kehrein, Wolfgang. 2017. 'There's No Tone in Cologne: Against Tone Segment Interactions in Franconian.' Pp. 147–94 in *Segmental Structure and Tone*, edited by W. Kehrein, B. Köhnlein, P. Boersma, and M. van Oostendorp. Berlin, Boston: Walter de Gruyter.

Kenstowicz, Michael. 1994. *Phonology in Generative Grammar*. Cambridge: Blackwell Publishers.

Kenstowicz, Michael. 1997. 'Quality-Sensitive Stress.' *Rivista Di Linguistica* 9(1):157–188.

Kiparsky, Paul. 1973. 'Phonological Representations.' Pp. 3–136 in *Three Dimensions of Linguistic Theory*, edited by O. Fujimura. Tokyo: TEK.

Kiparsky, Paul. 1993. 'An OT Perspective on Phonological Variation.' Presented at Rutgers Optimality Workshop 1993 and at NWAV 1994.

Kiparsky, Paul. 1997. 'LP and OT.' Handout. Ithaca, NY: Cornell Linguistic Institute.

Kiparsky, Paul. 2000. 'Opacity and Cyclicity.' *The Linguistic Review* 17:351–365.

Kiparsky, Paul, and Morris Halle. 1977. 'Towards a Reconstruction of the Indo-European Accent.' Pp. 209–38 in *Studies in stress and accent*, edited by L. M. Hyman. Los Angeles: Department of Linguistics, University of Southern California.

Kirchner, Robert. 1993. 'Turkish Vowel Harmony and Disharmony: An Optimality Theoretic Account.' Presented at the Rutgers Optimality Workshop I.

Knjazev, S. V. 2000. 'K Voprosu o Mexanizme Vozniknovenija Akan'ja v Russkom Jazyke.' *Voprosy Jazykoznanija* (1):75–101.

Knjazev, S. V. 2006. *Struktura Fonetičeskogo Slova v Russkom Jazyke: Sinxronija i Diaxronija*. Moskva: MAKS-press.

Kochetov, Alexei. 2002. *Production, Perception, and Emergent Phonotactic Patterns: A Case of Contrastive Palatalization*. New York and London: Routledge.

Köhnlein, Björn. 2017. 'Synchronic Alternations between Monophthongs and Diphthongs in Franconian: A Metrical Approach.' Pp. 211–36 in *Segmental structure and tone.*, edited by W. Kehrein, B. Köhnlein, P. Boersma, and M. Van Oostendorp. Berlin, Boston: Walter de Gruyter.

Koneczna, Halina, and Witold Zawadowski. 1956. *Obrazy Rentgenograficzne Głosek Rosyjskich*. Warszawa: Państwowe Wydawnictwo Naukowe.

Kraska-Szlenk, Iwona. 1995. 'The Phonology of Stress in Polish.' University of Illinois dissertation.

Kryvicki, A. A. 1959. 'Fanetyčnyja Asablivasci Adnoj z Havorak Poŭdnja Belarusi.' Pp. 98–104 in *Pracy instytuta movaznaŭstva AN BSSR, VI.* Minsk: Akademija Nauk Belaruskaj SSR.

Kurylo, O. 1928. 'Do Pytannja pro Umovy Rozvytku Dysymiljatyvnoho Akannja.' *Zapysky Istoryčno-Filolohičnoho Viddilu Ukrajins'koji Akademiji Nauk* 16:48–72.

Kuznecov, P. S. 1960. *Russkaja Dialektologija.* 3rd ed. Moskva: Prosveščenie.

Kuznecov, P. S. 1973. *Russkaja Dialektologija.* Moskva: Prosveščenie.

de Lacy, Paul. 2002a. 'The Formal Expression of Markedness.' UMass dissertation. [Also Rutgers Optimality Archive, Report No. 542].

de Lacy, Paul. 2002b. 'The Interaction of Tone and Stress in Optimality Theory.' *Phonology* 19(1):1–32.

de Lacy, Paul. 2006. *Markedness: Reduction and Preservation in Phonology.* Cambridge: Cambridge University Press.

de Lacy, Paul. 2007. 'The Interaction of Tone, Sonority, and Prosodic Structure.' Pp. 281–307 in *The Cambridge Handbook of Phonology*, edited by P. de Lacy. Cambridge: Cambridge University Press.

Ladefoged, Peter. 1968. *A Phonetic Study of West African Languages: An Auditory-Instrumental Survey (No. 1).* Cambridge: Cambridge University Press.

Lahiri, Aditi, and Vincent Evers. 1991. 'Palatalisation and Coronality.' Pp. 79–100 in *The special status of coronals: internal and external evidence. Phonetics and phonology, v.2.*, edited by C. Paradis and J.-F. Prunet. San Diego: Academic Press.

Lavitskaya, Yulia, and Bariş Kabak. 2014. 'Phonological Default in the Lexical Stress System of Russian: Evidence from Noun Declension.' *Lingua* 150:363–385.

Lehfeldt, Werner. 2010. *Akcent i Udarenie v Sovremennom Russkom Jazyke.* Moskva: Jazyki slavjanskoj kul'tury.

Lehiste, Ilse. 1970. *Suprasegmentals.* Cambridge MA: MIT Press.

Lehiste, Ilse. 1976. 'Influence of Fundamental Frequency Pattern on the Perception of Duration.' *Journal of Phonetics* 4:113–17.

Lehiste, Ilse, and Pavle Ivić. 1986. *Word and Sentence Prosody in Serbo-Croatian.* Cambridge MA: MIT Press.

Lehiste, Ilse, and Gordon E. Peterson. 1961. 'Some Basic Considerations in the Analysis of Intonation.' *Journal of the Acoustical Society of America* 33:419–25.

Lehiste, Ilse, and K. Popov. 1970. 'Akustische Analyse Bulgarischer Silbenkerne.' *Phonetica* 21:40–48.

Lehnert-LeHouillier, Heike. 2007. 'The Influence of Dynamic F0 on the Perception of Vowel Duration: Cross-Linguistic Evidence.' in *Proccedings of the 16th international congress of phonetic sciences.* Saarbrücken, Germany.

Levi, Susannah V. 2005. 'Acoustic Correlates of Lexical Accent in Turkish.' *Journal of the International Phonetic Association* 35(1):73–97.

Liberman, Mark, and Alan S. Prince. 1977. 'On Stress and Linguistic Rhythm.' *Linguistic Inquiry* 8:249–336.

Lightner, Theodore M. 1972. *Problems in the Theory of Phonology: Russian Phonology and Turkish Phonology.* Edmonton, Alberta: Linguistic Research Inc.

Lombardi, Linda. 1999. 'Positional Faithfulness and Voicing Assimilation in Optimality Theory.' *Natural Language and Linguistic Theory* 17:267–302.

Łukaszewicz, Beata, and Janina Mołczanow. 2018a. 'Leftward and Rightward Stress Iteration in Ukrainian: Acoustic Evidence and Theoretical Implications.' Pp. 261–80 in *Phonology, Fieldwork, Generalizations*, edited by B. Czaplicki, B. Łukaszewicz, and M. Opalińska. Berlin: Peter Lang.

Łukaszewicz, Beata, and Janina Mołczanow. 2018b. 'Rhythmic Stress in Ukrainian: Acoustic Evidence of a Bidirectional System.' *Journal of Linguistics* 54(02):367–88.

Łukaszewicz, Beata, and Janina Mołczanow. 2018c. 'The Role of Vowel Parameters in Defining Lexical and Subsidiary Stress in Ukrainian.' *Poznań Studies in Contemporary Linguistics* 54(3):355–75.

Łukaszewicz, Beata, and Janina Mołczanow. in prep. 'Metrical Phonology of Slavonic Stress.' in *The Oxford Guide to the Slavonic Languages*, edited by N. Bermel and J. Fellerer. Oxford: Oxford University Press.

Maddieson, Ian. 1984. *Patterns of Sounds.* Cambridge: Cambridge University Press.

Majors, Tivoli. 1998. 'Stress-Dependent Harmony.' University of Texas dissertation.

Martynaŭ, V. U., and A. I. Padlužny, eds. 1975. *Halosnyja Belaruskaj Movy: Akustyčny Analiz.* Minsk: Navuka i texnika.

Matisoff, James A. 1973. *The Grammar of Lahu.* Berkeley, CA.: University of California Press.

Mayer, Gerald L. 1976. 'The Stress of Foreign Place Names in Russian.' *Slavic and East European Journal* 20:451–59.

McCarthy, John J. 1999. 'Sympathy and Phonological Opacity.' *Phonology* 16:331–99.

McCarthy, John J. 2002. *A Thematic Guide to Optimality Theory.* Cambridge: Cambridge University Press.

McCarthy, John J. 2003. 'Sympathy, Cumulativity, and the Duke-of-York Gambit.' Pp. 23–76 in *The Syllable in Optimality Theory*, edited by C. Féry and R. van de Vijver. Cambridge: Cambridge University Press.

McCarthy, John J. 2007. *Hidden Generalizations: Phonological Opacity in Optimality Theory.* London and Oakville: Equinox.

McCarthy, John J. 2011. 'Autosegmental Spreading in Optimality Theory.' Pp. 195–222 in *Tones and Features: Phonetic and Phonological Perspectives*, edited by J. A. Goldsmith, E. Hume, and L. Wetzels. Berlin and Boston: Walter de Gruyter.

McCarthy, John J., and Alan S. Prince. 1995. 'Faithfulness and Reduplicative Identity.' Pp. 249–384 in *Papers in Optimality Theory. University of Massachusetts Occasional Papers in Linguistics. Vol. 18*, edited by J. L. Beckman, W. Dickey, and S. Urbanczyk.

McCarthy, John, and Alan Prince. 1993. 'Generalized Alignment.' Pp. 79–153 in *Yearbook of Morphology*, edited by G. Booij and J. van Marle. Dordrecht: Kluwer.

Melvold, Janis L. 1989. 'Structure and Stress in the Phonology of Russian.' MIT dissertation.

Miller, Patricia. 1972. 'Vowel Neutralization and Vowel Reduction.' Pp. 482–89 in *Papers from the Eight Regional Meeting of the Chicago Linguistic Society*, edited by Perenteau, Levi, and Phares. Chicago: Chicago Linguistic Society.

Mohr, B. 1971. 'Intrinsic Variations in the Speech Signal.' *Phonetica* 23:65–93.

Mołczanow, Janina. 2007. 'Russian Vowel Reduction and Phonological Opacity.' *Slavonic and East European Review* 85(2):201–30.

Mołczanow, Janina. 2012a. 'Tone and Vowel Reduction in East Slavic.' Poster Presented at the Workshop 'Tone: Theory and Practice', 28.09 – 29.09, Max Planck Institute for Evolutionary Anthropology, Leipzig, Germany.

Mołczanow, Janina. 2012b. 'Vowel Reduction in Slavic and Germanic.' Talk given on the 27th of January at the Linguistic Colloquium at the University of Marburg, Germany.

Mołczanow, Janina. 2015. 'The Interaction of Tone and Vowel Quality in Optimality Theory: A Study of Moscow Russian Vowel Reduction.' *Lingua* 163:108–37.

Mołczanow, Janina. 2017. *Tone-Sonority Interaction in Optimality Theory: East Slavic Vowel Reduction.* Warsaw: Instytut Lingwistyki Stosowanej UW.

Mołczanow, Janina, Ulrike Domahs, Johannes Knaus, and Richard Wiese. 2013. 'The Lexical Representation of Word Stress in Russian: Evidence from Event-Related Potentials.' *Mental Lexicon* 8(2):164–94.

Mołczanow, Janina, Ekaterina Iskra, Olga Dragoy, Richard Wiese, and Ulrike Domahs. 2019. 'Default Stress Assignment in Russian: Evidence from Acquired Surface Dyslexia.' *Phonology* 36(1):61–90.

Mołczanow, Janina, and Beata Łukaszewicz. 2021. 'Metrical Structure and Licensing: An Argument from Ukrainian.' *Linguistic Inquiry* 52 (3): 551–577.

Mołczanow, Janina, Beata Łukaszewicz, and Anna Łukaszewicz. 2018. 'Rhythmic Stress or Word-Boundary Effects? Comparison of Primary and Secondary Stress Correlates in Segmentally Identical Word Pairs.' *Proceedings of the International Conference on Speech Prosody* 908–12.

Mołczanow, Janina, Beata Łukaszewicz, and Anna Łukaszewicz. 2019. 'An Acoustic Study of Vowel Undershoot in a System with Several Degrees of Prominence.' *Proceedings of the Annual Conference of the International Speech Communication Association, INTERSPEECH* 1756–60.

Mołczanow, Janina, Beata Łukaszewicz, and Anna Łukaszewicz. 2021. 'Timing Patterns in a Hybrid Metrical System.' *Lingua* 255, 103066.

Morén, Bruce. 2003. 'The Parallel Structures Model of Feature Geometry.' *Working Papers of the Cornell Phonetics Laboratory* 15:194–270.

Mortensen, David R. 2013. 'Tonally Conditioned Vowel Raising in Shuijingping Mang.' *Journal of East Asian Linguistics* 22:189–216.

Mutaka, Ngessimo M. 1994. *The Lexical Tonology of Kinande.* Munich: Lincom Europa.

Myers, James, and Jane Tsay. 2003. 'A Formal Functional Model of Tone.' *Language and Linguistics* 4(1):105–38.

Nakonečnyj, M. F. 1969. 'Naholos.' Pp. 358–369 in *Sučasna ukrajins'ka literaturna mova. Vstup. Fonetyka*, edited by I. K. Bilodid. Kyjiv: Naukova Dumka.

Nazarova, T. V. 1961. 'Dejaki Fonetyčni Hiperyzmy v Ukrajins'kyx Hovirkax Nyžnjoji Prypjati.' *Dialektolohičnyj Bjuleten'* 8:18–30.

Nelson, James Platt. 1974. 'Vowel Phonology in Russian Dialects: First Pre-Stress Syllable in Dialects Characterized by Akan'e.' University of Illinois at Urbana-Champaign dissertation.

Nespor, Marina, and Irene Vogel. 1986. *Prosodic Phonology.* Dordrecht: Foris.

Nikolaev, S. L. 2006. 'Zametki o Vokalizme Zakarpatskogo Govora s. Sinevir.' Pp. 380–83 in *Issledovnija po slavjanskoj dialektologii. 12: Areal'nye aspekty izučenija slavjanskoj leksiki*, edited by G. P. Klepikova and A. A. Plotnikova. Moskva: Institut slavjanovedenija RAN.

Nikolaeva, T. M. 1971. 'Mesto Udarenija i Fonetičeskij Sostav Slova (Rasstanovka Udarenija v Neizvestnyx Slovax Inostrannogo Proisxoždenija).' Pp. 59–69 in *Fonetika, fonologija, grammatika: k semidesjatiletiju A. A. Reformatskogo*, edited by F. P. Filin. Moskva: Nauka.

Nitta, Tetsuo. 2001. 'The Accent System in the Kanazawa Dialect: The Relationship between Pitch and Sound Segments.' Pp. 153–185 in *Proceedings of the Symposium Cross-Linguistic Studies of Tonal Phenomena: Tonogenesis, Japanese Accentology, and Other Topics*, edited by S. Kaji. Tokyo: Tokyo University of Foreign Studies.

Odden, David. 1999. 'Typological Issues in Tone and Stress in Bantu.' Pp. 187–215 in *Cross-linguistic studies of tonal phenomena: tonogenesis, typology, and related topics*, edited by S. Kaji. Tokyo: ILCAA.

Odden, David. 2005. *Introducing Phonology.* Cambridge: Cambridge University Press.

Ohala, John J. 1973. 'The Physiology of Tone.' Pp. 3–14 in *Consonant types and tone*, edited by L. Hyman. Los Angeles: University of Southern California.

Ohala, John J. 1978. 'Production of Tone.' Pp. 5–39 in *Tone: A linguistic survey*, edited by V. A. Fromkin. New York: Academic Press.

Ohala, John J. 1981. 'The Listener as a Source of Sound Change.' Pp. 178–203 in *Papers from the Parasession on Language and Behavior*, edited by C. S. Masek, R. A. Hendrick, and M. F. Miller. Chicago: Chicago Linguistics Society.

Ohala, John J. 1986. 'Consumer's Guide to Evidence in Phonology.' *Phonology Yearbook* 3:3–26.

Ohala, John J., and William G. Ewan. 1973. 'Speed of Pitch Change.' *Journal of the Acoustical Society of America* 53:345.

van Oostendorp, Marc. 1995. 'Vowel Quality and Phonological Projection.' Tilburg University dissertation.

Orzechowska, Paula, Janina Mołczanow, and Michał Jankowski. 2018. 'Struktura Sylaby a Akcent Wyrazowy w Języku Rosyjskim: Badanie Korpusowe.' *Studia et Documenta Slavica* 1–2(5–6):79–91.

Padgett, Jaye. 2002. 'Feature Classes in Phonology.' *Language* 78(1):81–110.

Padgett, Jaye, and Marija Tabain. 2005. 'Adaptive Dispersion Theory and Phonological Vowel Reduction in Russian.' *Phonetica* 62(1):14–54.

Panov, M. V. 1967. *Russkaja Fonetika.* Moskva: Prosveščenie.

Parker, Stephen. 2002. 'Quantifying the Sonority Hierarchy.' UMass dissertation.

Paschen, Ludger. 2015. 'Datenbankgestützte Zugänge Zum Jakan'e in Der Südrussischen Peripherie.' Pp. 209–21 in *Junge Slavistik im Dialog IV. Beiträge zur VII.-IX. Slavistischen Studentenkonferenz*, edited by A. Weigl, N. Nübler, K. Naumann, and Y. Movchan. Hamburg: Dr. Kovač.

Pater, Joe. 2000. 'Nonuniformity in English Secondary Stress: The Role of Ranked and Lexically Specific Constraints.' *Phonology* 17:237–74.

Paufošima, R. F. 1980. 'Aktivnye Processy v Sovremennom Russkom Literaturnom Jazyke: Assimilativnye Izmenenija Bezudarnyx Glasnyx.' *Izvestija Akademii Nauk SSSR. Serija Literatury i Jazyka* 39(1):61–68.

Paufošima, R. F. 1981. 'O Proiznošenii Glasnyx Vtorogo Predudarnogo Sloga v Nekotoryx Russkix Govorax.' in *Dialektologija i lingvogeografija russkogo jazyka*, edited by R. I. Avanesov, S. V. Bromlej, and B. E. G. Moskva: Nauka.

Paufošima, R. F. 1983. *Fonetika Slova i Frazy v Severnorusskich Govorax.* Moskva: Nauka.

Pearce, Mary D. 2013. *The Interaction of Tone with Voicing and Foot Structure.* Stanford, CA: CSLI Publications.

Plapp, Rosemary K. 1996. 'Russian /i/ and /ɨ/ as Underlying Segments.' *Journal of Slavic Linguistics* 4:76–108.

Poser, William J. 1984. 'The Phonetics and Phonology of Tone and Intonation in Japanese.' MIT dissertation.

Potebnja, A. A. 1865. *O Zvukovyx Ossobenostjax Russkix Narečij. 'Filologičeskije Zapiski' 1.* Voronež.

Požarickaja, S. K. 2005. *Russkaja Dialektologija.* Moskva: Akademičeskij Proekt: Paradigma.

Prince, Alan. 1998. 'Paninian Relations.' Handout from Talk at the University of Marburg.

Prince, Alan, and Paul Smolensky. 1993. *Optimality Theory: Constraint Interactions in Generative Grammar.* Oxford: Blackwell. Available on Rutgers Optimality Archive, ROA-8/2002.

Pulleyblank, Douglas. 1996. 'Neutral Vowels in Optimality Theory: A Comparison of Yoruba and Wolof.' *Canadian Journal of Linguistics* 41:295–347.

Recasens, Daniel. 1991. *Fonètica Descriptiva Del Català.* Barcelona: Institut d'estudis catalans.

Revithiadou, Anthi. 1999. *Headmost Accent Wins: Head Dominance and Ideal Prosodic Form in Lexical Systems.* The Hague: Holland Academic Graphics.

Reynolds, William. 1994. 'Variation and Phonological Theory.' University of Pennsylvania dissertation.

Rischel, Jørgen. 1963. 'Morphemic Tone and Word Tone in East Norwegian.' *Phonetica* 10:154–64.

Rose, Sharon, and Rachel Walker. 2004. 'A Typology of Consonant Agreement as Correspondence.' *Language* 80(3):475–531.

Rose, Sharon, and Rachel Walker. 2011. 'Harmony Systems.' Pp. 240–90 in *The Handbook of Phonological Theory*, edited by J. A. Goldsmith, A. C. L. Yu, and J. Riggle.

Rubach, Jerzy. 1997. 'Extrasyllabic Consonants in Polish: Derivational Optimality Theory.' Pp. 551–81 in *Derivations and Constraints in Phonology*, edited by I. Roca. Oxford: Oxford University Press.

Rubach, Jerzy. 2000. 'Backness Switch in Russian.' *Phonology* 17:39–64.

Rubach, Jerzy. 2002. 'An Overview of Palatalisation-I.' *Studies in Phonetics, Phonology and Morphology* 8(2):169–86.

Rubach, Jerzy. 2003. 'Polish Palatalization in Derivational Optimality Theory.' *Lingua* 113(3):197–237.

Rubach, Jerzy. 2007. 'Feature Geometry from the Perspective of Polish, Russian, and Ukrainian.' *Linguistic Inquiry* 38(1):85–138.

Ryan, Kevin M. 2014. 'Onsets Contribute to Syllable Weight: Statistical Evidence from Stressed Meter.' *Language* 90(2):309–41.

Sagey, Elizabeth. 1986. 'The Representation of Features and Relations in Non-Linear Phonology.' MIT dissertation.

Sappok, Christian, Alexander Krasovitskij, Ludger Paschen, Katrin Brabender, Andreas Koch, and Nadja Kühl. 2016. 'RuReg: Russian Regions. Acoustic Database.' Available Online at Www.Rureg.De.

Savinov, D. M. 2013a. 'Arxaičeskij Dissimilativnyj Vokalizm v Razvitii.' Pp. 317–34 in *Russkaja fonetika v razvitii. Fonetičeskije 'otcy' i 'deti' načala XXI veka*, edited by M. L. Kalenčuk and R. F. Kasatkina. Moskva: Jazyki slavjanskoj kul'tury.

Savinov, D. M. 2013b. *Evoljucija Sistem Vokalizma v Južnorusskix Govorax.* Moskva: RAN.

Sawicka, Irena, and Stefan Grzybowski. 1999. *Studia z Palatalności w Językach Słowiańskich.* Toruń: Wydawnictwo Uniwersytetu Mikołaja Kopernika.

Šaxmatov, A. A. 1915. *Očerk Drevnejšego Perioda Istorii Russkogo Jazyka. (Enciklopedija Slavjanskoj Fillologii, 11.).* Petrograd: Imperatorskaja Akademija Nauk.

Ščerba, L. V. 1912. *Russkie Glasnye v Kačestvennom i Količestvennom Otnošenii.* St. Petersburg.

Schuh, Russel G. 1971. 'Ngizim Phonology.' Ms., University of California, Los Angeles.

Schuh, Russel G. 1978. 'Tone Rules.' Pp. 221–56 in *Tone. A linguistic survey*, edited by V. A. Fromkin. New York: Academic Press.

Selkirk, Elisabeth O. 1980. 'The Role of Prosodic Categories in English Word Stress.' *Linguistic Inquiry* 11:563–605.

Selkirk, Elisabeth O. 1984. 'On the Major Class Features and Syllable Theory.' Pp. 107–36 in *Language sound structure*, edited by M. Aronoff and R. T. Oehrle. Cambridge MA: MIT Press.

Selkirk, Elisabeth O. 1986. 'On Derived Domains in Sentence Phonology.' *Phonology Yearbook* 3:371–405.

Shapiro, Michael. 1968. *Russian Phonetic Variants and Phonostylistics.* Berkeley and Los Angeles: University of California Press.

Shih, Shu-hao, and Paul de Lacy. 2019. 'Evidence for Sonority-Driven Stress.' *Catalan Journal of Linguistics* 18:9–40.

Sievers, Eduard. 1881. *Grundzüge Der Phonetik.* Leipzig: Breitkopf and Härtel.

Spears, Richard A. 1968. 'Tonal Dissimilation in Maninka.' *Journal of African Languages* 7:88–100.

Stankiewicz, Edward. 1993. *The Accentual Patterns of the Slavic Languages.* Stanford, California: Stanford University Press.

Stroganova, T. G. 1955. 'Odna iz Osobennostej Južnovelikorusskogo Vokalizma.' *Voprosy Jazykoznanija* 4:94–103.

Suzuki, Keiichiro. 1998. 'A Typological Investigation of Dissimilation.' University of Arizona dissertation.

Szpyra-Kozłowska, Jolanta. 1998. 'The Sonority Scale and Phonetic Syllabification in Polish.' *Biuletyn Polskiego Towarzystwa Językoznawczego* 54:63–82.

Timberlake, Alan. 1993. 'Isochrony in Late Common Slavic.' Pp. 425–39 in *American contributions to the 11th International Congress of Slavists, Bratislava, August–September 1993: literature, linguistics, poetics*, edited by R. A. Maguire and A. Timberlake. Columbus: Slavica.

Timberlake, Alan. 2004. *A Reference Grammar of Russian.* Cambridge: Cambridge University Press.

Toc'ka, Nina. 1973. *Holosni Fonemy Ukrajins'koji Literaturnoji Movy.* Kyjiv: Vydavnyctvo Kyjivs'koho Universytetu.

Toc'ka, Nina. 2002. 'Fonetyka i Fonolohija.' Pp. 16–76 in *Sučasna ukrajins'ka literaturna mova*, edited by A. P. Gryščenko. Kyjiv: Vyšča škola.

Tolstaja, M. N. 2009. 'Pozicii Regressivnoj Akkomodacii i Garmonii Glasnyx v Zakarpatskom Govore s. Sinevir.' Pp. 115–43 in *Issledovnija po slavjanskoj dialektologii. 14: Fonetičeskij aspekt izučenija slavjanskich dialektov*, edited by L. E. Kalnyn'. Moskva: Institut slavjanovedenija RAN.

Trubetzkoy, Nikolaj S. 1939. *Grundzüge Der Phonologie*. Prague: Vandenhoeck and Ruprecht.

Vago, Robert. 1973. 'Abstract Vowel Harmony Systems in Uralic and Altaic Languages.' *Language* 49:579–605.

Vaillant, André. 1950. *Grammaire Comparée Des Langues Slaves, Vol. I: Phonétique*. Lyon: IAC.

Vajtovič, N. T. 1968. *Nenaciskny Vakalizm Narodnyx Havorak Belarusi*. Minsk: Navuka i Texnika.

Vanvik, Arne J. 1963. 'Some Problems in Scandinavian Tonemics.' *Phonetica* 10:165–73.

Vasiljev, L. L. 1904. *Glasnyje v Sloge Pod Udareniem v Moment Vozniknovenija Akanja v Obojanskom Govore*. Izv. ORJAS. Vol.9 (1).

Vaux, Bert. 2014. 'Language Games.' Pp. 722–50 in *The Handbook of Phonological Theory*, edited by J. A. Goldsmith, J. Riggle, and A. C. L. Yu. Malden, MA, and Oxford, U.K: John Wiley & Sons.

Vennemann, Theo. 1972. 'On the Theory of Syllabic Phonology.' *Linguistische Berichte* 18:1–18.

Vinogradov, G. S. 2005. 'Detskije Tajnye Jazyki.' *Russkij Jazyk (Ed. by Ivanova E. A., Rpt. from Irkutsk, Vlast' Truda, 1926)* 16(496):14–25.

Vojtovič, N. T. 1972a. 'K Voprosu o Putjax Razvitija Akan'ja v Vostočnoslavjanskix Jazykax.' Pp. 17–39 in *Obščeslavjanskij lingvističeskij atlas: materialy i issledovanija, 1970*, edited by R. I. Avanesov, S. B. Bernštejn, S. K. Požarickaja, and F. P. Filin. Moskva: Nauka.

Vojtovič, N. T. 1972b. 'O Svjazi Vokalizma s Ritmiko-Intonacionnoj Sistemoj v Russkix i Belorusskix Govorax.' Pp. 57–63 in *Russkoje i slavjanskoje jazykoznanije. K 70-letiju člena-korrespondenta AN SSSR R. I. Avanesova*, edited by F. P. Filin, V. G. Orlova, and V. F. Konnova. Moskva: Nauka.

Vyhonnaja, L. C. 1991. *Intanacyja. Nacisk. Arfaepija*. Minsk: Navuka i Texnika.

Vysotskij, S. S. 1973. 'O Zvukovoj Strukture Slova v Russkix Govorax.' Pp. 17–41 in *Issledovnija po russkoj dialektologii.*, edited by J. S. Azarx, S. V. Bromlej, and L. N. Bulatova. Moskva: Nauka.

Vysotskij, S. S. 1984. 'O Moskovskom Narodnom Govore.' Pp. 22–37 in *Gorodskoje prostorečije. Problemy izučenija*, edited by E. A. Zemskaja and D. N. Šmel'ov. Moskva: Nauka.

Walker, Rachel. 2000. *Nasalization, Neutral Segments, and Opacity Effects*. New York: Garland.

Walker, Rachel. 2005. 'Weak Triggers in Vowel Harmony.' *Natural Language and Linguistic Theory* 23(4):917–89.

Wee, Lian-Hee. 2019. *Phonological Tone*. Cambridge: Cambridge University Press.

Wiese, Richard. 1996. *The Phonology of German*. Oxford: Oxford University Press.

Wijk, N. van. 1934. 'Zur Entwicklungsgeschichte Des Akanje Und Jakanje.' *Slavia* 13:650–64.

Wilson, Colin. 2001. 'Consonant Cluster Neutralization and Targeted Constraints.' *Phonology* 18:147–97.

Withgott, Meg, and Per-Kristian Halvorsen. 1984. 'Morphological Constraints on Scandinavian Tone Accent.' Stanford: Center for the Study of Language and Information Report No. CSLI-84-11.

Yanushevskaya, Irena and Daniel Bunčić. 2015. 'Russian.' *Journal of the International Phonetic Association* 45:221–8.

Yip, Moira. 1980. 'The Tonal Phonology of Chinese.' MIT dissertation.

Yip, Moira. 1999. 'Feet, Tonal Reduction and Speech Rate at the Word and Phrase Level in Chinese.' Pp. 171–94 in *Phrasal Phonology*, edited by R. Kager and W. Zonneveld. Nijmegen: Nijmegen University Press.

Yip, Moira. 2002. *Tone*. Cambridge: Cambridge University Press.

Yu, Alan C. L. 2010. 'Tonal Effects on Perceived Vowel Duration.' Pp. 151–68 in *Papers in laboratory phonology (Vol. 10)*, edited by C. Fougeron, B. Kühnert, M. D'Imperio, and N. Vallée. Berlin: Mouton de Gruyter.

Zaliznjak, A. A. 1985. *Ot Praslavjanskoj Akcentuacii k Russkoj*. Moskva: Izdatel'stvo Moskovskogo Universiteta.

Zaxarova, K. F. 1959. 'Arxaičeskije Tipy Dissimiljativnogo Jakan'ja v Govorax Belgorodskoj i Voronežskoj Oblastej.' Pp. 6–55 in *Materialy i issledovanija po russkoj dialektologii. Novaja serija. Vol.1*, edited by R. I. Avanesov and V. G. Orlova. Moskva: RAN.

Zec, Draga. 1992. 'The Cyclicity of a Tonal Rule.' *Papers from the Annual Regional Meeting, Chicago Linguistic Society* 28(2):303–15.

Zec, Draga. 1999. 'Footed Tones and Tonal Feet: Rhythmic Constituency in a Pitch-Accent Language.' *Phonology* 16:225–64.

Zee, Eric. 1980. 'Tone and Vowel Quality.' *Journal of Phonetics* 6:247–58.

Zemskaja, E. A. 1973. *Russkaja Razgovornaja Reč*. Moskva: Nauka.

Zhang, Jie. 2002. *The Effects of Duration and Sonority on Contour Tone: Typological Survey and Formal Analysis*. New York and London: Routledge.

Zhang, Jie. 2004. 'The Role of Contrast-Specific and Language-Specific Phonetics in Contour Tone Distribution.' Pp. 157–90 in *Phonetically based phonology*, edited by B. Hayes, R. Kirchner, and D. Steriade. Cambridge: Cambridge University Press.

Ziłyński, Jan. 1932. *Opis Fonetyczny Języka Ukraińskiego*. Kraków: Polska Akademia Umiejętności.

Zlatoustova, L. V. 1981. *Fonetičeskie Edinicy Russkoj Reči*. Moskva: Izdatel'stvo Moskovskogo Universiteta.

Language index

Ancient Greek 61fn.

Bambara 61
Bantu 119–120, 160
Basque 106
Belarusian 2, 3fn., 8, 15, 16fn., 17, 36, 46, 59, 61, 65, 75fn., 87–88, 99, 101, 103, 107, 115, 134fn., 150, 155, 166
Bora 61fn.
Bulgarian 7, 106

Catalan 80fn., 106
Croatian *see* Serbo-Croatian
Czech 6

Dutch 1, 76, 101
  Baexem 101
  Weert 13, 101–102

Eastern Maninkakan 13fn.
English 1, 7, 160

Finnish 119
Foochow 12, 14
French 76
Fuzhou 12, 14

German 76

Hausa 61
Hungarian 119

Italian 57, 122

Japanese 12, 14–16, 88

Kera 57, 61–62, 119
Kinande 13fn.

Lahu 12, 14
Limburgian 13

Mixtecan 61fn.

Neo-Štokavian 15, 57fn., 88
Ngizim 12–13, 88
Norwegian 15, 57

Rengao 13
Russian
  Central Russian 2, 22, 28, 30, 38, 41, 113, 150, 152, 154–155
  Moscow Russian 15, 26fn., 171fn.
  Northern Russian 25, 64, 66, 83, 115, 122, 134fn., 151fn., 163
  Old Moscow 171, 176
  Regional Russian 114–115
  Southern Russian 2, 17, 23, 31, 34, 37–38, 40–41, 42fn., 63–65, 120, 132, 142, 150
  Standard Russian 1–3fn., 8–9, 15–20, 22–25, 28–30, 44–63, 65–67, 72–82, 84fn., 86–93, 108, 111, 116fn., 122, 134fn., 148, 150–153, 156–158, 160, 169–174, 178

Serbian *see* Serbo-Croatian
Serbo-Croatian 12, 15, 16, 57, 61fn., 87, 88
Shuijingping Mang 12–13
Slave 61
Slovene *see* Slovenian
Slovenian 14, 87–88, 106, 180
Spanish 57
Sri Lankan Portuguese 7
Swedish 12, 16, 57

Taiwanese 13
Tswana 160
Turkish 119
Tuvan 119

Ukrainian 16fn., 36, 46, 57–59, 60fn., 64, 66, 69, 83, 87, 99–100, 115, 154fn., 158
Upper Snov Basin dialects 87, 99–100, 103

Vladimir-Volga Basin dialects 102

Wenzhou 108
Western Cham 13

Subject index

accented *vs* unaccented stems 48–49, 60fn.
alternation [o] – [e] 29fn, 30, 172–173
assimilative-dissimilative reduction 4, 20–22, 38–41 (described), 56–57, 68–69, 111fn., 112, 120, 125, 137–146 (analyzed), 147, 149

Basic Accentuation Principle 48
blocking of reduction 2, 21, 26–28, 27fn., 76–80, 85, 91, 103, 150, 152, 166, 169, 177
borrowing 26, 34, 47, 61, 77fn., 92, 153fn., 172fn.

compound 49, 51, 63fn.
compound dissimilative reduction 4, 21–22, 36–38 (described), 44, 56–57, 68–69, 120–137 (analyzed), 140, 144, 146–148

default stress 45, 48–49, 51–53, 62
derivational levels 134–136, 146, 151, 170, 174–176
derivational OT *see* Stratal OT
dissimilative reduction 1, 2, 4, 17–18, 20–22, 30–36 (described), 37fn., 38–44, 61–63, 64fn., 66–72, 75–76, 86–89, 91, 93–99 (analyzed), 104–105, 108–109, 111–112, 115–121, 123–133, 136–138, 140, 144, 146–148, 178–179

Element Theory 82–84
empty onset *see* hiatus
extreme reduction 7–8, 19, 22, 25–27 (described), 42, 44, 72, 73–80 (analyzed), 81, 85, 97, 178

factorial typology 86, 111–115
feature agreement 2, 4, 122, 134fn., 147, 151–152, 156, 160, 165, 169, 177, 179
feature geometry 84, 152, 158
foot form *see* foot structure
foot structure 3, 45–46, 49–63, 66–72, 81, 86, 89–90, 96, 99, 104, 107–114, 123–126, 126, 133, 140–141, 143, 178
free variation 23, 78, 92, 98–99, 103, 106–108

hard stridents *see* non-palatalized stridents
harmonic alignment 3, 5–7, 9, 178
hiatus 26, 73, 76–80, 85, 165
hybrid metrical structure 60fn., 65–69, 72, 111fn.

language game 49, 53–56, 72, 111
lexical accent 1fn., 15–16, 25fn., 45–49, 50fn., 56–62, 64, 67–68, 70–72, 93, 110fn., 114
lexical stress *see* lexical accent
linguistic scales
  prosodic prominence scale 6–8, 74

sonority scale 3, 5, 8–9, 12, 74, 89, 93, 178
tonal scale 3, 7, 9, 12, 89, 93, 178
LP/OT *see* stratal OT

mixed rhythmic structure *see* hybrid metrical structure
mobile stress 47–48
moderate reduction 52, 72, 19, 25, 27, 79, 81, 86, 178
mora 61, 81, 106, 118

non-dissimilative reduction 4, 19–22, 27–30 (described), 31, 42, 44, 61, 66, 69, 71, 88–93 (analyzed), 94, 104, 111–112, 115–116, 117, 125, 148, 162, 178–179,
non-palatalized stridents 4, 21, 150, 169–177

opacity 133–134, 146, 151
opaque generalizations *see* opacity
optionality *see* free variation

perceived duration 101–102
phonetic undershoot 18, 64fn., 82
pitch accent 12–13, 15–16, 57fn., 59, 101–102, 180
positional faithfulness 56, 90, 95, 108, 115, 120, 135, 156
post-tonic reduction 19, 25, 68, 71
Potebnja's formula 63
pretonic length 3fn., 8, 58, 86–87, 99–110, 115–116, 142, 146
prominence reduction 7, 73–74, 82
prosodic head 7–8, 57, 61, 73–74, 84, 86, 108, 113
prosodic non-head 7–8, 61, 73–74, 84, 86, 113–114

reduction patterns
Aŭciuki 87, 99–110, 113
Bel'sk 20, 39–40, 44, 119, 137–138, 143–144, 147, 149
Čuxloma 22, 151, 163–164
Dmitrov 20, 36–38, 44, 119–121, 123–124, 126, 128, 129fn., 130–132, 147, 149
Don 20, 30, 32–36, 40, 44, 94–97, 109, 111, 120, 123fn., 131fn., 143, 146–149
Kidusovo 20, 39–40, 44, 119, 137–140, 144–146, 149
Kultuki 20–21, 39–40, 44, 119, 137–138,144–146, 149
Mosal'sk 20–21, 36–38, 40, 44, 119–121, 123–126, 128–132, 144–149
Novoselki 20, 39–40, 44, 119, 132, 137–140, 144–146, 149
Obojan' 20, 30–31, 33–36, 40–41, 44, 94–98, 105, 109, 111, 120–121, 123–124, 126, 128–130, 132, 138, 140, 144, 146–149
Orexovo 20, 39–40, 44, 119, 137–138, 144–146, 149
Ščigry 20, 36–38, 40, 44, 119–121, 123–124, 127–129, 132–136, 144–147, 149
Sudža 20, 36–38, 40, 44, 119–121, 123–124, 126, 128–130, 132–136, 144–149
Upper Snov Basin 87, 99–100, 103
Vladimir-Volga Basin 102
Zadon 31, 32fn., 33, 36, 98, 132
Žizdra 8, 20–21, 30–31, 33–36, 44, 75, 94–97, 109, 111, 120–121, 123–125, 144, 146–149, 163
reduction types
[a]-reduction 2, 8–9, 17, 18, 21, 28, 30–32, 40, 75, 82, 84, 86, 88, 93, 95–97, 102–103, 105–109, 113, 116, 127–128, 134fn., 136, 140–142, 144, 147–152, 154, 164–165
[e]-reduction 21–22, 28–30, 42, 44, 82–84, 91fn., 150, 152–153, 155, 160–165, 167–169
moderate [e]-reduction 22, 163–166

[i]-reduction 17, 22, 28–30, 42, 44, 127, 129–133, 136, 140, 146, 150–152, 156–158, 160–165, 167, 169
[ja]-reduction 18, 21–22, 31, 32fn., 37fn., 38, 98, 124, 126–127, 129, 131, 133, 143–144, 147–149, 155, 162
moderate [ja]-reduction 21–22, 41, 148, 150, 162–168, 170
strong [ja]-reduction 166
[o]-reduction 83–84
resyllabification 77
retraction
[ɛ]-retraction 133–134, 151
[i]-retraction 153
rhythmic stress *see* secondary stress
rhythmic structure 47, 52, 58fn., 63–66, 69, 116

secondary place of articulation 24, 28, 84, 148, 152, 177
palatalization 24–25, 83 , 134, 139, 152–153, 155, 158, 160, 169, 174, 177
velarization 24, 84
secondary stress 16fn., 58, 49, 50–51, 60fn., 63–66, 69
serial OT *see* stratal OT
spreading (H tone) 63, 87–88, 93
spreading (feature) 79, 83–84, 116, 120, 122, 159–160
stem-final hypothesis 49, 51, 52fn., 60
stratal OT 134, 174, 177
stress fixed on the inflectional ending 47
stress fixed on the stem 47
stringency 6fn, 9
substance-free phonology 82
Synevir vowel raising 158–159

two-pattern reduction *see* moderate reduction
typology 4, 12–16, 71, 120, 179

vowel harmony 4, 18, 21, 44, 56–57, 78, 103fn., 118–120, 122, 133–134, 137, 147, 158

www.ingramcontent.com/pod-product-compliance
Lightning Source LLC
LaVergne TN
LVHW021126110826
R19582500001B/R195825PG844660LVX00003B/3

9781800502345